INDIANA'S CITIZEN SOLDIERS

The Militia and National Guard
in Indiana History

Edited by
William J. Watt and James R. H. Spears

Published by
THE INDIANA STATE ARMORY BOARD
Indianapolis, 1980

Printed in the United States of America
First Printing 1980
Published by the Indiana State Armory Board
Military Department of Indiana
P. O. Drawer AO, Stout Field
Indianapolis, Indiana 46241
Library of Congress Catalog Card Number 80-620014

ACKNOWLEDGMENTS

A comprehensive history of the Indiana militia and National Guard last was attempted in 1901, primarily to commemorate the Guard's involvement in the Spanish-American War. Since then, Hoosier National Guardsmen have served in two world wars, other national emergencies, and in scores of incidents of state duty for domestic emergencies. Few people are aware of the extent of the Indiana Guard's contributions to the nation's defense and to the state's well-being.

Indiana's Citizen Soldiers was undertaken at the suggestion of Major General Alfred F. Ahner, who believed that a modern history of the Indiana militia and National Guard would stimulate a better understanding of the importance of the state's volunteer soldiers and would promote a greater sense of pride in their heritage among Indiana's Guard personnel.

Indiana's Citizen Soldiers could not have been published without the active support of the Indiana State Armory Board, whose members are:

> Governor Otis R. Bowen
> Major General Robert G. Moorhead
> Major General Alfred F. Ahner
> Brigadier General Clyde C. Wright
> Brigadier General Ervin H. Bucher
> Colonel Judson H. West
> Captain Robert O. Jackson, USNR

The editors are indebted to our contributors, who volunteered their time and talent. In addition to inspiring this book, General Ahner offered helpful critiques on several chapters and provided valuable assistance to the editors and contributors in gathering information.

Several other individuals and institutions merit acknowledgment: the Indianapolis *Star* and *News*, the Associated Press, Brigadier General Bruce Jacobs and Colonel Leslie Cross of the National Guard Association of the United States, the Indiana State Library, Major General Wendell C. Phillippi, Major General Robert D. Weliver, Major General Kenneth W.

iii

Brewer, Colonel William A. Scott, Lieutenant Colonel Joseph Delaney, Major Herbert Allison, Captain H. Michael Goss, Captain James Mier, Chief Warrant Officer Howard Light, Chief Warrant Officer John Simpson, John Selch, Thomas Joyce, and Lieutenant Colonel Harry Grube. Mrs. Mary McIntyre, Mrs. Mary Lundy, and Mrs. Viola Walker provided valuable assistance in the preparation of the manuscript.

The writers have attempted to maintain a high standard of scholarship while presenting a narrative in a manner that would not prove to be too foggy for readers lacking a military background. It is our hope that *Indiana's Citizen Soldiers* will generate increased interest in Indiana's military history, because the state's military heritage is a rich one, indeed.

William J. Watt
James R. H. Spears
Military Department of
Indiana, Indianapolis

April 1, 1980

TABLE OF CONTENTS

APPENDICES:

A section of photographs follows page 106.

Photographs are courtesy of:

The Indianapolis *News.*
The National Guard Association of the United States.
38th Infantry Division Public Affairs Office.
Military Department of Indiana.
120th Public Affairs Detachment.

Maps and cover design by Barbara Scheitlin
and David Chesak

THE MILITIA AS A NATIONAL INSTITUTION

William J. Watt

The militia, the able-bodied men of a community ready on short notice to stand together in its defense, is a notion as old as tribal society that has been sustained down the centuries as trained civilian-soldiers have joined together to confront common danger. As society changed, the militia gave way to professional standing armies in some nations, while in others, like the United States, it came to occupy a special place in the system of defense.

The idea of a universal obligation to serve is recorded in some of the earliest Anglo-Saxon annals, where the militia was defined to include able-bodied males from young manhood to middle age. Although the obligation theoretically touched every man, even at this early date a subtle distinction was made between the militia as an all-encompassing levy of manpower and the *organized* militia as a special local military institution with individuals enrolled as members and trained, however rudely, in the principles of soldiering. In the ninth century Britain of King Alfred, citizen soldiers already were being organized to learn the art of war and to stand ready for first callup to repel an attack upon community or kingdom. These trained bands of militiamen acquired the designation "trainbands" during the reign of James I. By that time the process had become refined to the extent that trainband members were issued arms in advance on the condition that they gather at a common meeting point when alarms of danger were raised. Eventually, trainbands in larger cities became the core of unrest that broke loose as Cromwell's revolution. Soon after the Cromwellian revolt—in part because English regimes were wary of armed civilian threats to their tenure—the militia began disintegrating in the British Isles, although it has survived in the British Territorial units which are direct institutional descendants of the trainbands.

Meanwhile, the militia was thriving in Switzerland, which inaugurated universal military training and coupled it with specialized units of younger men who were recognized as a first-line reserve.

1

Although the onset of professional European armies stunted, then withered the militia in continental nations, Englishmen colonizing North America adapted the institution to a radically different environment, where it has prevailed, despite occasional setbacks, to the present day. The task of hacking a new nation out of a wilderness infested with hostile Indians while at the same time developing a seaboard that was vulnerable to foreign interference required the work of all colonists sturdy enough to contribute to it. Available manpower was needed for clearing, planting, and town-building. The impoverishment of the early colonies did not allow for the extravagance of a standing army, despite these ever-present dangers. Furthermore, it would have required a substantial standing army to guarantee that regulars effectively could respond to Indian attacks which threatened settlements scattered along the coastal region from Massachusetts to the Carolinas. Virginia nourished the militia through colonial times, in part because of the success of the organized defenses of Jamestown colony during its fledgling years. Its strong defense deterred Indians from undertaking hostile enterprises. As Virginia colonies expanded from the tidewater to the piedmont, militia districts were created and the colonial assembly provided by statute for an armed citizenry. The process was repeated at Plymouth and at Massachusetts Bay, where all adult males were required to arm themselves and to organize units for training. Specialized contingents ready for action on short notice were antecedents of the minutemen of the Revolution.[1]

A considerable volume of folklore has surrounded the presumed skills of shooting, forest lore, and fighting possessed by America's pioneers. These skills were honed to a keener edge in tense living on the frontier fringe; but, as settlement edged westward, men in the established colonies were not inclined to maintain them. As the immediate danger to family and community receded, the art of fighting lost its importance and its appeal. Although militiamen proved valuable in fracases with Indian raiders on the western border, they were not especially effective when used in an organized fashion on expeditions away from home. Historian Russell Weigley observed:

> Few men came to America to be soldiers. More likely, they came in part to escape soldiering. They would fight when they had to, to preserve the homes and farms and way of life they had crossed the ocean to find. But they did not wish to abandon

homes and farms for months, or a season, to go off soldiering in
pursuit of objects only remotely connected with their own aspirations or security. Militia training did not prepare them for extended campaigns, nor did militia organization befit the maintenance of long expeditions.[2]

Even though the need for a local defense force had diminished, enrolled militia companies and regiments remained
active, in the words of Walter Millis, playing a role in local
politics and community affairs not unlike that of many volunteer fire companies in rural communities today.[3]

During the Revolution, Washington sought to raise a professional army, drawing upon militia units to flesh it out.
Throughout the fighting the new nation's forces—both Continental Army and militia—were strapped by inadequate training, poor logistics, and short-term enlistments that made it
nearly impossible to mount campaigns of long duration. Repeatedly, Washington endeavored to create his Continental
Army on the British pattern, with enlistments to carry on as
long as the war lasted. He was unable to convince the Continental Congress to ratify this policy. In fact, such a measure
probably would have proved unacceptable to the citizenry.
The general ultimately advocated annual quotas from the
states' militias.

The revolutionary experience altered the relationship between citizen, state, and military institutions. Colonial America
experienced a people's war, rather than one conducted as a duel
of professional armies. It was apparent that more was at stake
than the limited objectives of traditional eighteenth-century
warfare and politics. If war was to be waged in the broader
interests of the people, rather than for the political objectives
of monarchs, the government was in a position to call upon the
mass citizenry for assistance on a greater scale than previously
had been the case.[4]

How the new country's military system was to be defined
turned out to be a central issue in the debates surrounding the
nation's constitution-making. There was, to begin with, a
smouldering resentment against large standing armies of professionals. They were symbols of oppression and despotism
that had caused many Americans to flee the old world. They
were viewed as a threat to civil liberties in a fragile new nation.
Colonists remembered all too vividly the forced quartering of
British regulars in their homes. In the compromise language

that emerged in the Constitution, the notion of a citizen army was included, in part, because the government saw only limited objectives for a regular army—garrisoning the seacoast forts and arsenals, and stationing a modest force on the Indian frontier. Although the performance of the militia had been both praised and damned during the Revolutionary conflict, a realistic appraisal of the nation's resources argued against the expense of keeping a large force of regular troops because, outside the city limits of principal eastern seaports, America remained a poor nation, still struggling on a vast new continent. These factors influenced the language of the Constitution.

Despite their rather conservative attitude concerning military affairs, the framers of the Constitution made provision for considerable flexibility in the maintenance of a regular army. Congress was given the power to declare war, to raise armies, and to activate the militia for federal service to "execute the laws of the union, suppress insurrections and repel invasions." The legislative branch was granted authority to supervise the organization, arming, and discipline of the militia while it was in federal service. The document further strengthened the status of a citizen-based army in the Second Amendment, which states: "A well-regulated militia being necessary to the security of a free state, the right of the people to keep and bear arms shall not be infringed."

Since the power to maintain an army was an awesome one, analysts have seen the preservation of the state militias as a means of striking a compromise between federal and state sovereignty. The militia underscored the precept that the states retained at least a dual sovereignty in military affairs. It has been suggested that the militia articles actually were necessary to insure the Constitution's ratification by the states.[5]

The Constitution provided a broad legal foundation for the architecture of the nation's defense system, but it was up to Washington and his colleagues actually to define the form and structure of the Army. The process begun by these early leaders at the close of the eighteenth century is not complete even in the 1980s. Throughout the intervening decades the recurring theme of American military debate has been that of seeking to resolve the appropriate organization and development of the nation's armed forces.

Frustrated at times by the miscarriage of tactical adventures resulting from a lack of adequate manpower, or of promising

4

campaigns aborted because militia enlistments expired, Washington occasionally had harsh words for the citizen-soldiers:

> Men just dragged from the tender scenes of domestic life; unaccustomed to the din of Arms; totally unacquainted with every kind of military skill, . . . when opposed to Troops regularly trained, disciplined and appointed, superior in knowledge, and superior in Arms, makes them timid and ready to fly from their own shadows. . . . Again, Men accustomed to unbounded freedom and no control, cannot brook the Restraint which is indispensably necessary to the good order and Government of an Army. . . . To bring Men to a proper degree of subordination is not the work of a day, a month, or even a year.[6]

However, Washington had been a militiaman, aware of the occasional spectacular successes of an armed citizenry against a Gentleman Johnny Burgoyne, or at King's Mountain, and he ultimately advocated a strong militia. Initially, Washington called for a regular army of 2,631, considering it to be barely adequate for patrolling the western frontier and for garrisoning the nation's northern and southern borders. It soon was obvious that this wouldn't be enough. A cluster of distinguished Revolutionary War generals—Washington, Steuben, Knox, Pickering, Heath, Hand, and Rufus Putnam—called for the uniform organization of the militia among the states and the effective training and equipping of militia units.

Washington drafted a memorandum, "Sentiments on a Peace Establishment," that, unfortunately, was not widely circulated until the twentieth century. In it he called for a standing army to garrison Indian posts, West Point, the Canadian border, and arsenals. It was to be augmented by "a well-organized Militia; upon a plan that will pervade all the states and introduce similarity in their Establishment, Manoeuvres, Exercise and Arms." The general argued that the nation was too poor to maintain a regular army; and, even if that option proved to be an affordable one, "still it could not be done without great oppression of the people."[7]

In years to come, critics of the militia would quote Washington's comments disparaging the militia as reasons for abandoning it, not knowing that, despite his misgivings during the Revolution, he considered an effective militia to be essential to the nation.

At the time Washington's memorandum was written the militia was decaying in the older colonies, its units becoming ceremonial gathering points for a proliferation of officers, little more than dandies, swelling the ranks of the titled but untrained. To counter this, Washington recommended the creation of light infantry companies made up of younger, better-trained men who would function as the leading edge of the enrolled militia. This would provide the nucleus of an effective reserve while avoiding a politically difficult overhaul of the militia that would have required the jettisoning of numerous high-ranking officers and the reduction of the number of units to something approaching realism.

General Steuben, a militia supporter well acquainted with its potential after five years of service as inspector general of the Continental Army, proposed a Continental Militia comprised of young volunteers from the enrolled militia who would enlist for three years and who would receive a month's field training each year. Initially, he would have pegged its strength at 21,000, scattered geographically.

Meanwhile, Secretary of War Knox suggested the retention of universal military service by segregating the militia into three categories. Young men would train six weeks each year, before graduating at age 21 to the "main corps" which would include enrollees up to age 45. As militiamen passed that age boundary they would be placed in a reserve corps where they would be eligible for call until age 61. This ambitious plan got nowhere and a watered-down version was submitted in 1790.

Congress rejected each of these approaches, instead opting for the Militia Act of 1792, which became the statutory basis of the militia system until the twentieth century. It required the enrollment in state militias of able-bodied male citizens aged 18 to 45. Soldiers were to equip themselves with essential weaponry. The system was organized from the company level on up through division formations. The President had the authority to order militiamen to active service for no more than three months in any one year. States were supposed to monitor enrollment and training, but no federal standards were established.

Twentieth century critics would term the act a catastrophe. General John MacAuley Palmer, whose opinions on Army organization influenced Army policy from World War I through World War II, observed:

> Its passage actually made our military system worse than it was before the bill was introduced. The old militia organization with its phony regiments and divisions now had federal sanction

6

and was made uniformly bad throughout the nation. Washington had proposed militia in terms of 'gilt-edge bonds,' Congress issued it in terms of 'watered stock'. . . . The Militia Act of 1792 did more than kill a well-organized militia. It gave federal sanction to an ill-organized militia. By the time of Jefferson's administration this had become a gigantic nationwide organization. It formed a vast array of territorial regiments, brigades and divisions, generally untrained and entirely free from national supervision or control. In the new states on the frontier, some of its regiments under vigorous leaders like Andrew Jackson were actually assembled and trained. But most of the host assembled only once a year for the 'annual muster' which was always an 'annual spree' and generally nothing more.[8]

Weigley, on the other hand, reflected that, given the limited resources of a young nation, it is doubtful that Congress could have done much better. Although the Militia Act of 1792 did not improve the militia, at least, he claimed, it kept the tradition alive. In years to come, that would prove beneficial to the nation.[9]

However, the decades following enactment of the militia law were ones in which evidence rapidly accumulated that the "ill-organized" approach brought on a near-bankrupt militia system. The militia return for 1808 indicated the extent to which the militia had dwindled from a flesh-and-blood fighting force to one whose substance largely consisted of mildewed rosters. It showed on paper that the militia counted 674,827 among its members (a bigger force than the National Guard of the 1970s) and included 80 major generals, 226 brigadier generals, 1,033 infantry regiments, 8,892 infantry captains, and 473 cavalry captains. It was obvious that the militia was doing little more than adding an extra squiggle or two to the signatures of frontier-era status seekers.

This state of affairs guaranteed that the militia system generally would be a failure during the War of 1812. Critics of the militia are quick to recount the battle at Bladensburg in August, 1814, in which a contingent of ill-prepared militiamen broke and fled before the British, bringing derision and disgrace upon the system. Many tended to forget, though, that the British left 2,000 veterans of the Peninsular War dead on the battlefield at New Orleans where they had encountered better-trained western militiamen under the command of Andrew Jackson. Coupled with the fact that the majority of militia units had deteriorated as trained fighting forces was the further disadvantage that short terms of enlistments for federal active duty did not give any of them the chance to show their mettle. Unfortunately, what was considered to be an inadequate performance by militia outfits during the War of 1812 colored federal military planning for the remainder of the nineteenth century.

When John C. Calhoun became Secretary of War in 1817, it was his task to reshape the post-war Army, in part because Congress, for reasons of economy, wanted to cut the regular forces from 10,000 to 6,000. In earlier times military planners might have fallen back on the militia to cover the deficit, but attention now was focused on professionalizing the Army. While advocating a stronger Navy to undertake the role of coastal defense, Calhoun in 1820 pursued the concept of an "expansible" Army, utilizing a small regular force that would function as a cadre of veterans into whose ranks raw recruits would be added in time of war. He envisioned as many as five recruits for every experienced soldier.

Calhoun explained his view of the militia in a report to Congress:

> I am aware that the militia is considered, and in many respects justly, as the great national force; but, to render them effective, every experienced officer must acknowledge that they require the aid of regular troops. Supported by a suitable corps of trained artillerists, and by a small well-disciplined body of infantry, they may be safely relied on to garrison our forts and to act in the field as light troops. In these services, their zeal, courage, and habit of using fire-arms, would be of great importance and would have their full effect. To rely on them beyond this, to suppose our militia capable of meeting in the open field the regular troops of Europe, would be to resist the most obvious truth, and the whole of our experience as a nation. War is an art, to attain perfection in which, much time and experience, particularly for the officers, are necessary.[10]

The trend toward professionalization of the Army would continue through the Mexican War and Civil War and on into a post-war period in which isolated bands of regulars, operating from remote posts in the west, functioned as an Indian-fighting constabulary. The attitudes of professionals found their catalyst in the writings of Brevet Brigadier General Emory Upton, whose treatise, *The Military Policy of the United States*, was widely circulated among the higher ranks of policy-makers in manuscript form until it was published by the War Department in 1904. Upton, an ardent professional who had become even more enamored of professional standing armies after a tour as observer of European armies on maneuver, lavished praise upon the U. S. regulars while abusing the whole idea of a militia. He attacked the performance of militia units on the battlefield, criticized the dual structure of state and federal control of the institution, and complained that reliance upon citizen soldiers brought on both extravagance and disaster. Upton called for an administrative reorganization of the Army along the lines of the German general staff. The regulars would be the primary force, augmented in time of war by the "expansible" approach outlined by Calhoun. A system of national volunteers, organized locally but under federal control, would fuel the war-time expansion. The militia would be relegated to third-line status, supported exclusively by the states, and utilized solely as a civil defense force. Upton's testy defense of the regulars and his scorn for the citizen soldier became gospel for many Army officers through World War I.[11]

The nation's experiences during the War with Spain stimulated intensified talk of reorganization, since the new role of the United States as a world power argued in favor of an Army befitting that stature and equipped for the task. Scandals involving food, logistics, and medical care added to the clamor for modernization. Even though enthusiasm for the doctrine of professionalism was in full bloom, the visibility of the National Guard during the Spanish conflict entitled it to a role in the nation's defense establishment.

The reorganization process was spurred by Secretary of War Elihu Root, who perceived the many inadequacies of the existing system. Root observed that there seemed to be two fundamental principles guiding consideration of Army organization: first, that the real object of having an army is to provide for war and, second, that the regular forces could not, by themselves, carry out the war effort.[12] In 1902, he called for the enactment of legislation to restructure the militia system:

> It is really absurd that a nation which maintains but a small regular army and depends upon unprofessional citizen soldiery for its defense should run along as we have done for one hundred and ten years under a militia law which never worked satisfactorily in the beginning, and which was perfectly obsolete before any man now fit for military duty was born. The result is that we have practically no militia system. . . . The National Guard organizations of the several states have grown

9

up in default of any national system and to meet local requirements. Their relations to the Federal Government have never
been defined or settled. The confusion, controversy, and bad
feeling arising from this uncertain status were painfully apparent
at the beginning of the war with Spain; and it must always be
the same until Congress shall exercise its constitutional power
over the subject.[13]

The Militia Act of 1903 resolved some of these problems,
although the disciples of Emory Upton still were endeavoring
to reduce the militia to third-rate status. Commonly known as
the Dick Act, after Congressman Charles W. Dick of Ohio, the
law revamped the militia by segregating it into two classes.
The Organized Militia constituted National Guard formations,
while the Reserve Militia was the non-enrolled, able-bodied
manpower of the states. Under its provisions the federal government was to arm and equip the Guardsmen. In turn, National Guard units had to hold 24 drill periods and a five-day
encampment each year. The regular Army would provide in-
structors and inspectors. Federal service was limited to nine
months, although Guardsmen might extend that service by
volunteering as a unit.[14]

Reaction was mixed. Many Guard outfits demonstrated
marked improvement. Unfortunately, promised federal equipment often arrived in dribbles, and inspection reports written
by regular officers tended to be unnecessarily harsh. In 1908
the law was amended explicitly to provide for the use of the
National Guard in foreign service. Then, in 1912 Attorney
General George W. Wickersham issued an opinion that the
militia could not be obligated to serve outside the nation's
borders. That opinion, coupled with the pervasiveness of
Upton's writings, rekindled the controversy. In 1915 Secretary of War Lindley Garrison proposed a doubling of the regular Army, formation of a Continental Army as the principal
ready reserve, and the downgrading of the National Guard to
third-line status. Guard interests fought back energetically, as
did a number of congressmen; a compromise was reached in the
National Defense Act of 1916. The new law expanded the
regulars, increased the strength and the federal supervision of
the National Guard, designated the Guard as the principal reserve force, and created an enlisted reserve for the regular
Army. This was coupled with the creation of the Reserve Officers Training Corps and the Officers Reserve Corps.

Even the standout performance of citizen soldiers during World War I failed to dilute the drive by professionals to reduce them to a minor role in the defense system. Palmer, who had been an advisor to Secretary of War Henry L. Stimson, argued against the Uptonians and in favor of a citizens' army. His testimony so impressed the Senate Military Affairs Committee that he was attached to it as an advisor and did much to shape the form of the National Defense Act of 1920. It reduced the peacetime strength of the regular Army and placed the foundation of military preparedness on the National Guard and the Organized Reserve. Where Upton had rejected the citizen soldier, Palmer believed that the citizen army was the only organization reflective of American heritage and in tune with national aspirations. He wrote:

> The problem of military organization has two aspects, a dynamic aspect and a political aspect. The measure of military force required to meet any given emergency is purely dynamic, while the form of military institutions must be determined on political grounds, with due regard to national genius and tradition. There can be no sound solution of the problem if either of these fundamental aspects is ignored. . . . The practical military statesman must recognize both of these elements of the problem. He does not propose impracticable or foreign institutions, but seeks to develop the necessary vigor and energy within the familiar institutions that have grown with the national life.[15]

In short, the professionals had been ignoring American history in their endeavors to shape a model army. It would be far better to strengthen the capabilities of a citizen army that was in harmony with democratic traditions. Although peacetime budget-cutting would dissipate some of the National Guard's vigor, passage of the 1920 law provided an enduring foundation for its future. The essential precepts of the 1920 law remain in force today, despite an era of world wars and ongoing global confrontations between superpowers. Although slogans about the "Total Force" haven't fully jelled the partnership, the relationship between the full-time professional soldier and the citizen who has devoted sufficient time to make soldiering a second profession is a stronger one that is based on mutual respect. Critics still are heard. As late as 1978, Department of Defense planners were considering reorganization schemes that included, as one option, the reduction of the National Guard to company-sized units to be integrated into the regular Army

11

structure if war came. At the same time, others in the Department of Defense were striving to shave days off of the anticipated mobilization schedules for National Guard units because they saw an urgent need to place Guardsmen in battle alongside the regulars within a few weeks' time.

Although the federal government now exercises pervasive influence over the training and qualifications of Guardsmen, the citizen soldiers continue to take great pride in their other role as state domestic emergency forces. Throughout our history this duality has been the subject of scrutiny and occasional criticism. As one writer put it:

> Each unit of the Guard is responsible to two distinct governments and serves both alternately. Each unit receives financial support from two distinct appropriations recommended by two distinct chief executives and passed by two distinct legislatures. In consequence, each unit of the Guard has, presumably, two distinct loyalties at the same time. Indeed, for nearly 200 years, the American militia with its multi-headed organization and multi-directed loyalties has completely cleaved the military axiom of a unified command.[16]

The critic is in error. Duality may be the Guard's greatest strength. During peacetime, Guardsmen train for war while serving the states. If war comes, they do not abandon their ties to community and state, but the transition to a foreign battlefield transforms them into soldiers of the nation.

---

[1] See Russell F. Weigley, *History of the United States Army* (New York: Macmillan, 1967).

[2] Ibid., p. 12.

[3] Walter Millis, *Arms and Men* (New York: Putnam, 1956), p. 23.

[4] Ibid., pp. 26-27.

[5] William H. Riker, *Soldiers of the States* (Washington: Public Affairs Press, 1957), p. 2.

[6] John C. Fitzpatrick, ed., *The Writings of George Washington* (Washington: Government Printing Office, 1932), p. 106.

[7] Washington's treatise is most easily found in appendix to General John MacAuley Palmer's *Washington-Lincoln-Wilson* (Garden City, N.Y.: Doubleday, 1930).

[8] General John MacAuley Palmer, *America in Arms* (New Haven: Yale Universiy Press, 1941), p. 65.

[9] Weigley, *History of the U. S. Army*, p. 94.

[10] John C. Calhoun, Message to the House of Representatives, December 12, 1820.

[11] Emory Upton, *The Military Policy of the United States* (Washington: Government Printing Office, 1904).

[12] Elihu Root, *Military and Colonial Policy of the United States*, ed.

Robert Bacon and James B. Scott (Cambridge: Harvard University Press, 1916), pp. 351-352.

[13] Ibid., pp. 445-446.
[14] Weigley, *History of the U. S. Army,* pp. 320-322.
[15] Palmer, *America in Arms,* p. 141.
[16] Riker, *Soldiers of the States,* p. 1.

INDIANA'S FRONTIER MILITIA

George W. Geib and William J. Watt

As scattered settlements gained toeholds in the wilderness northwest of the Ohio River, the militia began to emerge as a bulwark against the threat of marauding Indians and to help counter possible adventures by the British. The government of the Northwest Territory provided the basis for creation of the militia in the region that ultimately would encompass Indiana.

In 1788 Governor Arthur St. Clair promulgated an act to organize the militia, specifying that all males aged 16 to 50 be enrolled and provide themselves with firearms, powder, and shot. Units were organized into 64-man companies under the direction of a captain, lieutenant, and ensign. The units also included four sergeants and four corporals. Battalions consisted of eight companies, and were led by a lieutenant colonel, a major, and an adjutant. Regiments comprising two battalions were commanded by colonels. The law required that companies parade at 10 o'clock each Sunday morning near the local church and stipulated fines for non-attendance. In 1791 the act was changed to adjust parade day to Saturday and to require two hours of drill. In January, 1790, William Clark of Clarksville was named justice of the peace and captain of the militia in the Clark's Grant area, which had been reserved for veterans of George Rogers Clark's Revolutionary War expeditions in the western regions. Later that year the militia was organized at Vincennes under the command of Francis Vigo, who was commissioned a major. Militiamen enrolled in 1790, who did not qualify for a land grant under some other governmental program, were allotted 10 acres in anticipation that their services would be needed in campaigns against hostile tribes. Only 560 regulars were available to police the far-flung communities; however, only a few hundred militiamen actually would have been available for Indian-fighting duty from the settlements located in what was to become Indiana.[1]

During the 1790s a number of expeditions were mounted against Indian tribes in the Great Lakes region, but they were

14

carried out by regulars augmented by militia units from Pennsylvania and Virginia. Few Hoosier citizen soldiers were involved.

In 1800 the Northwest Territory was subdivided, with the region west of a line near the present Indiana-Ohio border becoming Indiana Territory. William Henry Harrison, who had been the Northwest Territory's delegate to Congress, was named governor. The only substantial towns were Vincennes, Kaskaskia, Cahokia, and the enclave at Clark's Grant. Settlements existed at Peoria and at Michilimackinac, a long-established outpost at the connecting channel between Lake Michigan and Lake Huron. Small trading stations functioned at Green Bay and at Prairie du Chien. An 1800 census placed Indiana's territorial population at 6,550. Initially, population growth was slow, except at Clark's Grant, because land was not available for sale to immigrants since it was public land reserved by treaty to the Indian tribes. However, after 1805 the Whitewater valley was opened to settlement and received a burgeoning influx of pioneers, while numerous hamlets began to develop on the north bank of the Ohio.

During the next decade Ohio, Michigan, and Illinois territories were formed, reducing Indiana to approximately its present state boundaries by 1809. A census taken in 1810 placed Indiana's population at 24,520.

Governor Harrison didn't arrive at Vincennes until January, 1801. Meanwhile, Indiana Territorial Secretary John Gibson began to structure the government and had organized the Indiana militia in August, 1800. Indiana's territorial militia was founded under provisions of a Northwest territorial act of 1791. It was amended by Indiana Territory in 1806 and altered substantially in 1807. The law required that able-bodied male citizens aged 18 to 45—except preachers, jail-keepers, and certain territorial officers—enroll with the captain commanding the company in their militia districts. The citizen soldier was to arm himself with musket, bayonet, extra flints, cartridges, balls, one-fourth pound of powder, knapsack, and pouch. Militia units were organized to the division level, with a major general in command. Each battalion included a company of younger men who drilled more frequently than the others and who functioned as light infantry or grenadiers. Each brigade was to create an artillery company, although cannons generally were lacking, and a troop of cavalry. Militia-

15

men provided their own uniforms, although the style was prescribed by a regimental board of officers.[2]

Provision was made to rotate militiamen for callups, since most officials believed that they would be employed frequently against Indian bands. Initially, squads within companies were assigned on a rotating basis, generally with one-eighth of the membership in each increment. Eventually, whole companies were rotated on active service. In 1811 the militia laws were amended to enable militiamen to pay an annual fine of five dollars and thereby exempt themselves from militia service. That legislation also repealed an exemption for Quakers that had been enacted only a year earlier.[3]

Militia muster days became the focal point of community social life as well as provided opportunities for the men to drill and to receive tactical instruction. Musters were less frequent, usually every two months, but they occupied nearly an entire day. Fines for non-attendance were stiff ones, potentially as high as $6 for a private and $100 for an officer. Since muster days provided the few occasions on which the majority of a community's citizens gathered together, they became events which took on political significance. Elections to militia offices provided springboards for many frontier-era political careers while the muster gathering afforded opportunities for political discussions and candidates' electioneering. Militia musters also seemed to stimulate a good deal of carousing—to the point that territorial officials prohibited whiskey salesmen from vending spirits within two miles of a militia gathering.[4]

The early military history of Indiana is inextricably linked to the War of 1812, in which the exposed western territory played a distinctive role. Most interpretations of that conflict place emphasis upon its maritime origins and conduct. The causes of the war are found in such maritime grievances as impressment of sailors, and the important battles of the war are often portrayed as naval engagements involving such warships as the frigate *Constitution*. These views, in turn, reflect the opinions of many contemporaries. One need only to read the war message of President James Madison in June, 1812, or the editorial pages of American newspapers as far west as the states of Ohio and Kentucky to realize that many landlocked Americans shared a revulsion against the abuses which the British government had perpetrated upon American sailors and shipping after 1805.[5]

16

In the Indiana Territory, on the other hand, a very different British abuse dominated popular opinion. There, in the sparsely settled area that many still called the "western country," the great question that agitated pioneer opinion was the renewal of Indian hostilities. Many had hoped that the 1795 Treaty of Greenville would bring an era of perpetual peace to the western country, but those hopes largely had been dashed after 1807. Instead, Indiana pioneers had experienced a variety of hostile Indian acts. Livestock was stolen, trade goods were plundered, and some isolated settlers were even attacked.[6]

Indian leaders themselves often attributed these hostile activities to the rapid expansion of American settlement and to the excessive hunger for land and for trade which they contended characterized most western settlers. However, the American pioneers generally rejected these interpretations and argued instead that the renewal of Indian hostilities appeared to be proof of British plots directed against American pioneers and designed to keep Americans from realizing the potential of the western country.

Although the Americans saw the hand of the British in such ways, the fact remained that the primary object of their concern had become the Shawnee Prophet and his brother, Tecumseh. Moving to the Indiana Territory from Greenville, Ohio, in 1808, the brothers had established an increasingly large Indian community along the banks of the Tippecanoe River near its junction with the Wabash. Although continually professing that their desire was merely to return to the old Indian ways and to avoid the corruption which was endemic in the existing tribes of the period, the activities of the two leaders had created increasing concern on the part of white settlers. Tecumseh was known to have traveled widely among both the western and southern Indian tribes and was known on many occasions to have spoken on behalf of a renewed Indian confederacy that would act to oppose any further white expansion. Although he normally avoided direct threats of violence, most settlers saw an obvious implication of violence.

Tecumseh, moreover, increased such fears when, in both 1810 and 1811, he held widely publicized councils with Territorial Governor William Henry Harrison during which the Indian leader assumed a threatening adversary position. By 1811, the combination of widespread Indian threats, occasional Indian violence, and Tecumseh's provocative activities had proved

17

too much for Indiana territorial authorities. Seeking and obtaining authorization from worried federal officials, Governor Harrison prepared to lead a military expedition against Prophet's Town. The expedition was to recover stolen goods, intimidate the Indian tribes, and (although Harrison denied it) probably force military action before significant British assistance could reach Tecumseh.[7]

Harrison began by assembling a force from at least three sources. First, he secured the transfer to the Indiana Territory of the Fourth Regiment of United States Infantry, a regular unit numbering approximately 400 effectives. Second, exploiting Kentucky's continued antagonism toward Indian tribes of the northwest, he obtained a number of Kentucky volunteer companies. Finally, reflecting the concern of the territory of which he was governor, Harrison obtained a modest number of Indiana militia.

The small number of Indiana militiamen who participated in the Tippecanoe campaign is a reflection not only of the small population of the territory, which numbered under 10,000 families at that time, but also of the defensive character of Indiana's militia arrangements. Beginning about 1807, when Indian troubles had begun to escalate, Harrison had requested that pioneers band together into small bodies of men who would construct fortified homes, often called stations, to which a number of families could repair in time of crisis. By 1811, the construction of such stations was widespread across the eastern, southern, and western portions of the territory; and most Indiana militiamen were providing their annual service in the construction or in the temporary garrisoning of these posts. Their utility in repelling potential Indian raids was good, but the effect of so many stations was to absorb most men who might have engaged in the upcoming campaign. In consequence, the troops who presented themselves to Harrison normally came as volunteers from the more settled areas of the state. Corydon, for example, contributed the most famous of the Tippecanoe units: Captain Spier Spencer's distinctively garbed Yellowjackets.

Harrison had learned the soldier's trade under General Anthony Wayne in the 1790s, and the preparations which the governor now undertook reflected the influence of Wayne's leadership.[8] First among these was the need for secure bases. Harrison not only refurbished the rundown fortifications at

18

Vincennes, but more important, built for himself two fortified bases north of the Indiana territorial capital. The more important of these, constructed near the site of modern Terre Haute, was named Fort Harrison. The second was a small block house constructed north of there on the Wabash River. With his lines of retreat secured, Harrison next addressed himself to the question of discipline. Earlier experiences with western volunteers had convinced him that the greatest danger to any volunteer force lay in the possibility of Indian attack upon poorly disciplined men. Accordingly, Harrison concentrated considerable emphasis upon maintaining exact formations in march and in camp and upon avoiding any stragglers who might encourage an Indian attack. Using the Wabash River to transport supplies as far north as possible, and carefully avoiding any hilly or broken country which might encourage Indian ambush, Harrison's force began moving northward in the late fall of 1811, and successfully reached Prophet's Town on the afternoon of November 6.

Arriving at a time when Tecumseh was absent seeking other allies, Harrison was greeted by representatives of the Prophet, who assured him of their peaceful intentions and who offered no resistance as Harrison occupied a high and relatively dry patch of ground some three-quarters of a mile from Prophet's Town. Deploying his forces in an irregular hollow square on that partly wooded terrain, Harrison encamped for the night. There, shortly before dawn on the morning of November 7, he was attacked by several hundred Indian warriors.[9] Later Indian accounts leave doubt why the decision was made to attack Harrison. Some blame the Prophet himself, arguing that the presence of Harrison's troops caused him to launch an attack which his brother had carefully counseled against. Other accounts stress the hotheadedness of several of the warrior bands who were living within Prophet's Town, and still other accounts stress the presence of Canadian representatives who allegedly stirred the tribes to action. Whoever made the decision, however, the bulk of the Indians in the town decided to launch three attacks upon Harrison's forces: one each from the northeast, the northwest, and the south.

In the ensuing battle, Harrison's preparations stood him in relatively good stead. His troops, sleeping with their arms, were in most cases able to leap into position before the Indians reached the encampment, and the handful of warriors who did break into the camp were quickly slain with little loss. Less satisfactory was Harrison's practice of allowing his men to maintain large campfires to ward off the autumn chill, as a number of his men were apparently injured or killed while silhouetted against those fires in the early moments of the battle. Once their initial rush had proved unsuccessful, the Indians proved remarkably tenacious in their subsequent attacks. They continued to fire into the camp even after Harrison launched a series of uncoordinated infantry and cavalry charges against them. Finally breaking off the engagement after about two hours, and taking most of their dead and wounded with them, the Indians withdrew northward, leaving Harrison in possession of the battleground. Technically, at least, the victory was his. However, Harrison's comparatively large casualties, numbering approximately one-fifth of his force, and his inability to pursue the fleeing Indians rendered the victory fairly inconclusive. He did, however, burn Prophet's Town, while his personal bearing and his successful conduct of the withdrawal to Vincennes earned widespread approval from the volunteer units of his army and went far toward explaining the commission that he later received from the Kentucky government during the War of 1812.

Although an undercurrent, the events of the western country undoubtedly had their bearing upon the final decision for war and were given mention in President Madison's war message. As the west found itself being drawn into the conflict, the Indiana Territory tended to take on less importance than the Michigan Territory to the north, where the primary American defensive positions were located at Detroit and Mackinac. To assure their defense, the government transferred the Fourth Regiment from Vincennes to Detroit early in 1812 and placed the Indiana Territory's defense once again upon its volunteer and militia units. Harrison, although hungry for military command, remained in the territory until the declaration of war actually was made.

This is not to say that the American government left the Indiana Territory totally undefended. Far to the north, well in advance of the line of settlement, were two federal Indian defense fortifications. One was the old and long-established Fort Wayne on the Maumee River; the other, the recently constructed Fort Harrison on the upper Wabash. Each was placed under the command of one company of the First United States

Infantry. These two fortresses, together with the fortified stations held by the Indiana militia, shielded the territory at the outset of the fighting.[10]

As the war began, most of the Indian tribes withdrew north toward Canada; and, as the American settlers had long prophesied, a British and Indian alliance now formed, with considerable success. A combined British and Indian force easily surprised and captured Fort Mackinac, and another Indian force massacred the retreating garrison of Fort Dearborn on the south shore of Lake Michigan. Much more serious was the disastrous failure of the projected American offensive into upper Canada (modern Ontario). Instead, little more than two months after war had been declared, the American garrison at Detroit, including the Fourth Regiment, surrendered to the British. Suddenly, in place of the conquest of Canada that many western politicians had prophesied, the War of 1812 turned into a defensive struggle in the northwest.[11]

It was at this point that the most serious military threat in Indiana's early history developed. Buoyed by their victories at Mackinac, Dearborn, and Detroit, a large Indian council held on the St. Joseph's River in late August now decided to launch an offensive against the American positions in Indiana. It is a comment upon both the defensive preparations of the Indiana settlers and the influence of the British agents among the Indian tribes that the Indians decided to launch their attacks against American military installations rather than against the numerous settlers' stations scattered across the southern part of the territory. At this time, only one isolated Indiana community was directly assaulted by the advancing Indians. This was Pigeon Roost, in modern Scott County, named after the vast number of passenger pigeons which often nested there. The Pigeon Roost settlement had mistakenly failed to erect a suitable settler fortress, even though it lay on the exposed fringe of northward settler penetration. Local legend suggests that at least some of the inhabitants had committed the further error of personally offending important Indian leaders of the time. As a consequence, some ten residents were either slain or captured in early September, 1812, and the Pigeon Roost Massacre, as it was quickly called, became the most serious atrocity in Indiana during the British and Indian War.[12]

The bulk of the Indian offensives, however, struck against the two small and lightly garrisoned posts at Fort Harrison and

21

Fort Wayne. Each fort successfully resisted the attacks launched against it, but the manner of their resistance varied considerably.

At Fort Harrison, for example, the conduct of the American defense was sufficiently impressive to vault into national prominence Captain Zachary Taylor, the fort's commander. Taylor's post should have fallen easily. It had been surrounded by some 500 hostile tribesmen and, due to an outbreak of malaria which had weakened a number of the garrison, some of the attackers had been able to crawl up to one of the fort's block-houses and set it afire at night to herald the outbreak of the siege. Taylor, however, had risen from a bout of fever, extinguished the fire, erected new breastworks, and for two days thereafter maintained a defense of the post which prevented any further Indian attacks, while limiting the garrison's losses to those of one or two men who unsuccessfully attempted to escape from the fort.[13]

Fort Wayne, on the other hand, was less blessed with its commander, James Rhea. Rhea, a captain of some 20 years service in the Army, had contracted rheumatism and with it an excessive addiction to alcohol. When another 500 tribesmen moved to surround his fort, he was able to do little except sit in his quarters yelling that the garrison would be massacred, emerging only to offer one of the Indian leaders a 50-cent bribe to withdraw from the attack. Rhea's subordinates at Fort Wayne, however, including two youthful lieutenants and a well-informed Indian agent, were able to rally the garrison's defenders and maintain a successful defense of the post for ten days. Their exploits became even more impressive when the Indians tried several ruses during the siege, including the creation of two imitation cannon, which they rolled toward the fort and fired several times before the wooden tubes exploded.[14]

In both cases, it was necessary to lift the siege by raising relief forces. Those relief forces, interestingly enough, were raised largely in Kentucky, rather than in Indiana. With the bulk of the Indiana militia still pinned down holding their fortress stations and with many Indiana residents fleeing back across the Ohio for safety as word of Pigeon Roost and other alleged atrocities began to circulate, it was necessary to turn to Kentucky for most of the forces that were used in the remainder of the year. Kentucky responded enthusiastically. A state for 20 years, with a population numbering over one-half million

people, it showed an ardor for the War of 1812 which was un-
equaled in America. The Kentuckians were not, of course, the
veterans of earlier conflicts. But, perhaps more dangerous for
the foes, they were the children of those veterans. Eager to
gain glory equal to that of their fathers, and therefore willing
to take exceptional risks and chances, 5,000 Kentucky volunteers
turned out in the summer and early autumn of 1812 for service
in the Indiana and Michigan territories.[15]

These forces were divided into two parts. One, raised in
eastern Kentucky, was to rendezvous near Newport, Kentucky,
and was then to march north through western Ohio toward
the Maumee River and Lake Erie. The other force, raised in
western Kentucky, was to rally at Vincennes, Indiana, and was
then to march north, either into the Wabash valley or out
across the prairies of Illinois as the situation should warrant.

Of these two forces the more famous, undoubtedly, is the
one that rallied at Newport, Kentucky, because this force became the nucleus of the new Northwestern Army. This army,
for the next year and one-half, would bear the responsibility
for recapturing Detroit and for initiating the long-delayed
American offensive in Canada. Wishing to promote the American cause, utilize his own experience, and participate in the
victories that he hoped would be forthcoming, William Henry
Harrison hurried to join that army. Using his reputation from
the battle of Tippecanoe, as well as his numerous political contacts in the west, Harrison was able to secure a commission as a
major general in the Kentucky militia. This commission,
coupled with his political contacts in Washington, subsequently
earned him command of the Northwestern Army in the Michigan and Ontario theaters. Many people associate the Northwestern Army with the war in Indiana. In reality, however,
the Northwestern Army generally avoided the territory of Indiana. Instead, it pushed northeast in a memorable campaign
that culminated late in 1813 with the recapture of Detroit and
the subsequent destruction of the British and Indian forces at
the Battle of the River Thames, where Tecumseh was slain.

On two occasions, however, the Northwestern Army made its
presence felt in the Indiana Territory. One of these was in
September, 1812, when the army stopped long enough on its
northward advance to lift the siege of Fort Wayne, reinforce
the garrison, and allow Harrison to remove Captain Rhea from
command. The other, more serious involvement came in De-

23

cember, 1812, when the army launched a punitive expedition against the Indian towns of northern Indiana.

Such expeditions had become a feature of western Indian war. Although it is common to associate Indians with nomadic hunters, the tribes of the old northwest were largely sedentary farmers. They lived in well-established towns, where they grew a large portion of their food supplies. Because the tribes were agricultural, it was a common practice of American expeditions to weaken a tribe's ability to resist by burning their towns and crops. In particular, post-harvest expeditions had long been considered an effective military means of subjugation. The Indian towns that most concerned the Northwestern Army were obviously those that lay along its western flank in the Indiana Territory. These towns, many of them occupied by the Miami or the Potawatami, were viewed as a natural source of recruits and as a base of operations from which the Indians could raid against the exposed supply lines that lead north from Cincinnati and Dayton.

Accordingly, late in 1812, Colonel Thomas Campbell and a mixed force of troops from the Northwestern Army, including regular Army units, volunteer units from Pennsylvania and Kentucky, and small bands of scouts, were sent west with orders to burn the Indian towns along the Wabash and Mississinewa rivers. Campbell, who had undoubtedly discussed tactics with Harrison before leaving, followed a plan of operations quite similar to that used before Tippecanoe. Every effort was made to prevent surprise raids on march or in camp, and Campbell's force had penetrated far into the Indiana Territory when, on the night of December 12, 1812, he was subjected to an attack very reminiscent of that launched against Harrison a year earlier. Attacking in the pre-dawn darkness, several hundred tribesmen struck at the northwest corner of Campbell's lines, overrunning a small advance post and then repeatedly firing into the American lines. Campbell's men, many of them mounted troops, huddled behind small breastworks or behind their horses and suffered some 35 to 40 casualties while inflicting a similar number upon their enemies. As at Tippecanoe, dawn caused the Indians to break off their attack and the American forces did not pursue them—a decision probably encouraged by worsening weather and by the loss of a number of horses. Instead, Campbell's force withdrew into Ohio, suffering greater

24

casualties from frostbite than it had suffered in the inconclusive battle.[16]

While the Northwestern Army was maneuvering on Indiana's eastern borders, the other relief force of Western Kentucky volunteers rendezvoused at Vincennes and launched two campaigns into the interior. Commanded by Samuel Hopkins, a Kentucky congressman and a major general of militia, the Vincennes force decided to strike against other important Indian towns. These towns, located along the Illinois and Tippecanoe rivers, played the same role for the western forces that the Mississinewa towns had played for Campbell's expedition. Unfortunately, Hopkins's volunteers proved less agreeable to discipline or a protracted campaign than had been true of Harrison's force. Subsequent accounts of the first, unsuccessful expedition onto the Illinois prairies laid stress upon the inadequacy of the guides, upon the appearance of terrifying prairie fires set possibly by Indians, and upon Hopkins's own weaknesses as a commander. Wherever the blame lay, Hopkins's force withdrew to Vincennes prematurely and most of the Kentucky volunteers returned home. Before disbanding his force, Hopkins mounted an additional expedition which marched up the Wabash River in the late fall of 1812 and burned a number of towns along the Wabash and Tippecanoe Rivers before the campaign ended in a costly Indian ambush along Wildcat Creek near modern Lafayette.[17]

The war in Indiana Territory subsequently lapsed into comparative obscurity during 1813, but the continued needs of the settlers for protection produced another significant feature of the war, the United States Rangers. "Ranging" was the early nineteenth century term for scouting, and the creation of small companies to "range" the frontier was a frequent practice. Harrison, for example, had maintained several small companies of Indiana rangers when hostilities erupted in 1807. Recognizing the popularity of rangers, the United States government early in 1812 had authorized four mounted companies in the northwest and subsequently expanded this to approximately 18 companies. Of this force, roughly one-fourth was designated for the Indiana Territory. Each ranger company consisted of 40 to 60 mounted troops, enlisted for one year and intimately acquainted with the terrain and geography of their own area. The Indiana ranger units were placed under the command of William Russell, colonel of the Seventh United

25

States Regiment, and were based in such towns as Vincennes and Vallonia, where they became the basis of defense for the remainder of the war.[18]

In theory, the purpose of each ranger company was to divide into small groups across a broad area of terrain looking for Indian sign and, if finding it, to go rapidly to notify local settlements. Should Indians appear in large numbers, the rangers were expected to consolidate, move to whatever fort or station was threatened, and become the core of defense against the attackers. Local militia units were expected to co-operate with the rangers in at least two ways. First, if they would volunteer, the militia would garrison such ranger forts as Vallonia and hopefully cooperate in scouting operations. Second, local units were certainly expected to defend the small forts and stations which might be the target of Indian raids.

Some of the western ranger units, notably in the Missouri and Illinois territories, engaged in well-publicized campaigns. In Indiana the rangers were little tested because few Indians returned to the state after 1812. Their absence could be traced to the serious defeats being suffered by the British along Lake Erie in 1813, as well as the burning of many Indian towns in 1812. When Indians did return to Indiana, moreover, they returned as small war parties seldom numbering more than 20 men from such tribes as the Potawatomi and the Kickapoo. These small war parties presented little threat to any except the most exposed settlements and produced only isolated casualties of one or two settlers per month during 1813 and 1814. So overwhelming was the settler and ranger presence by late 1813 that many of the more docile Indian tribes which had escaped burning and punishment in the early days of the war, now arrived at informal peace arrangements with the local settlers and crossed over to accept the protection of the American forces.

Only once in this period did any serious activities result from Indian raids. In March, 1813, a small Indian force was detected north of Vallonia in Jackson County. Learning of them, a mixed force commanded by John Tipton, a veteran of the Battle of Tippecanoe and a future United States Senator, hurried north in pursuit. A small portion of the Indian party was overtaken on the Driftwood River, (the modern east fork of White River) and the so-called Battle of Tipton's Island ensued where a few of the Indians were slain or injured before escaping.[19]

The comparatively small number and docile behavior of the Indian tribes in Indiana encouraged the rangers to take the offensive. Late in the summer of 1813, a force massed at Vallonia to carry on further expeditions against the Indian towns. Uniting regular troops from Fort Harrison, ranger companies, and mounted volunteers from both Indiana and Kentucky, Colonel Russell made a 500-mile sweep that circled most of Indiana. He burned the few remaining hostile towns, destroyed most of the remaining Indian crops, and confirmed that most hostile Indians had fled the state.[20]

The larger war dragged on for another inconclusive year until ended by a negotiated *status quo ante bellum* peace settlement at Ghent. However, the war's results were already clear in Indiana, where the Indians had been defeated.

Indiana's state constitution, adopted in 1816, declared able bodied men aged 18 to 45 as members of the militia, although blacks and Indians were exempted. The General Assembly was given the authority to prescribe their arms, equipment, and training; lawmakers also were empowered to allocate the number and location of units and to set the ranks of staff officers. The governor's chief military subordinates were designated the adjutant general and quartermaster general. Officers' commissions were to be issued by the governor and be valid for "good behavior" or until the officer reached the age of 60. Conscientious objectors could avoid militia enrollment and duty, but were required to pay an annual fine equal to the lowest fines assessed militia privates for failure to attend drills.

Although Indiana's population had nearly tripled during the short period of time between the 1810 census and the achievement of statehood, settlement remained concentrated in the Ohio River borderlands and the hill counties of southern Indiana. In the years that followed, the remaining Indians gradually were displaced through a series of cessions and treaties, which usually provided modest annual payments to the tribes in turn for their agreement to withdraw westward out of the state by a specified time. As the tribes gave way a stream of immigrants worked northward into the river valleys of central and western Indiana; new towns flourished during the decade following statehood.[21]

Although state government devoted considerable attention to

27

militia affairs by perfecting existing legislation and by diligently compiling annual muster rolls for transmission to the War Department, the frontier militia already had passed its high water mark. In 1819 the last garrison of regulars was withdrawn from frontier outpost duty at Fort Wayne. Even though northwest Indiana was only sparsely settled, it was clear that the end of the frontier era was close at hand. Only small groups of Indians remained in the state. While most whites' hostility toward them continued to be violent, the threat of raids and warfare had diminished.

The last great Indian scare occurred during the Black Hawk War, which was not fought on Indiana soil. Black Hawk, who sympathized with the British, led a group of Sauks in northwestern Illinois. Although the Sauks technically had ceded tribal lands to the government, the elderly leader took offense when squatters occupied his fields and townsites while the tribe was absent on a winter hunt in 1831. During the ensuing months, tension mounted and the anti-Indian attitudes of regular soldiers and Illinois politicians stiffened. In the spring of 1832 Illinois Governor John Reynolds considered the Sauks' threats against the squatters and the tribe's refusal to leave to be tantamount to acts of war. The Illinois militia was activated and regular forces under General Henry Atkinson prepared to move against the tribe.

Reports of skirmishes and Indian raids, both real and rumored, triggered panic in the settlements along the Wabash and in the frontier prairie regions northwest of that river. On May 18, 1832, an alarm was raised that hostile Indians were on the warpath and were headed east to Lafayette. Local militia units responded to the emergency and moved to engage them, encountering a torrent of refugees from rural areas and small towns in western Indiana and eastern Illinois. A similar panic swept settlements in the Lake Michigan region as families made hasty departures for points well to the east and south. Governor Noah Noble activated the militia of Marion, Johnson, and Hendricks counties and dispatched them to Lafayette. Neither this contingent nor the local militiamen from the frontier areas encountered any Sauks during the course of their reconnaissances. Meanwhile, Congress had authorized the levying of several companies of rangers to patrol the frontier region until the emergency passed. Indiana raised two companies, but they did not see any fighting because Black Hawk's

28

band was all but annihilated at the battle of Bad Axe on the Mississippi River near the present site of Victory, Wisconsin.[22]

Aside from being one of the more regrettable episodes in white-Indian relations, the Black Hawk War had the effect of solidifying the animosity of frontier dwellers against the tribes. Never again, whites argued, should they be exposed to the dangers of an Indian uprising. Removal of the remaining clusters of Indian bands from their lodgments in northern Indiana was an outgrowth of the hatred generated by the Sauk conflict, piled on top of a dark tradition of incidents of massacre and terror in remote frontier settlements.

During 1833 Indian agents began negotiations to secure the tribes' departure, through persuasion, payment, or intimidation. The Potawatomies, historic dwellers of the lands bordering Lake Michigan's south rim, proved to be stubborn. Although a group of commissioners succeeded in achieving contract purchases of certain lands (at 50 cents an acre), the government refused to approve the transactions. In 1836 the tribe was bought out at one dollar per acre on the condition that the Potawatomies would have two years to leave the state. However, in anticipation of their removal and the land sale that might follow, squatters began to occupy tribal lands. Occasional violence resulted. Colonel Edward A. Hannegan brought a militia company to the region of present-day Marshall County in hopes of restoring order; he was not successful. Hints of trouble with both the Potawatomies and Miamis stimulated Governor David Wallace to call out the militia of Cass and Miami counties under the command of John Tipton. Tipton's men arrived at Twin Lakes on August 30, 1838, where about 200 Indians were meeting in council with the Indian agent, Colonel Abel C. Pepper. Despite Tipton's urgings, the Indians refused to leave. Tipton disarmed them and sent patrols to scour the region for other natives. The patrols gathered about 700 Indians, destroyed their lodges, and confiscated their property.

Under the guns of militiamen, the Indians were forcibly removed, first to Logansport, then west to the Tippecanoe battleground, and then to Danville, Illinois, where Indiana militiamen turned over the group to federal authorities who transported them to Kansas. The westward trek through Indiana became known as the "trail of death" because food and wagon transport were inadequate. The elderly and children became exhausted; many died. By the time they reached the

29

state line, nearly half of the 800 Indians were unfit for travel. More than 150 died before the trail of death ended in the Osage River region of Kansas.[23]

Only miniscule Indian settlements remained in Indiana after the enforced removal in 1838. Indiana's frontier period was over. No longer required for what had been its fundamental reason for being, the Indiana militia entered a period of decline, leaving independent companies to carry on the tradition of citizen soldiering, while the district militia system largely consisted of paper organizations.

[1] Logan Esarey, *A History of Indiana* (Indianapolis: Bowen, 1918, 2 vols.; reprint ed., Indianapolis: Hoosier Heritage Press, 1970), pp. 165-167.

[2] *Laws of Indiana Territory* (Springfield: Illinois Historical Society, 1930, 2 vols., reprint ed., Indianapolis: Indiana Historical Bureau, 1931), Vol. I, p. 213; 399-425.

[3] Ibid., Vol. II, p. 280.

[4] Esarey, *History of Indiana*, pp. 166-167.

[5] The conflicting visions stirred by the declaration of war can be seen in Bradford Perkins, *The Causes of the War of 1812* (New York: Holt, Rinehart, Winston, 1962).

[6] Early frontier conditions are captured in William Cockrum, *Pioneer History of Indiana* (Oakland City: Journal Press, 1907).

[7] See the Vincennes *Western Sun,* Indiana's only newspaper at that time; also Logan Esarey, ed., *Messages and Letters of William Henry Harrison,* 2 vols. (Indianapolis: Indiana Historical Commission, 1922).

[8] George W. Geib, "William Henry Harrison," *Dictionary of American Military Biography,* Roger Spiller, ed. (New York: Greenwood, 1980).

[9] Robert McAfee, *History of the Late War in the Western Country* (Lexington: Worsley & Smith, 1816).

[10] Alec R. Gilpin, *The War of 1812 in the Old Northwest* (East Lansing: Michigan State University Press, 1958).

[11] Harry L. Coles, *The War of 1812* (Chicago: University of Chicago Press, 1965).

[12] Carl Bogardus, *The Pigeon Roost Massacre* (Austin, Ind.: Muscatatuck Press, 1962).

[13] Holman Hamilton, *Zachary Taylor: Soldier of the Republic,* 2 vols. (Indianapolis: Bobbs-Merrill, 1941).

[14] George W. Geib, "Fort Wayne in the British and Indian War: The Siege of 1812," *Indiana Military History Journal,* October, 1977.

[15] James Hammack, *Kentucky and the Second American Revolution,* (Lexington: Kentucky Bicentennial Commission, 1976).

[16] Elizabeth J. Glenn, *Ethnohistorical and Archaeological Descriptive Accounts of the War of 1812 Mississinewa Campaign and Aftermath,* Ball State University Archaeological Reports, November 16, 1977.

[17] "The Expeditions of Major General Samuel Hopkins up the Wabash, 1812," *Indiana Magazine of History,* Vol. 43, No. 4.

[18] An entertaining, popular account is Herbert R. Hill, "Vallonia Area is Scenic and Historic," *Outdoor Indiana*, October, 1978.

[19] Nellie Robertson and Dorothy Riker, *The John Tipton Papers* (Indianapolis: Indiana Historical Bureau, 1942).

[20] An outstanding source is Richard Knopf, ed., *Document Transcriptions of the War of 1812 in the Northwest*, 11 vols. (Columbus, Ohio: Anthony Wayne Parkway Board, 1957-62).

[21] Esarey, *A History of Indiana*, pp. 223-30, 323-325.

[22] Ibid., pp. 325-332; Sandford C. Cox, *Old Settlers: Recollections of the Early Settlement of the Wabash Valley* (Lafayette: Courier Printing, 1860; reprint ed., Indianapolis: Hoosier Heritage Press, 1970), pp. 86-97.

[23] Esarey, *A History of Indiana*, pp. 333-339; Irving McKee, "The Trail of Death," Indianapolis: Indiana Historical Society Publications, 1941), Vol. 14.

THE MEXICAN WAR ERA

George W. Geib

Prior to 1835 Indiana's military affairs had been dominated by the state's frontier and pioneer character, close to the world of the Indian, far removed from the centers of American civilization, and often governed in large measure by proximity to the British presence in Canada. After 1835 this character changed rapidly. New canals, new roads, and a resulting rapid influx of new settlers quickly filled the state from south to north.[1] By 1860 Indiana was being quickly integrated into the new and bustling life of the aggressive young American republic.

Those changes were accompanied by changes in the Indiana militia, which tended to alter and to develop slowly, sometimes in unusual ways, in the 25 years that preceded the Civil War. During this period, Indiana continued to maintain and to develop the type of two-level militia system which had become general in the United States under the operation of the federal Militia Act of 1792.[2] At one level, at least in theory, all adult Indiana males continued to enjoy a militia obligation, a responsibility to appear at an appropriate county or township center for a certain number of days of training each year, and an obligation to turn out in a time of crisis, rebellion, or invasion to protect the state against any foreign or domestic enemies that might appear. At the same time, however, Indiana law after 1842 permitted any individual who chose to do so to serve his militia obligation not through the district system, but to serve it instead through separate volunteer or, as they were called in Indiana, independent companies. These had gradually organized in a number of the more established cities and counties of the state, and like their volunteer counterparts throughout much of the rest of the United States, were organizations made up of individuals who had agreed to provide some military contribution beyond the legal minimum. Most commonly this took the form of added time devoted to drill and preparation, or of additional money spent in the purchase of uniforms, accoutrements, and entertainment during their days of drill.[3]

Both systems remained in operation throughout the period from 1835 to 1860. With the removal of the clear and imminent danger that once made the militia necessary, the district system went into a rapid and ultimately terminal decline.[4] Attendance at training days, for example, plummeted rapidly. After 1832, no Indiana militia unit was able to maintain an accurate muster roll, despite the state law which required such a report to the state's adjutant general. Even where small numbers of individuals did continue to appear on training days, local observers repeatedly recorded the lack of discipline and the general holiday spirit that increasingly characterized the time. Even though federal shipments of arms to the state of Indiana continued to be made on an annual basis for the equipment of the militia, commentators similarly reported that most militia men who appeared were armed with little more than rakes and cornstalks, looking not to the defense of their state but merely to the fulfillment of an obligation that was increasingly irrelevant to most citizens.

The system, however, did not totally die. Small numbers of Hoosiers continued to honor the obligation Indiana law still imposed upon them; and, probably of considerably more importance, politically ambitious men throughout the state continued to recognize opportunities for public advancement in a militia system that offered captive audiences on training days, as well as titles of rank for officers. State officials encouraged these practices by regular exhortations to the citizenry and, perhaps more effectively, by regularly granting commissions to those individuals who secured election as officers and thereby maintained a shadowy, paper organization up to the days of the Civil War.

The future, however, clearly lay with the independent companies. Initially composed of the more socially elite and prestigious individuals of the community who possessed both the time and the wealth necessary to provide the special additional commitments that such company membership imposed on them, their organizations had become a regular feature of the parades and hoopla that characterized the bustling society of early Indiana. Clad in uniforms of blue or gray, whose styles increasingly reflected the new, vibrant romanticism of the nineteenth century, these were the units which encompassed the increasing number of individuals who made a true commitment to the militia. By the late 1840s, the numbers of commissions in the independent companies that were issued each year by the governor of Indiana surpassed the number of commissions granted to the district system. After 1842, these "old" companies, as many of the independent volunteers had come to be called, represented the core around which any serious military recruitment or military activity would need to be conducted in the state.

The key test of the Hoosier volunteer, however, took place not in Indiana but far away in Mexico in the years between 1846 and 1848.[5] To this day, the roots of the Mexican War remain clouded in controversy and in obscurity. Bred out of the exuberant expansionism of the American republic in the 1830s and 40s, begun under controversial and disputed circumstances along the Rio Grande in the spring of 1846, the war with Mexico was welcomed enthusiastically by the ruling Democratic party and was supported by sizeable majorities in both houses of Congress. Although a vocal minority voiced deep suspicions of the war's alleged ties to the expansion of slavery, and the emergence of a southern "slave" power, the dominant mood in Indiana in 1846 was clearly one of support for the war.[6] It was a mood of support that was quickly put to the test through the federal government's need to raise these troops by expanding the regular Army; and several Indiana companies were, in fact, raised for the 16th Infantry Regiment whose recruiting area lay within the territory of the old Northwest.

In the summer of 1846 the government decided that a majority of the troops who would be used to fight in Mexico would be raised through the traditional system of short-term volunteers, recruited within the various states of the Union that had shown political support for the war. To that end, the War Department informed the governor of Indiana, James Whitcomb, that his state was requested to contribute three regiments of one-year volunteers to be recruited in a manner appropriate to the state of Indiana and sent to participate in the battles of the northern Mexican theater. Later commentators, who generally delighted in expressing the difficulties and disadvantages that the decaying militia system suffered, were quick to point to the obstacles that stood in the way of fulfilling the government's request. Apart from the governor himself, the only officer within state government who was charged with responsibility for the militia was the adjutant general, a political appointee named David Reynolds. Living on a salary of $100 per year, and operating from a small office in the state capitol building without clerical assistance, Reynolds, like his predecessors, held his position as political preferment. He had little responsibility in peacetime other than that of processing the 100 to 200 requests that came in each year for military commissions in the district and independent militia companies.

Now, however, these two officials were suddenly and abruptly faced with the responsibility of raising a major combat force. Volunteers were essential, thanks to the practice common to the time of limiting by law the obligation of most militiamen to service within the state of their residence. Thus, while independent or district companies could be invited to participate in the war, it would not be possible to compel service once the troops had left the state of Indiana. To meet this challenge, Whitcomb and Reynolds decided to employ traditional methods of open recruiting. They hoped to locate numbers of ambitious young potential officers seeking political advancement, personal recognition, or public service, who could be called upon to go within their communities and recruit the 70 to 80 privates who would constitute each of the needed companies.

The state's recruiting regulations were simple in outline. Basically, any individual who chose to do so could strive to recruit others to join him to form a company. Once any 70 to 80 individuals had met together and agreed that they would constitute a company, they had the opportunity to elect a captain and two lieutenants to command it. Once that election had taken place, it was the responsibility of the captain to communicate to the governor and the adjutant general the fact of the company's creation; and it was, in turn, the governor's responsibility to accept the first 30 companies who reported themselves to him as the Indiana forces in the war.

Informally, the methods of raising a company apparently varied from area to area. Although county histories are not clear as to the methods of recruitment, it would appear that in some locations "old" companies proved to be the basis of recruitment, being largely absorbed into the new volunteer companies. In still other locations, it appears that politically prominent individuals who had once held commissions within the district militia system used their community and personal positions and influence to recruit friends and connections to form new companies separate from the existing militia structures. At still other locations, evidence suggests that independent, patriotically motivated citizens who had few, if any, ties with a local power base, let alone that of the militia, chose to go out and raise the company on their own.[7] The best account we have is that of Lew Wallace, then a youthful Hoosier residing in Indianapolis. In his memoirs, Wallace recounts that, upon hearing of the declaration of war and of the call for volunteers, he personally visited the governor to inquire the method of raising a company. The governor outlined the procedure; and Wallace, acting upon that information, proceeded to rent a small downtown office and to hire an artist who prepared color transparencies urging men to fall in for the war. Then Wallace hired, again from his own funds, a drummer and fifer who were to follow him about the city as he went from place to place urging men to join. To Wallace's surprise, some 75 men responded to those calls; though, as an indication of the policies of the time, Wallace himself was only elected second lieutenant of the company. The captaincy passed to one of the early recruits who, in Wallace's words, "sat well upon a horse."[8]

By such varied methods, 52 companies offered their services to Whitcomb in 1846. In accordance with the published procedures, Whitcomb accepted the first 30 and instructed them to travel by the most expeditious means to the site of old Fort Clark near Jeffersonville, a location the troops renamed Camp Whitcomb in his honor. There the governor quickly appeared, interviewed the officers, and divided the companies along geographic lines into three regiments, the first from the northern region of the state, the second from the southeast, and the third from the southwest.

Once the regiments had been formed, Whitcomb and Reynolds in turn called for the election of regimental officers. As loyal Democrats they were careful to prepare in advance an approved list of candidates, assuring that an overwhelming majority of the senior officers would share Governor Whitcomb's political preference. The only difficulty which occurred in this smooth election process came from the success of one of the newly elected colonels, Joseph Lane, who was appointed brigadier general by President Polk to assume overall command of the Indiana forces. The vacancy which Lane thereby created within the Second Indiana Regiment was quickly filled through the election of a Paoli physician, William Bowles. The Bowles election, however, was curiously clouded. Bowles was chosen in a battle with another Democrat who apparently would have won the balloting if one company's ballots had not been withheld from the count by a dissatisfied officer. The confusion was so great that a second election had to be held when the regiment reached Texas, and Bowles himself was later to assert that his authority was compromised for the remainder of the war by the resulting confusion. If the purpose was, as most observers believed, to ensure Democratic rather than Whig control of the Indiana units, this purpose was indeed achieved.[9]

As the elections were being completed, Whitcomb and Reynolds attempted to complete the equipment and supplies that were necessary for the troops. In most cases, the volunteers had arrived with many of the possessions they would need for the war already in hand. Cash advances from various state banks permitted the purchase of most routine camp items as cooking utensils and blankets, while government military arsenals along the Ohio and Mississippi armed the men. Ultimately, eight of the ten companies of each regiment were armed with muskets and the remaining two with rifles from the arsenal at Baton Rouge.

Once equipped, the troops were rapidly moved to the theater of war, as steam navigation made possible a fast trip along the Ohio, the Mississippi, and the Gulf coast. Only at points of trans-shipment were the movements of troops delayed. Thus, when steamboats were to unload them in New Orleans, it was discovered that transportation along the Gulf was not yet available; and the first real taste of camp life that most Indiana volunteers experienced was in the boggy fields south of New Orleans near the site of the battles of 1815. As Hoosier troops moved later toward the American camps near the mouth of the Rio Grande, adverse wind conditions caused a portion of them to be stranded for periods of time on sand bars and gave to those who had expected little more than a lark a sense of the rigor of campaigning in the deep south. Much more serious than the problem of transportation was that of disease, which soon beset the Indiana forces. Coming from isolated areas which had been relatively untouched by the epidemics of the nineteenth century, many began to fall prey to such killers as measles.

The fact that accounts of such camp problems dominated the

37

memoirs of the Indiana volunteers is indicative of a larger problem that they faced. Although the regiments were recruited promptly, and although they did in fact arrive in the war theater earlier than units from several other states, the Indiana units initially saw little military action. The First Regiment, for example, spent its entire year of service under Colonel James P. Drake with nothing but garrison duty and the hope, always frustrated, of being transferred to the actual scene of the war. Arguing that it was necessary to protect his lines of communication, General Zachary Taylor, commander of American forces in that northern Mexican theater, placed the First Indiana in or about Matamoris, near the mouth of the Rio Grande, to guard his communication and supplies. The First Regiment vigorously protested, and, in one instance, exploited confused orders from subordinates in the hope of marching to the scene of combat, but were always denied in this regard. Even the Second and Third Indiana regiments, although they were ultimately to see combat, initially found themselves left far behind. When the battles around Monterey took place, Indiana troops were still in camp or in routes of march across northern Mexico.

To this day, the question arises as to why General Taylor did not choose to make more use of the Indiana forces. His argument at the time, frequently repeated to the unhappy troops, was that someone had to guard the supplies and communications, and that it had simply fallen to Indiana by the luck of the draw to perform that function. Indiana leaders, on the other hand, became increasingly suspicious that politics may have had something to do with it. In a brigade that was overwhelmingly Democratic in composition, it was no doubt easy to see political motives in the behavior of a general who would soon be a Whig candidate for President. Whatever the case, the fate of the Indiana troops was the fate of all troops relegated to garrison and supply duties. Boredom, fatigue, and camp disorders dominated their lives.

The situation of the Second and Third regiments, however, altered abruptly early in 1847 as a consequence of strategic decisions made outside the northern theater. These decisions were primarily those of President James K. Polk and represented a basic shift of the theater of war. Initially, Polk had hoped to win the war through battles fought by Taylor along the northern frontier. As the war in the north proved increasingly inconclusive and as Taylor's star continued to rise within the opposition Whig party, Polk decided to shift the theater of operations south to Vera Cruz and along the National Road to Mexico City. The President further decided to give that command to General Winfield Scott and began to shift to Scott many of the units that originally had fought with Taylor. "Old Rough and Ready" soon found himself with no more than a dozen units spread along the entire northern frontier, among them the three regiments of the Indiana Brigade. The First was still at Matamoris; but the Second and Third were now added to his main field force in the area around Monterey and Saltillo, well into the interior of northern Mexico.

American strategy envisioned Taylor's force as little more than a corps of observation, but the Mexican forces under Santa Anna quickly recognized the small size of Taylor's command. Early in 1847 the Mexicans decided to take advantage of Taylor's numerical weakness by pushing north with a large force that would, it was hoped, destroy Taylor, reassert Santa Anna's reputation in Mexican military affairs, and thereby improve morale for the defense of the National Road against Scott's far larger army. To face Taylor's 4,500-member American force, Santa Anna accordingly brought together approximately 22,000 Mexican troops. Many of those were relatively low quality militia; but others represented good regular units of the Mexican army, including several high quality cavalry regiments.

The geography of northern Mexico made the natural northward advance of Santa Anna's army that of the road between Saltillo and San Luis Potosi. To that end, Taylor had moved most of his forces to the Saltillo road. Uncertain as to the size of the Mexican force, but recognizing that he would be outnumbered and placed on the defensive, Taylor chose a defensive location some miles south of Saltillo, which he felt best suited the needs of the American forces. The location, now named for the Buena Vista ranch, lay in a north-south direction between two high ranges of peaks. Through the valley ran the road to Saltillo, intersected on either side by deep ravines cut by the heavy rains which fall in other seasons. Taylor chose the site primarily because the high peaks protected his flank from all but relatively light skirmishing units and because the ravines and the few hills that lay between them offered excellent positions behind which his infantry could shelter themselves or upon which his artillery could be mounted for maximum effectiveness.[10]

In deploying his troops, Taylor attempted to hold the mountain flanks by posting to them small skirmishing units. He chose for the eastern, or left flank, of the American forces several rifle companies, including four companies of the Second and Third Indiana regiments. To the center, where he believed the bulk of the Mexican forces would ultimately be committed, Taylor placed most of his artillery and, in a thin and somewhat disconnected line that extended over a mile from west to east, the remaining regiments that were available to him. Among them, the Third Indiana Regiment was posted near the Saltillo road and the Second Indiana was placed at the far left of the valley, guarding the American line between the mountain and the road. Taylor apparently had anticipated that the main Mexican assault would fall upon the area near the road and, accordingly, had left the Second Indiana with little support apart from a three-gun battery of artillery.

Noting this weakness, when Santa Anna arrived and deployed his forces, he chose instead to launch the first major Mexican attack of the battle against that exposed flank position. Thus, after some light skirmishing on the mountain peaks in the late afternoon of February 22, 1847, Santa Anna on the morning of the 23rd massed a number of his infantry regiments, backed them by a portion of his lancers, concealed them as best he could in other ravines that ran across the mountain valley, and moved them toward the Second Indiana's position. Word of the impending Mexican advances was late to reach the American forces and upon reaching them apparently resulted in some confusion.

The confusion owed a good deal to the fact that the Second Indiana was in doubt that day as to who its actual commander was. Present on the field, and officially responsible for the conduct of the regiment, was Colonel William Bowles, the Paoli physician who had been chosen in the disputed election some months earlier. But present also and attached personally to the Second Indiana was General Joseph Lane. Lane, who had quarreled heavily with the commander of the Third Indiana, generally absented himself from those troops and, since the First Indiana was far away in Matamoris, had in large degree reassumed effective command of the Second from Bowles. The two men, moreover, had apparently had a personal falling out

40

which caused them on the day of the battle to take positions at opposing ends of the long line occupied by the 400 men of the eight companies that stood in the valley. Bowles was positioned at the far right and Lane at the far left, each apparently out of hearing of the other, when the Mexican assault struck their small force.

For the next 20 minutes one of the more intense small unit engagements of the war ensued. The Second Indiana, reinforced by its artillery battery, initially stood its ground well. Firing between 20 and 25 rounds at the enemy, they apparently inflicted casualties on the Mexican force that may have totaled between 500 and 600 men. So great were those casualties that at one point several of the more forward Mexican units were seen to fall back and to be held in the engagement only by bayonet-wielding units of their own army, who forced them back into action.

But at this point, the Second Indiana suddenly and abruptly broke. Beginning with the companies on its far right flank, one after another they began falling back from the action despite the best efforts of several officers, including Zachary Taylor himself. Once the withdrawal began, they were rallied only with great difficulty, a small number of the men retreating all the way to Buena Vista ranch before they were reorganized and another portion seeking refuge with the nearest American unit, the Mississippi regiment under the command of Jefferson Davis.

The disorderly withdrawal of the Indiana regiment presented General Taylor with the greatest crisis of the battle of Buena Vista. Fortunately for his later reputation, there were two other units near the scene that were able to rally the faltering Hoosiers and to present a front that was able to repulse the Mexican advance. One was Davis's Mississippi regiment; the other was the Third Indiana which marched across the field to join them. Numbering about two-thirds of the total men committed, the Third Indiana laid considerable claim after the battle to being the true heroes of the engagement.

In his subsequent report, Taylor attributed the Second Indiana's withdrawal to those momentary panics which he argued all volunteer units were subject to at one point or another. He further indicated that he bore no animosity against the Second Indiana, which he pointed out had in large measure rallied and which he had himself placed in the front of the American lines

41

should the action have continued on February 24. In fact, the entire episode might soon have been forgotten had it not attracted wide attention in the American press. A staff officer attached to Taylor, by the name of Kingsbury, produced immediately after the battle a highly colored account under the name "Buena Vista." He submitted it to New Orleans papers, from which it was widely reprinted around the country. The account, written in the romantic and exaggerated style of the mid-nineteenth century, placed heavy stress upon the cowardice of the Second Indiana Regiment while ignoring withdrawals made by several other units during the course of the battle. When the account reached Indiana it apparently produced a storm of criticism directed against the troops of that regiment. Embarrassing as those criticisms might be to the enlisted men, they were particularly embarrassing to the politically ambitious officers involved.

As a consequence, a search quickly ensued to ascertain the true cause for the regiment's retreat.[11] At least within the minds of the reigning Democratic party, the responsibility for that retreat was quickly fastened upon the head of the unfortunate William Bowles. Bowles, it was discovered, had in fact ordered the regiment to retreat. Later testimony in a court of inquiry showed that Bowles had, at least twice, given the command "cease firing and withdraw," without designating a place further back upon the battlefield to which they should withdraw. The companies nearest to Bowles had apparently acted upon his instructions and others, although not hearing the command, had apparently followed suit when they saw their supporters to the right falling back from the field. In particular, Bowles found himself hounded for these shortcomings by General Lane, whose political ambitions were commensurate with his rank and who was particularly insistent that some form of court martial or court of inquiry be convened, if only to clear Lane's reputation. Ultimately, such a court was held, but the result was not wholly to Lane's liking. The court did conclude that Bowles's long absence from his regiment, primarily in search of protection for his commission, had in fact robbed Bowles of the experience necessary to command companies and battalions in the field. However, the court did not choose to treat Bowles as a coward and joined, to a degree, with General Taylor in commending Bowles for his personal presence and bravery upon the battlefield.

42

Several factors probably explain why other officers upon the scene at Buena Vista did not join with the Indiana Democratic leaders in heaping opprobrium upon Bowles's character. For one thing, they noted in Lane's initial report of the engagement that he had made no adverse mention of Bowles and had only raised the charges after subsequent publicity and politics had made the issue significant. Many apparently shared General Taylor's belief that the entire affair was motivated more by political necessity than by any consideration of military discipline. For another thing, the officers on the field were apparently reluctant to press too deeply into the conduct of the Indiana forces lest such an inquiry spill over to encompass other officers involved. An inquiry into the Second Indiana's behavior would ultimately have to ask why the unit had been placed in such an exposed position. While this might not have reflected on General Taylor, it would almost certainly have involved General John Wool, who had given the specific orders which placed the unit at the point from which they later withdrew. Finally, any inquiry which attempted to place the blame fully upon Bowles would have left unanswered the behavior of the several Indiana companies which had not been within hearing of the colonel. They had been part of the line under General Lane's personal command, and although General Lane had ordered an advance at almost the exact same moment that Bowles ordered retreat, no company within hearing of Lane had obeyed the order to advance. Their withdrawal without orders and their subsequent failure to rally promptly and effectively, even when offered the protection of the Mississippi regiment, tend to suggest that Bowles deserved only a portion of blame.[12]

General Taylor certainly had no desire to see his very impressive victory over an opposing force nearly four times his size compromised by the petty politicking that seemed to follow it. In consequence, the entire affair tended to be downplayed by the other American forces. It might even have been entirely forgotten if a year later Taylor had not presented himself for the Presidency. Then, in the state of Indiana, the ruling Democratic party would obviously use any opportunity available to embarrass and to dispute his candidacy. The fact that Taylor had not joined with the Democratic leadership in placing the blame upon the unfortunate Colonel Bowles, and the assumption that General Taylor thereby seemed to cast at

43

least some aspersion on the Indiana troops, proved to be an attractive campaign issue. Throughout the 1848 campaign the behavior of the entire Second Indiana Regiment was one of the central and debated issues of the campaign. Whether it was ultimately decisive in determining the Indiana vote is questionable, but General Taylor did lose the Indiana electoral vote.[13]

Whatever the political ramifications may have been, the battle of Buena Vista marked the effective end of any combat that the first three Indiana regiments were likely to see. In the ensuing months, they retained responsibility for guarding a now quiet northern frontier, engaging in little more than small skirmishes with bands of Mexican guerrillas who began to operate in the areas. In the late spring, when their one-year enlistments expired, they were promptly taken back to the American camps at the mouth of the Rio Grande to retrace the steps that had brought them a year earlier into the Mexican theater. Greeted by enthusiastic crowds in the Ohio valley upon their return, most were mustered out along the Ohio River although many units retained their integrity until they reached their home towns where they could engage in a final victory parade and where, on numerous occasions, they could be presented by the ladies of the town with an appropriate souvenir flag.

Disbanding the three Indiana regiments did not, however, end Indiana's participation in the Mexican War. With the issue in Mexico still in doubt because Scott's army was bogged down along the road to Mexico City, it was decided in Washington in 1847 that additional regiments should be raised, among them two more from Indiana.[14] Recruitment began in the spring of 1847 when the War Department asked Governor Whitcomb to duplicate the procedures of the previous year. Reynolds and Whitcomb repeated these procedures but stipulated that any company organized too late to participate in the 1846 campaign could have precedence in being accepted for the 1847 campaign. Of the 22 companies that had been organized too late to take part in 1846, two availed themselves of this opportunity and became the first two companies of the Fourth Regiment.

Eight additional companies were organized, some of them apparently incorporating in their numbers veterans who had returned from the Rio Grande theater in the preceding weeks. The presence of those veterans in the army probably explains the difference in the names the companies took for themselves. Where in 1846 companies had called themselves the "Blues" or the "Grays" or the "Guards," by 1847 they were using such labels as the "Shelbyville Hards" and the "Grabbers No. 2." Once raised, the regiment under Colonel W. A. Gorman retraced the familiar path of the earlier Indiana units. Rapidly transported down the Ohio, Mississippi, and the Gulf, it was initially placed under the command of General Taylor and became part of the army of observation that he continued to maintain along the northern frontier.

Shortly thereafter, Indiana was called upon to add a fifth and final regiment of infantry for the war. But in the case of this regiment, the government adopted a somewhat different procedure. Rather than ask the governor to raise the troops, it turned instead to the commander of the most successful of the three Indiana regiments of 1846, Colonel James Lane of the Third Indiana.[15]

Lane was known to be a Democrat, but apparently had deep personal animosities toward many of the other figures who had been active during the period, including General Joseph Lane. James Lane was now called forth to personally organize a new Fifth Regiment, with the interesting additional stipulation that he should give precedence, and attempt in every way possible, to recruit the regiment from veterans who had returned from the war in previous months. Lane apparently encountered some difficulties in this regard. He was forced to leave one of the ten companies of his regiment behind when it moved south because inadequate numbers of recruits had been raised, and was compelled to turn to Whitcomb and Reynolds for assistance in recruiting the necessary numbers of men to fill out his regiment. But it ultimately was organized, went through the formalities of confirming Lane as colonel, and in turn moved south toward garrison duty in Mexico.

With the Fourth Regiment initially posted along the Rio Grande, and with the Fifth not organized until the late autumn of 1847, it might have seemed that Indiana's effective participation in the war had come to an end. However, in the interim, changes in Washington again were to produce changes in the fortunes of at least some Indiana volunteers. Specifically, the Polk government continued to show animosity toward Taylor, who they felt was continuing to hoard unnecessarily large numbers of troops on the now extremely quiet northern frontier.

Accordingly, in the summer of 1847, as Taylor made preparations to launch his presidential campaign, the government decided that many of the units which had initially been assigned to Taylor should be transferred to the support of General Scott. By the time this decision was made, the striking force which General Scott would use to advance upon Mexico City already had moved into the mountains and would soon capture the capital city.

The troops that were being transferred from the Rio Grande were not being brought for the primary offensive, but instead were to serve another essential need of the southern theater, that of guarding the communications of Scott's army. By the early fall of 1847, this need had become considerable. Although Scott's army had been able to defeat the Mexican forces which were formally out in the field against it, everywhere that Scott's army passed it left behind it broken Mexican units which were joined by local citizens to form small bands of guerrillas. In the summer and fall of 1847 they began launching increasingly large and annoying attacks upon the lengthy wagon trains that were necessary to keep Scott's army properly supplied in the Mexican highlands. Thus, when a number of units, including the Fourth Indiana, were transferred to the area around Vera Cruz, they were intended primarily as wagon guards to keep the supply routes open. These recent arrivals were placed under the command of Brigadier General Joseph Lane, whose accomplishments at the battle of Buena Vista had done nothing to hurt his stock politically with the Polk administration. In fact, Lane and the Fourth Indiana arrived at Vera Cruz in time to participate in the last major organized military operations of the 1847 campaign.[16]

This 1847 campaign centered around the relief of a small American garrison, mostly invalids, who were holding the city of Pueblo well up in the highlands on the road to Mexico City. The garrison, although not actively threatened, had been surrounded and was being subjected to a constant harassing siege by a number of partisan Mexican units who were being gradually joined by the remnants of the defeated forces from Mexico City itself. As the intensity of the siege mounted, and as the problem of supplies increased, it became apparent that some form of relief would be necessary. To that end Lane and the bulk of the forces from the Rio Grande were ordered to take a large two-mile train of wagons into the mountains, to

46

disperse the besiegers, and to resupply the Pueblo garrison. Lane originally anticipated relatively low levels of opposition, and some of his critics were later to allege that he had placed inadequate stores of ammunition in the wagon train for the support of his own troops.

But Lane's forces did begin moving into the mountains along the National Road in time to encounter the last organized Mexican resistance. This resistance was organized by the same man that Lane had opposed at Buena Vista, General Santa Anna. Defeated at Mexico City and seriously considering withdrawal from Mexican affairs, Santa Anna was apparently persuaded by elements of the Mexican military to take command of the remnants of the forces around Pueblo and to seek a final military victory that might in some way recoup his fortunes or improve Mexico's position in the upcoming peace negotiations. Bringing small numbers of Mexican artillerymen and cavalry, Santa Anna responded. In addition to reinforcing the garrison around Pueblo, he began to block the main roads into Pueblo from the coast, chief among them the road which passed through the Mexican city of Huamantla.

That city became the focus of the ensuing campaign, as Lane's forces advancing from the east and Santa Anna's forces advancing from the northwest, engaged in a race to see who would control its walls and marketplace. By a narrow margin the Mexicans won the race, placing their cannon within the city and reinforcing the cannon with a small number of cavalry. Then American, Mexican, and more American units arrived in succession. The sequence involved American cavalry and American infantry, led by the Fourth Indiana, marching in to recapture the town. One of the Fourth Indiana's later and prouder boasts was that it was the first to reach the walls of Huamantla and, as such, was the first American infantry unit to place its flag in that beleagured city. Poorly led and characterized by extremely low morale as a result of their earlier defeat, the Mexican forces quickly broke and scattered in the face of the final American infantry offensive. This permitted the Americans to lift the siege of Pueblo and, in ensuing days, to march several miles in each direction bombarding and capturing several Mexican towns and dispersing any Mexican units that might seriously threaten communications in the area.

Thereafter, Lane's brigade went into garrison duty similar to that which the earlier regiments had experienced. When,

47

some weeks later, the Fifth Indiana completed its movement down the Gulf, it joined those final garrison forces. They again experienced little except the monotony of camp, occasional skirmishes with guerrillas, and the invariable harrassment of disease and climate which once again took a greater toll of the Hoosier forces than any they suffered in battle. With Senate ratification of a peace treaty negotiated under questionable conditions, American forces were then withdrawn in the spring of 1848. As the summer progressed, the later Indiana regiments once again retraced the route up to the Ohio River, once again experienced the round of parades and celebrations that had become commonplace in the previous year, and thereby brought to an end Indiana's participation in the great volunteer war against Mexico.

The Mexican war made its mark in Indiana primarily on the careers of the indivduals who participated in it. For some, and especially for the discredited, the contribution was primarily negative. Colonel Bowles did return to Paoli to resume the practice of medicine, but in ensuing years became increasingly involved with dissident organizations within the state and ultimately in the 1860s achieved perhaps his greatest fame by becoming associated with the Knights of the Golden Circle. Others, who had been more fortunate in their military careers, were similarly more fortunate in their subsequent political careers. Many of the colonels of Indiana's regiments passed on to other states. There, most were to build distinguished political careers, culminating in seats as either senators or governors. For the younger men who had participated in the Indiana regiments, there was a legacy of military experience that in many cases would express itself in positions of command in the Civil War or, at the very least, in positions of prominence in the still-growing independent companies that characterized much of the state in the 1850s.[17]

Contemporary commentators who sought to find long-term consequences of the Mexican War observed that the most obvious was to provide many independent companies throughout the state with a hard core of veterans who had developed a taste for the soldier's life and were able to bring a sense of experience and expertise back to their local communities. It became a particularly common practice for the officers of the five Indiana regiments to form small independent companies of their own, to uniform them, and to drill them from the

48

manuals that they had learned in camps that ranged from Madison, Indiana, to the highlands of Mexico. Typical of these were the Wallace Zouaves. Raised in the Indianapolis area by Lew Wallace, they were garbed in the elaborate Zouave costumes that had first been borrowed from the French experiences in Africa and were now an expression of the romantic zeal in North America; and they were drilled in such a way that when the Civil War came a number of them would quickly assume leadership positions in different regiments of the Indiana volunteer infantry. Beginning in 1861 those regiments would be numbered consecutively from six rather than from one in recognition of the regiments which served in Mexico. It was indicative of the role which the war with Mexico played in confirming and advancing the volunteer experience in Indiana.

[1] R. C. Buley, *The Old Northwest, Pioneer Period, 1815-1940*, 2 vols. (Indianapolis: Indiana Historical Society, 1950).

[2] An excellent introduction is found in Walter Millis, *Arms and Men* (New York: Putnam, 1956).

[3] *A History of the National Guard of Indiana* (Indianapolis: Pratt, 1901), pp. 73-86.

[4] See, for example, Logan Esarey, *A History of Indiana*, 2 vols. (Indianapolis: Bowen, 1918; reprint ed., Indianapolis: Hoosier Heritage Press, 1970).

[5] The indispensible introduction to this era is Oran Perry, *Indiana in the Mexican War* (Indianapolis: Burford, 1908). It contains most relevant documents except Whig newspaper accounts.

[6] The standard modern account of the war, with a good bibliography, is K. Jack Bauer, *The Mexican War, 1846-1848* (New York: Macmillan, 1974).

[7] Interesting accounts are included in *History of Greene and Sullivan Counties* (Chicago: Goodspeed, 1884), pp. 567-570; and *History of Lawrence, Orange, and Washington Counties* (Chicago: Goodspeed, 1884), pp. 794-796.

[8] Lew Wallace, *An Autobiography*, 2 vols. (New York: Harper, 1906).

[9] R. C. Buley, "Indiana in the Mexican War," *Indiana Magazine of History*, Vol. 15, No. 4, pp. 261-326, 46-48.

[10] Modern accounts of the ensuing battle include David Lavender, *Climax at Buena Vista* (Philadelphia: Lippincott, 1966); and Edward Nichols, *Zach Taylor's Little Army* (Garden City: Doubleday, 1963).

[11] George W. Geib, "The Case of Colonel William Bowles," *Indiana Military History Journal*, July, 1976: 30-32.

[12] Perry contains most of the pro-Lane domuments. For the Whig rebuttal, consult the *Indiana State Journal*; and the *St. Joseph Valley Register* (September and October, 1848).

[13] The most detailed assessment is Herman T. Viola, "Zachary Taylor

and the Indiana Volunteers," *Southwestern Historical Quarterly* 72, January, 1969: 335-346.

14 For an assessment of numbers involved, note Jim Dan Hill, *The Minute Man in Peace and War* (Harrisburg: Stackpole, 1964).

15 Wendell Holmes Stephenson, *The Political Career of General James H. Lane,* Publications of the Kansas Historical Society, III (Topeka, 1930).

16 These operations and the rest of the war are well detailed in Justin H. Smith, *The War with Mexico,* 2 vols. (New York: Macmillan, 1919).

17 For examples, see W. R. Holloway, *Indianapolis* (Indianapolis: Indianapolis Journal Printing, 1870).

HOOSIER MILITIAMEN AND THE CIVIL WAR

James R. H. Spears

In the period between the end of the Mexican War and the mid-1850s there was very little militia activity in Indiana. By the mid-50s, there was a resurgence of interest in the militia which was greatly increased in 1860 by the national tour of Elmer Ellsworth's Zouave Cadets of Chicago. The Zouaves, with their gaudy Algerian style uniforms and their silent drill, were a great attraction wherever they performed on their tour, and by 1860 there were at least six Zouave militia companies in Indiana. By the beginning of the Civil War, Indiana had between 20 and 30 militia companies, all of which were infantry, and none of which received state funds or arms.[1] These units were independent militia, not organized militia, which would have been entitled to receive state support. There were probably no organized militia units in Indiana in 1861. The members of independent militia units bought their own uniforms and equipment, or were supported by well-to-do patrons, or by a combination of both. While excellent in close order drill and the social graces, few spent any time on marksmanship or field soldiering.

On April 15, 1861, three days after the firing on Fort Sumter, President Lincoln called on the states for 75,000 militia to put down the rebellion. Lincoln acted under the Militia Act of 1795 which gave the President the authority to call upon the states for militia to serve not in excess of 90 days.[2] Since Congress was not in session and could not be quickly summoned, this was the only means available to the President to raise troops. Indiana's quota was set by the War Department at six regiments of infantry totaling 4,683 officers and men. Each regiment was to consist of ten companies of 74 men and three officers. A regiment was commanded by a colonel who had a staff of a lieutenant colonel, major, four company grade officers, a sergeant major, and three non-commissioned officers. On April 16, after receiving the state quota from the secretary of war, Governor Oliver P. Morton issued a proclamation calling the loyal men of the state to organize themselves into companies and report by telegraph when organized. The office of adjutant general was vacant and Governor Morton appointed Lewis Wallace, a Crawfordsville lawyer, to fill the vacancy. Wallace, just turned 34, was a former state senator and the son of a former governor. He had served as a second lieutenant in the First Indiana Volunteer Infantry in the Mexican War and had been prominent in the unorganized militia throughout the 1850s. Wallace commanded the Montgomery Guards of Crawfordsville and had organized and drilled the Wabash College Cadets, both uniformed and drilled as Zouaves. Both units enlisted to a man and became cadre for companies of the 11th Indiana Volunteer Infantry. During the war, three former Wabash College Cadets received the Medal of Honor, and two became general officers before the war ended.[3]

The response to the governor's call was very quick and overwhelming. By the end of seven days, there were 12,000 volunteers in the State Fairgrounds in Indianapolis, which was renamed Camp Morton. The question became not who will go, but who will be lucky enough to get to go. Hundreds who were not able to enroll in companies in their own counties came to Camp Morton singly and in groups, by train, by horse, and on foot. To Governor Morton, the response was both gratifying and frustrating. Not only did the state have no uniforms, no equipment, nor many arms—Indiana had no money. The state treasury contained less than $10,000, most of which was held for trust funds, and the state's credit was, at best, poor. However, Morton and Wallace accomplished near miracles in the next 30 days.

Oliver P. Morton had been elected lieutenant governor on the Republican ticket in 1860, but was elevated to the governorship one day later when the legislature elected Henry S. Lane to the United States Senate. Morton was a native Hoosier, just 37, powerfully built, handsome, and a magnetic speaker. He was certainly the most able and energetic of the northern war governors. When the federal government could not supply ammunition, he started the Indiana State Arsenal and Indiana sold, at a profit, ammunition to the United States at a price lower than federal officials could purchase it elsewhere. Having a true and deep empathy for the soldiers in the ranks, Morton saw that Indiana did more for the welfare of its troops in the field than any other state. He also made certain that both the soldiers and the electorate knew the source of their support. Always a goad to the War Department, he was a man of great zeal—and no patience. For all of his many virtues he had a certain pettiness, and he refused to tolerate any opposition. Within a year, he and the equally ambitious Lew Wallace would become bitter lifelong enemies.

The six three-month regiments were organized, drilled, and provided locally made uniforms—which were gray. On April 25, although they were not yet completely equipped or uniformed, the first six regiments were mustered into federal service.[4] In remembrance and honor of the five regiments that Indiana had sent to the Mexican War, the Civil War regiments were numbered beginning with six, probably at Adjutant General Wallace's suggestion. The muster consisted of a physical examination of the soldiers, usually by a local physician under contract, and the swearing-in by a federal mustering officer. To examine the volunteers, the physician and the mustering officer inspected them in ranks, occasionally questioning one of doubtful age or physique, and making sure that all had a trigger finger and two upper and two lower matching front teeth, so that they could bite off the end of a paper cartridge. That the exams were not too thorough is attested to by the fact that several women passed muster, some serving for over a year before being detected. After the muster the officers were elected, it being generally understood that those who had been instrumental in recruiting would become officers. However, more than a few avid recruiters were disappointed. The field grade officers usually were elected by the company grade officers, with the exception of the colonel, and sometimes the lieutenant colonel, who were selected by the governor. Since these regiments were militia, they were volunteers and not a part of the regular Army. All of the officers were commissioned by the governor of the state that organized them, and even after the unit—regiment or battery—was mustered into United States service, the officers were commissioned throughout the war by the governors of the respective states, not by the federal government.[5]

On the day of the muster, Lew Wallace resigned as adjutant general and was commissioned colonel of the 11th Indiana Volunteer Infantry which he had carefully assembled from the best of the prewar militia companies, such as the National Zouaves of Indianapolis and the Montgomery Guards and Wabash College Cadets of Crawfordsville. The 11th adopted the Zouave drill, and a Zouave uniform of gray trimmed with red—designed, of course, by the regimental commander, the future author of Ben-Hur. Of the 36 officers of this unique regiment, five became general officers before the war ended, as did the regimental sergeant major, Wabash College student John C. Black, who, with his brother was among the five soldiers of this regiment who were awarded the Medal of Honor. Within two weeks Wallace's Indiana Zouaves were off by rail to Evansville where they inspected river traffic for contraband goods before finally leaving the state for Cumberland, Maryland, on June 10. The other five regiments went to western Virginia in increments between May 30 and June 19, where they served together as the Indiana Brigade under Brigadier General Thomas A. Morris, a West Point graduate of the class of 1834. Morris was a railroad president in Indianapolis and had been prominent in the Indiana militia. All six of the three-month regiments saw combat before the expiration of their short term of service.

While the first six regiments were being equipped and drilled, Governor Morton and the legislature were taking steps to enlist the services of the multitude who still wanted to join. After the mustering of the three-month regiments, there were still 29 complete companies at Indianapolis, and 68 companies in various parts of the state that had tendered their service.[6] Morton and the new adjutant general began organizing these companies into regiments of infantry for 12 months state service, or for federal service, if called. On May 6, the legislature, which was meeting in special session, passed the Six Regiment Bill which authorized the governor to form six regiments of infantry for state service. One regiment, the 14th, was to be encamped at Terre Haute, the 15th at Lafayette, and the 16th at Richmond. The other three, the 12th, 13th, and 17th, were to be organized at Camp Morton. These six state regiments formed another brigade, giving Morton the opportunity to appoint another brigadier general. To fill this vacancy, he chose the commander of the 10th Indiana Volunteer Infantry, Colonel Joseph J. Reynolds, who had recently been a wholesale grocer in Lafayette. Reynolds, an alumnus of both Wabash College and West Point, was a veteran of the Mexican War who had resigned his commission in 1857 to teach civil and mechanical engineering at Washington University in St. Louis. By the end of the war, he had risen to the grade of major general and was a corps commander.

The new regiments did not long remain in state service. Ten days after they were formed, the secretary of war called for four regiments of volunteer infantry to serve for three years or the duration of the war. Those men in the state regiments who did not wish to serve under these terms were discharged. Those remaining were consolidated into the 13th, 14th, 15th, and 17th infantry regiments and mustered into federal service, and from July 1-5, this four-regiment brigade left for western Virginia. The 12th and the 16th remained in state service until July 18, when, at the insistence of Governor Morton, they were taken into federal service for the unexpired term of their 12-month enlistment and sent east to serve with the Army of the Potomac.

Before the six three-month regiments had returned from the east, their officers and the governor had begun to recruit them for the three-year service. By mid-September, all six had reenlisted for federal service for three years or the war's duration. When they returned to federal service as three-year regiments, they all bore the same numerical designations, six through 11, and all returned in gray uniforms, for it was not until late October, 1861, that the War Department ordered that all units entering federal service be uniformed in blue, and specifically *not* gray. All six regiments returned under the same commanders, although many of the company commanders and NCO's had taken advantage of the many opportunities to obtain advancement in the new regiments that were forming. By mid-summer, the state had War Department authorization to begin forming batteries of light artillery and regiments of cavalry. By the end of 1861, Indiana had fielded 12 light artillery batteries and three cavalry regiments, and infantry regiments through number 59. The infantry regiments that went for "three-or-the-war" usually were organized within a congressional district and were larger than the three-month regiments. Each regiment still consisted of ten companies plus the field grade officers and staff, but each company now counted 98 men and NCO's, and each regiment, until October, 1861, had a regimental band of 24 men, making a total complement of 1,046 men. The cavalry regiments consisted of two battalions of three squadrons. Each squadron contained two companies, so that the complete cavalry regiment of 12 companies contained 1,168 officers and men. Early in the war each mounted soldier and officer furnished his own horse and equipment, for which he was paid 40 cents a day. The artillery batteries contained five officers and 143 men and NCO's. These units were all recruited with great ease, for more men offered their services than could be accepted at any given time.[7]

A week after enacting the Six Regiment Act the legislature, on May 11, passed the far-reaching and important Act For the Regulation and Organization of the Indiana Militia. This act divided the militia into the sedentary militia, which consisted of all able bodied white males who were subject to bear arms under the Indiana Constitution, and the active militia, which encompassed those white males 18 to 45 who voluntarily enrolled as members of recognized uniformed companies. The active militia was to be known as the Indiana Legion, a name that it kept until 1895 when it became the Indiana National Guard. This act, while very important, had one very major defect in that it only *invited* enrollments. The law offered no inducements to attract—nor any penalties to compel. Yet, for its weakness, it was remarkably effective as long as the war lasted. Once the war ended, the Legion collapsed. However, throughout the war the Legion provided a channel for recruiting and a cadre of at least partially trained officers and men. It performed a unique and valuable service along the Ohio River, as well as provided some restraining influence on those Hoosiers who were secession minded.

John Love of Indianapolis, who had been brigade inspector of General Morris's three-month brigade in western Virginia, was appointed major general and commander of the Legion. Love, a West Pointer and Mexican War veteran, set out to organize the Legion into companies and regiments, normally one regiment per county. Enthusiasm ran high in the summer of 1861 and large numbers enrolled, but the state and the federal government could not arm and equip all of those volunteering for federal service. Lacking arms, many units melted away; others volunteered as units for the Army. In Posey County, Judge Alvin P. Hovey raised a battalion which in late summer became a part of the 24th Indiana Volunteer Infantry, of which he became the colonel. The same story, on different levels, was repeated many times.

By late autumn, enough muskets were available to begin arming Legion companies, and the first to be armed were those in the 13 counties along the Ohio River.[8] As arms were issued companies again became active, and most drilled at least once a week, some daily. Both officers and men of the Legion provided their own uniforms and were paid only when called out by order of the governor. Throughout the war, the Legion was never furnished with first-class arms. As the federal forces in the field obtained better arms their turn-ins were issued to the states for militia use. Many Legion companies carried 71-caliber Prussian muskets, or Austrian or Belgian muskets which were obsolete in Europe. The most common arm throughout the war was the Harpers Ferry or Springfield 69-caliber smoothbore converted flintlock. By the end of the year, the Legion was well under way toward becoming a reasonably efficient home guard, considering the constraints due to lack of arms and the constant turnover in force. As 1861 ended, loyal Hoosiers could look back on a year of remarkable military achievement. The state had recruited, armed, equipped, uniformed, and sent forth 53,035 soldiers for three years service, with a bare minimum of help or supervision from the federal government, which had neither the organization nor the personnel for the task. In addition, Indiana had begun a militia for state defense, that, however indifferently armed, would prove remarkably valuable in the three trying years ahead.

In retrospect, 1861 was the year of the improvised war—organized by amateurs who sent forth armed and uniformed patriots, but not trained soldiers. However, a legacy had been established which provided a firm foundation for future operations. If 1861 was the year of improvisation, 1862 was certainly the year of turmoil for Indiana. The year began with bitter cold and deep snow which slowed recruiting. However, in January Union troops won a morale boosting victory in Kentucky at Mill Springs, in which Indiana troops played a significant role. This was followed in February by Major General U. S. Grant's significant victories at Fort Henry and Fort Donelson, in which Hoosier troops had an important role, led by Lew Wallace, who had been a brigadier general since the previous September. These Union victories also brought the war closer to home to the people of Indiana, for 3,700 rebel prisoners-of-war were sent to Camp Morton. Since Camp Morton could not accommodate all of them, part were sent to Terre Haute, and others were taken to Lafayette. Prison guards had to be hastily assembled, and for this task Morton used two partially recruited infantry regiments that were in camp in various parts of the state—the 53rd under Colonel Walter Q. Gresham, who later would become President Grover Cleveland's secretary of state, and the 66th under Colonel Richard Owen of New Harmony, who became commandant of the prison camp. A greater shock came on April 3, when, without warning, Secretary of War Edwin Stanton stopped all recruiting for the Army. This was probably the greatest blunder that the Lincoln administration made during the entire war, as military operations in Virginia and Tennessee proved in the next three months. During this hiatus, Governor Morton continued to complete the units that Indiana had under way. Stanton stopped recruiting, but Morton did not. The federal government resumed recruiting on July 2, 1862, with a call for 300,000 for three years, but the momentum had been seriously impaired throughout the North, and it went slowly, especially in eastern states, and in August the President called for 300,000 militia to serve for nine months. This militia call was to be filled by a *draft* in those states that did not meet their quota. Indiana's combined quota was 42,500 men, and although by October 6, the date of the draft, Indiana had 93,041 volunteers in service, the state was still 3,003 men short, the number that was drafted.[9]

While Governor Morton was struggling with the manifold problems of raising manpower, the Confederacy provided a surprising external stimulus to recruiting for both the volunteer service and the Legion. In early July, Brigadier General John Hunt Morgan began a cavalry raid through the bluegrass region of Kentucky which was denuded of federal troops. On the 10th, Brigadier General Jeremiah Boyle, commander of the District of Kentucky, wired Governor Morton requesting troops. The next day Indiana sent the 55th Indiana to Frankfort, Kentucky, while the same day the commander of the post at Henderson, Kentucky, asked the Legion commander at Evansville for 200 men of the Legion to help garrison Henderson, which was threatened by large bodies of Confederate Partisan Rangers, or guerrillas. Feeling that Evansville was just as exposed, he, of course, declined. The real shock of the month was yet to come.

On July 18, Adam R. Johnson, a former resident of Henderson, crossed the Ohio River and occupied Newburgh, a village 16 miles upriver from Evansville. Newburgh had a small military hospital that served about 90 sick and wounded Union soldiers. In the hospital building were stored about 250 muskets belonging to the Legion. Nearby were stockpiled ammunition and 150 new pistols. Learning of this from some of the disloyal citizens of the town, Johnson and about 60 men seized the ferry boat and rowed across the river about noon. The unguarded hospital was occupied and the leading citizens were captured and informed that the safety of the town and its inhabitants depended on their cooperation. To reinforce his threat, Johnson pointed across the river to two artillery pieces, which he said would shell the town to rubble if the citizens did not comply. If the citizens could have taken a closer look, they would have seen that the cannons were the rear wheels of a wagon and sections of stovepipe. Henceforth, Adam R. Johnson was known throughout the Confederacy, and the North, as "Stovepipe" Johnson.[10] The soldiers at the hospital were forced to sign paroles. Stovepipe Johnson, commissioned colonel of Partisan Rangers and brigadier general in 1864, remained in Newburgh until late afternoon. The town was pillaged. Horses and food were taken and ferried across the river. After Johnson and his raiders left, two citizens of Newburgh who had been instrumental in aiding the raiders were murdered by the outraged citizens. Within one hour after news of the raid reached Evansville, 2,000 Legion members had assembled under arms.[11] Two steamboats were commandeered and the force proceeded upriver to Newburgh, arriving after the raiders had left. The next day Stovepipe Johnson and his Partisan Rangers forced the small federal garrison out of Henderson, Kentucky, 12 miles below Evansville.

Recognizing that neither the U. S. forces, nor the government of Kentucky had control of the situation, Governor Morton ordered the Legion in the counties along the river to duty and called for Legion volunteers from other counties. At Greensburg, Colonel James Gavin, of the Seventh Indiana Volunteer Infantry, and Colonel John T. Wilder, of the 17th Indiana Volunteer Infantry, were home recruiting. Within a few hours, they had 600 volunteers from the Legion of Decatur County.[12] Companies volunteered from all over the state—twice what was needed. Two companies from Terre Haute and two from Lafayette were added to make a full regiment, which was mustered into United States service for 30 days as the 76th Indiana Volunteer Infantry. Colonel Gavin of the 7th Indiana Infantry had the unique distinction of being commissioned colonel of *two* regiments simultaneously, the Seventh and the 76th, while Colonel Wilder had the equally unique distinction

59

of being colonel of the 17th and lieutenant colonel of the 76th. Leaving the Warrick and Vanderburgh County Legion units to guard the numerous fords of the Ohio, the 76th crossed the river on July 22, occupied Henderson, and sent detachments into the countryside to break up Confederate recruiting stations and disperse guerrillas. The 76th stayed in Kentucky until the expiration of its 30-day service and had several sharp skirmishes with guerrilla forces. The 76th scarcely had entered Kentucky before Indiana began raising another regiment of infantry from the Legion for similar duty. A seven-company regiment, the 78th Indiana Volunteer Infantry, was mustered into federal service on August 5 for 60 days. Following its sister regiment, the 76th, through Henderson and into Kentucky, the 78th spent its 60 days breaking up guerrilla camps and Confederate recruiting stations. During its stay in Kentucky, the 78th lost one officer and three enlisted men killed in skirmishes.

While Indiana soldiers were trying to restore order along the Ohio River, far to the south the Confederate high command was planning more mischief for Kentucky in the form of a two-pronged invasion that brought them to within sight of the Ohio River. In the East, General E. Kirby Smith bypassed Cumberland Gap and entered Kentucky through Pound Creek Gap. To the West, General Braxton Bragg bypassed Nashville, Tennessee, and General Don Carlos Buell's Army of the Ohio, and headed toward Louisville. Once again, General John Hunt Morgan began a Cavalry raid into Kentucky to operate against the Union Army communications—railroads and the telegraph.

North of the Ohio River in Indiana and Ohio, anxiety increased daily as the Confederate armies advanced into Kentucky leaving the Union defenders behind them. Few federal troops were available to throw into the breach and Governor Morton already had pressed much of the Legion into service on the river and as prisoner-of-war guards. The national government could not provide troops from the east, for the Army of the Potomac was hard-pressed to hold General Lee at bay. The only solution was to recruit the existing quotas and forward green troops as rapidly as possible.

The public response to the urgent call for volunteers was prompt. However, like the spring of 1861, more men came forward than could be rapidly uniformed and armed. There was also a shortage of officers, especially those with any prior

60

experience. Lew Wallace, now a major general at home in Crawfordsville awaiting reassignment, was commissioned provisional colonel of the 66th Indiana Volunteer Infantry and took the unit to Lexington, Kentucky, on August 22, where he assumed temporary command of the district.[13] The 66th was certainly the only regiment in the war whose colonel was a major general. By August 21, Indiana had sent 16 regiments of infantry, three batteries of light artillery, and one cavalry battalion across the river into Kentucky. The Fifth Indiana Volunteer Cavalry also was mustered into service and sent to the counties along the Ohio River to guard the fords against unwanted trespassers from the south. In addition to not being able to provide arms and equipment, Washington was not able to advance the money to pay the volunteers their enlistment bounty and their initial pay. Many of the recruits had enlisted on the spur of the moment, were depending on this payment to sustain their families, and were reluctant to leave the state until paid. The incomparable Morton arranged loans of over $500,000 from private citizens and from Indianapolis and Cincinnati banks. The soldiers were paid. Some units that had left the state were paid in Kentucky. The 71st Infantry was paid at Richmond, Kentucky—an hour before it went into a battle in which the entire regiment was captured.

By the end of August, General Kirby Smith's Confederate troops were within 30 miles of Lexington, Kentucky. Near the village of Richmond, they met a two-brigade force of the newly created Army of Kentucky. One brigade consisted of four Indiana volunteer regiments commanded by Mahlon Manson, formerly the commander of the 10th Indiana Infantry, and now a brigadier general. The other brigade commanded by Brigadier General Charles Cruft of Terre Haute, contained two Indiana infantry regiments, one from Ohio, and one from Kentucky. None of the federal regiments had been in service longer than 12 days! Against a larger veteran force, the completely green troops probably did as well as could be expected—but, the result was disaster. The Union loss was 203 killed, 844 wounded, and 4,303 captured out of the small force of a little over 6,300 men.[14] The captured were paroled on the field and sent north to await exchange. Three days later Kirby Smith occupied Lexington, and the roads to either Louisville or Cincinnati were clear. Kirby Smith chose to go north and in a few days was in the outskirts of Covington, Kentucky, across the river from Cincinnati. After spending a week in the suburbs of Covington, Kirby Smith decided that Cincinnati could not be taken and marched south to occupy Frankfort, the state capital.

On September 5, Governor Morton declared martial law in the 13 Indiana counties bordering the Ohio River. All places of business were to close at three o'clock each afternoon except post offices, telegraph stations, and pharmacies. All able-bodied white males from 18 to 45 were to report to the nearest polling place, organize companies, elect officers, and arm themselves with whatever weapons they could obtain. Each company, under the control of the Legion, was to drill daily.[15] Although this *levee en masse* turned out over 20,000 minutemen (as they were called), few were properly armed and it is fortunate that they never met the Confederates. However, they did important service in guarding the fords of the Ohio, for Kentucky was swarming with guerrillas and lawless bands of deserters from both armies.

While General Smith occupied Frankfort, to the west the other Confederate force under General Bragg was racing the Union Army of the Ohio under General Buell to be first to gain the prize of the campaign—Louisville. Directly in the path of Bragg's army lay the Union garrison of Munfordville, Kentucky. The garrison was well situated and dug in on a bluff overlooking the Green River. On September 14, the Munfordville garrison was attacked by an advance Confederate brigade, which they easily fended off. Two days later Bragg threw his entire army at the small garrison. This small attack of pride cost him two days, for this relatively small detachment easily could have been bypassed. The loss to the Union was 15 killed, 57 wounded, and 4,076 captured—all Hoosiers. Again, as at Richmond, the captured were paroled on the field and sent back to Indiana to await exchange. The Confederates lost 35 killed, including one colonel, and 252 wounded. The price had been very high—for Buell had gained two days march, and on the 24th the Army of the Ohio arrived at Louisville, while Bragg veered off to Bardstown.[16]

August, 1862, had been a busy and difficult month in Indiana, and September brought more than its share of grief and humiliation. In August, the state had recruited and sent forward over 30,000 troops, but over 10,000 had been captured and returned home awaiting exchange. The month had seen almost

300 Indiana soldiers killed in Kentucky and over 900 wounded. In the east, with the Army of the Potomac, three weeks after the second battle of Bull Run five Hoosier units were engaged on September 17 in the battle of Antietam, a day in which more Americans were killed or wounded than in any other single day in American history, including the Second World War.

After a week of rest and re-equipping, General Buell moved out of Louisville on October 1. Seven days later his Army of the Ohio met the combined forces of Bragg and Kirby Smith near Perryville, Kentucky, about 35 miles southwest of Lexington. Ten Hoosier infantry regiments and four light artillery batteries were engaged in a bitter and indecisive one-day battle in which casualties on both sides were high. The 14 Indiana units suffered a total of 134 killed, 526 wounded, and 69 missing.[17] One regiment, the 22d Indiana Infantry, had 53 percent casualties.[18] The next day Bragg withdrew toward Cumberland Gap. Buell, declining to pursue, started his army back toward Nashville, Tennessee.

With Perryville and Antietam, military operations wound down for the year in both the east and in the Mississippi Valley, but recruiting and support of the troops in the field did not stop. October 6 brought the draft—which did not go off well. In fact, in several counties mobs prevented any attempt to administer it. The October elections, the first statewide balloting since the war began, gave the Democrats majorities in both houses of the Indiana legislature, indicating a deep popular dissatisfaction with the course of the war. The Mississippi River still was controlled by the Confederates below Memphis, Tennessee, which meant that southern Indiana, which was the state's most populous region, had to send the products of its farms and factories to eastern markets by railroad at a much higher cost than that of transporting them downriver to New Orleans. As discontent increased, recruiting became increasingly difficult, for the eager and the adventuresome already were in the Army, while the long casualty lists and those returning with empty sleeves and broken health reminded people at home of the great sacrifices being made by soldiers in the field.

In the west, where the majority of Indiana troops served, the last months of 1862 were relatively quiet, but the year ended noisily. At Chickasaw Bluffs, Mississippi, within sight of the courthouse in Vicksburg, on December 29 Major General William T. Sherman made an unsuccessful assault, and on the last

63

day of the year the Army of the Cumberland, commanded by Major General William S. Rosecrans, was engaged with General Bragg's Confederate Army of Tennessee at Murfreesboro, Tennessee, in an indecisive but politically timely victory.[19] Following the two days of heavy fighting, which occurred on December 31 and January 2, 1863, the Confederate forces withdrew into Alabama behind the Cumberland River, leaving all of middle Tennessee in federal hands. At Murfreesboro, or Stone's River, as it is sometimes called, 26 Indiana regiments and five batteries were engaged and they suffered a total of 2,500 casualties.[20]

The Army of the Cumberland's supply line from Louisville, Kentucky, to Nashville, Tennessee, was 190 miles long—and four feet, eight-and-one-half inches wide. The small locomotives were easily derailed. Bridges were made of timber and provided inviting targets for secessionists with arsonist tendencies. The rail line's vulnerability was an invitation to the daring and ambitious Brigadier General John Hunt Morgan, who had twice before proved his ability as a Confederate cavalry raider. During his Christmas raid in 1862 he burned railroad bridges extensively, and even torched the timber supports of one tunnel. At Muldraugh Hill between Elizabethtown and Louisville, where he burned the famous long bridge, he captured and paroled the 71st Indiana Volunteer Infantry, which only recently had been exchanged after having been captured on August 30, 1862, at Richmond, Kentucky. After being exchanged again, they were very prudently mounted and redesignated the Sixth Indiana Volunteer Cavalry and as such served until the end of the war without being again captured.[21] Morgan began his great Indiana-Ohio raid on June 11, with 2,400 men and four pieces of light artillery. General Morgan's orders were to destroy as much railroad as possible between Louisville and Nashville, and, if possible, make a dash on Louisville and burn all or part of the large federal depot there.[22] For several weeks Morgan's division successfully eluded federal troops as the raiders worked their way north. Their arrival on the banks of the Ohio at Brandenburg, Kentucky, on July 8 was not a surprise to the authorities in Indiana, for they had been watching Morgan's northward progress with keen interest. In the week prior to Morgan's crossing of the Ohio River, Governor Morton had sent to Kentucky the only organized troops in Indiana, at the request of Brigadier General Jeremiah Boyle, commander of the District of Kentucky.

About mid-morning on July 8, while Hoosiers were still celebrating the twin Union victories of Vicksburg and Gettysburg, Morgan's main body arrived at Brandenburg, a small village on the river due south of Corydon, Indiana.[23] He immediately began ferrying his troops across on two small steamboats that an advance detachment had captured by ruse the previous afternoon. The crossing was not unopposed, for the Indiana Legion, having learned of the capture of the two steamers, managed to place a six-pound smooth-bore cannon to contest the attempt. The Confederate artillery, four six-pounders, unlimbered and soon silenced the single piece of Legion artillery, killing one Legion officer and a citizen volunteer. The rebel artillery then began firing on the Legion infantry, some 400 in number under Colonel Lewis Jordan, who were just arriving, and drove them back. The raiders then crossed the river unmolested. By dark, all of the men and horses were on the Indiana side of the river. After crossing, Morgan burned one of the two steamers, the *Alice Dean;* the other, the *J. T. McCoombs,* managed to escape upriver. The rebel horsemen then went into bivouac for the night, after burning a gristmill on Buck Creek and murdering an unarmed civilian and setting fire to his home. The news that Morgan was in Indiana reached Indianapolis late on the evening of the eighth—and the effect was electrifying. In the governor's office the mood was close to panic. Reports from Harrison County and from federal authorities in Kentucky estimated Morgan's force from 4,500 to 6,000. At Camp Morton were 1,500 Confederate prisoners of war,[24] and the state arsenal held a considerable number of small arms and a large amount of powder, since it was a manufacturer of small arms ammunition. The only U.S. troops available were two companies of the 63d Indiana Volunteer Infantry, and a few hundred recently exchanged prisoners of war of the 63d and 73d Indiana Volunteer Infantry, and a few hapless recruits.

Unlike the dark days of October, 1862, Governor Morton did not declare martial law, although he was urged by federal authorities to do so. He did issue a general military order requiring all able-bodied white males in the counties south of the National Road (present U.S. 40) to form themselves into companies of at least 60 members, arm themselves the best way possible, and report to the local Legion commander. All except military business was suspended on the railroads and telegraph circuits. The response to this *levee en masse* was astounding. Not since Tippecanoe and the episodes of 1812 had Hoosiers been required to defend their own homes. The second week of July, 1863, proved that the spirit had not died. By the evening of July 11, 20,000 men had been mustered at Indianapolis, and more than 45,000 had volunteered and were standing ready at other points in the state.[25] Considering that Indianapolis had a civilian population in 1863 of only about 23,000, the capitol city must have had much of a circus atmosphere. These volunteers were Minutemen and were not a part of the regularly enrolled militia, the Legion, which already had turned out armed and uniformed. The Minutemen who were mustered at Indianapolis and other places were armed, but not uniformed. They were organized into regiments which were numbered from the 102d to the 114th Indiana Volunteer Infantry. Ten of these 13 regiments were sent south from Indianapolis, three of them on July 13 to Hamilton, Ohio, and the other seven to Vernon, Indiana, where they helped the Legion successfully block Morgan. Help from other states was offered and was quickly and gratefully accepted. A company of sharpshooters from Mattoon, Illinois, handsomely uniformed and armed with Henry 16-shot rifles, was assigned to the 103d Regiment. Two other Illinois companies, one from Charleston and the other from Ashmore, served with the 104th Regiment of Minutemen. The commander of the Military District of Missouri sent the 10th Kansas Infantry and the 12th Kansas Light Artillery Battery, both of which were used in the region between Mitchell and Seymour to guard railroad bridges.[26] While organizing Minutemen Governor Morton was not unmindful of the river barrier that now lay between Morgan and his freedom. Morton telegraphed Fleet Captain Pennock, USN, at Cairo, Illinois, commanding the Ohio River Squadron, and advised him of the situation and requested assistance on the river. Pennock immediately dispatched six gunboats upriver to guard the shoals and fords, and to destroy flatboats and scows that would be useful to Morgan in recrossing the river.

While Morton was busy in Indianapolis organizing troops, John Hunt Morgan also was active. Leaving their bivouac in early morning, the Confederates' three-brigade force moved

66

up the Mauckport Road toward Corydon, past the smouldering ruins of the grist mill and farmstead that they had burned the previous evening. Colonel Jordan and his 400 Legion infantry, joined by a few citizen volunteers, had formed a barricade of fencerails across the road about a mile south of town. Behind this obstacle, the defenders waited in line of battle. About ten o'clock the rebel advance appeared and immediately attacked from its march column without deploying. Twice the Confederate cavalry attacked, and twice the citizen soldiers repulsed them with some loss to the attackers, but without fatalities to the defenders. A spirited skirmish was sustained for longer than 30 minutes, during which time the entire Confederate column arrived on the scene. Morgan then unlimbered his four pieces of artillery and sent one regiment to flank the short line of defense, which had no artillery, and take the militiamen from the rear. Under the circumstances Colonel Jordan prudently surrendered, and Morgan paroled the 345 citizen soldiers who had stood and fought. Three of the Legion's citizen volunteers were killed outright, and two died later. The Confederate loss was eight killed, and 33 wounded, three of whom subsequently died in Corydon. Under the circumstances the militiamen gave a good account of themselves.[27]

After the surrender Morgan's cavalry moved into the town and immediately began plundering. Contributions of $1,000 were levied against each of the town's three flour mills, in lieu of burning them, and the county treasury was robbed. The raiders gathered more than 500 fresh horses in Harrison County before departing late that same afternoon. Leaving 11 seriously wounded in Corydon, Morgan went north up the Mauckport Road toward Salem, the county seat of Washington County. Traveling all night without guides, over unmarked dirt roads past farmsteads now deserted, the long dusty column arrived at Salem about nine o'clock the next morning, in time to capture a company of the Washington County Legion which had just mustered to receive ammunition. Again, Morgan levied $1,000 in greenbacks against each of the local mills while the troops plundered freely and without any restraint from their officers. While at Salem Morgan tapped the telegraph line to learn of federal activity and locations—an intelligence gathering technique he used whenever possible.[28] Previously in Kentucky spurious messages frequently had sent his pursuers in the wrong direction. He then burned a railroad bridge and the local railroad depot and quickly departed. Sending a large detachment up the Mauckport Road toward Brownstown (the direct route to Indianapolis), the main body headed east toward Vienna, a small village on the Jeffersonville and Indianapolis Railroad. The Brownstown feint had some of the desired effect, for later in the day it was reported by telegraph to Indianapolis that 500 of Morgan's men were near Brownstown, with the main body in their rear. When it was learned that Morgan actually had turned east, it was accepted as an indication that Indianapolis was not his objective, to officials' relief, but it opened the possibility that he might attack Jeffersonville or New Albany, both of which contained large amounts of military supplies, or that he might go eastward and attempt to cross the Ohio River at Grassy Flats, near Madison. For the federals, with limited resources, trying to checkmate the wily Morgan was an exasperating game, but time was on the federal side.

Brigadier General Edward Hobson, commanding a 2,500-man brigade of U.S. cavalry, had been pursuing Morgan through northern Kentucky since July 6. Hobson arrived at Brandenburg, on the Ohio River, a scant 12 hours behind the Confederates, but was delayed in getting steamboats to cross.[29] By the time that Morgan reached Vienna, Hobson was less than a day behind and gaining, but slowly, a fact that Morgan probably knew. Morgan stayed in Vienna only long enough to tap the telegraph line to intercept federal messages, and to burn the railroad station. He then moved on east to Lexington, the small county seat of Scott County, where the tired raiders spent the night. Learning that Madison was strongly defended by 3,000 Legion infantry supported by artillery, Morgan sent a detachment toward Madison as a feint while his main column moved toward Vernon, a tempting railroad target.

When the Confederate raiders turned east from Salem, Major General Orlando Wilcox, the commander of the recently created Military District of Indiana, immediately took measures at Indianapolis to defend Vernon—a county seat town on the Madison branch of the Jeffersonville and Indianapolis railroad. Three miles north of Vernon and its two large and vulnerable bridges, the Madison branch crossed the Ohio and Mississippi Railroad, the main line from Cincinnati to St. Louis. Destruction of the bridges and facilities at these two points would certainly damage the northern war effort, as well as retard pursuit by entrained U.S. troops. To protect these vital centers, General

Love's Legion force at Seymour was moved east over the O and M. A small Legion infantry regiment with light artillery was placed in each town. Morgan arrived at Vernon in mid-afternoon with his advance column and immediately demanded a surrender. Colonel Hugh Williams, the Legion commander, replied "that he was abundently able to hold the place, and if Morgan gets it he must take it by hard fighting."[30] Brave words for a militia commander with only 400 men and two cannon. In Kentucky and Tennessee, Confederate and U.S. forces in general had a considerable degree of contempt for the Home Guard. As John Hunt Morgan was learning, the Indiana militia seemed to march to a different drum.

The perplexed Morgan began to throw out a skirmish line, while the main column moved off toward Dupont to the south. Morgan later sent a flag of truce with another demand for surrender, but while the parley was taking place General Love arrived by train from the north with 800 Minutemen and Legion infantry. Love asked for two hours of time to remove women and other non-combatants and Morgan granted him 30 minutes, during which time the non-combatants were moved to a nearby woods. The Legion and Minutemen prepared for the attack. It never came. After a brief skirmish which produced only Confederate casualties—and very few of these—Morgan withdrew. The Confederates received an obvious check at Vernon. The citizen soldiers—Legion and Minutemen—though vastly inferior in number were not lacking in pluck. Morgan certainly could have overcome them but the casualties and time were not worth the price. After dark, General Lew Wallace, interrupted at home in Crawfordsville while continuing to await new orders and again pressed into emergency service, arrived by rail with 2,000 more Legion and minutemen infantry.[31]

The Confederates, by now quite jaded, spent the night in Dupont where they burned the railroad depot and water tank, along with two large bridges. Mayfield's Packing House was plundered, and, when the raiders moved out before dawn next morning, each trooper had at least one ham slung on his saddle. By moving north Morgan again confused the federals as to his true intentions. The Confederate advance party dashed into Versailles about noon the next day, Sunday, July 12, and again captured the local Legion commander and about 300 of his men who were mustering. Also caught unaware was the Ripley

County treasurer who had $5,000 in county funds which Morgan promptly took. The stay in Versailles was necessarily short. Although the rebel soldiers impressed every horse that they could find in their path, leaving few for General Hobson and his pursuing federals, the horses confiscated usually were work animals and not the fine saddle horses that the Kentucky cavalrymen were accustomed to. As their ride across southern Indiana progressed, the Confederates' mobility decreased markedly. Although the Hoosier citizenry of the Legion-Minutemen force pursued with vigor, the railroad-bound militia could not quite corner the Southern invaders, however poorly they were now mounted. From Versailles, they moved east down the Ohio and Mississippi line to Milan, burning every bridge along the route, and then turned north toward the Indianapolis and Cincinnati Railroad. Late that night the main body arrived at Sunman's Station, only to find that about 2,500 armed Hoosiers were there. After a brief skirmish in the darkness the Confederates turned east and bypassed the village. As Morgan left Sunman's Station, Colonel Lawrence Shuler, one of the defenders of Vernon, arrived close on the heels of the rebel rear guard. After Morgan had abandoned Vernon, Colonel Shuler mounted about 200 Legion soldiers on impressed horses and began to pursue the Confederate force. The redoubtable Shuler was no stranger to horses or to John Morgan. He was the first colonel of the Fourth Indiana Cavalry and commanded the regiment from August, 1862, until May, 1863, when he left the service because of disability. As commander, Shuler successfully fought Morgan on Christmas Day, 1862, at Munfordville, Kentucky.[32]

On the evening of July 11, Shuler's small but determined band had joined General Hobson's brigade of U.S. cavalry and had become its advance detachment. At Sunman's Station Colonel Kline G. Shryock, commanding the 104th Regiment of Minutemen, joined Shuler's provisional cavalry and marched to give him infantry support if the fox could be brought to bay. Like Colonel Shuler, Colonel Shryock was no stranger to providing infantry support, nor to marauding Kentucky cavalrymen. He had helped organize the 87th Indiana Volunteer Infantry and had commanded the regiment from August, 1862, until March, 1863, when he resigned. As commander of the 87th, he led his regiment in the pursuit of General Bragg in northern Kentucky and at the Battle of Perryville.[33] Shuler

70

caught the rear of the fleeing Confederates at the state line in Harrison, Ohio, next afternoon, but the rebels declined to stand and fight. Shuler rested his impromptu command for a few hours and then followed as far as Batavia, Ohio. Finding the Buckeyes able to protect themselves, he returned to Indiana. Discontinuing their support at Harrison, Shryock marched his force to Lawrenceburg. On the night of July 13 word was sent to Lawrenceburg that Morgan had doubled back and was advancing on the city. Colonels Gavin and Shryock both moved their regiments east to meet the latest threat but, on a sharp curve along the towpath of the Whitewater Canal, the head of one column mistook the tail of the other force for the non-existent enemy and fired. Before the shooting stopped, six were killed and 18 were seriously wounded—12 hours after the last of the Confederate invaders had crossed into Ohio.[34] By noon on July 13 the last of Morgan's band had entered Ohio and certain capture, which came 13 days later in eastern Ohio. Morgan left behind in Indiana burned mills, railroad stations, and railroad bridges, along with a long trail of worn-out and broken-down horses. The raiders also left a legacy that has become a venerable part of the folklore of southern Indiana, and a proud episode in the history of the Indiana militia that does credit to the tradition of the citizen soldier.

As the war dragged on into its third year the output of northern farms and factories exceeded all expectations. Due in large part to new labor saving inventions such as the reaper and improved threshing machines, agricultural production actually increased in the North, in spite of the great drain of manpower from the farms, while industrial production reached unheard of levels. No longer were the armies of the United States restrained for lack of muskets, food, or uniforms. The shortage was manpower. Due to high combat losses, extensive thinning by disease, and the increased requirements for service troops as the Union forces occupied more territory, the government's need for men could no longer be filled on a nation-wide basis by voluntary enlistments. Indiana, however, had met her quotas, but with ever-increasing difficulty. Reluctantly facing the problem, Congress in March, 1863, finally passed the National Conscription Act. Its consequences were far-reaching but they were more important politically than militarily, at least to Indiana troops, for the majority of soldiers raised in Indiana after national conscription remained volunteers, even

71

if reluctant ones. For the first time the act asserted the power of the national government to raise troops without state assistance. The law ignored the states and created enrollment districts that coincided with congressional districts. Each district was headed by an assistant provost marshal, an officer of the Army assigned by the War Department who had the power to arrest those who obstructed enrollment or the subsequent draft. Each state was supervised by an assistant provost marshal general, and each district by an assistant provost marshal, both officers of the Army. Both were appointed by the War Department and were empowered with the authority to arrest.[35] All white male citizens from age 20 to age 45 were required to register. A weakness, and a great one, was that anyone could be exempt upon the payment of $300 commutation, or by furnishing another person as a substitute. The section of the law allowing commutation was repealed in July, 1864, but substitutes were accepted until the end of the war.

Perhaps the greatest weakness of conscription was that it raised *new* regiments, when the actual need was for individual replacements to fill vacancies in existing regiments in the field. The real value of conscription was that it encouraged voluntary enlistments. Enrollment began in Indiana on May 28, 1863, and proceeded slowly, for there was widespread opposition to another draft. The first draft call came on July 18, but since Indiana previously had furnished more than her quotas, more were not required. The next call came on October 17, 1863, when the President issued a request for 300,000 men. This number was increased to 500,000 during the following February and ultimately was raised to 700,000 in March. Under these three calls Indiana's total quota was 45,529. During this period 37,011 Hoosiers enlisted and their numbers, added to an excess from previous calls of 11,102, resulted in a surplus. No draft was required.[36] In July, 1864, the President directed the raising of still another 500,000 and Indiana's new quota was set at 25,662. However, at this time in Indiana and throughout the North, wages were very high and labor was scarce. These factors, together with a polarization of public sentiment, made it impossible to fill the quota and Indiana had to resort to drafting 12,476 men to meet the requirement.[37] The last call of the war was made in December, 1864, for another 300,000. Indiana's share was 22,582 and this was met in part by volunteers, although the state

72

was forced to resort to a draft in March, 1865, to fill the last 2,424 vacancies.[38] Prior to July, 1864, all of the levies had been for new regiments. However, all of the men drafted in 1864 were sent to depleted veteran Indiana units in the field, where they easily were assimilated and quickly became old soldiers.

In the spring of 1863 the War Department came to the realization that the war would not end before autumn, 1864. By then, more than half of the regiments currently in the field would have reached or exceeded the expiration of their enlistments and would be mustered out. After May, 1861, all Indiana regiments, except for three one-year regiments, had been enlisted for three years, but all of the units raised under the draft of July, 1862, were for nine months. Many eastern states had furnished 12-month regiments. In an effort to retain one half of the Army, the War Department issued a general order in April, 1863, that any soldier who re-enlisted would be granted a 30-day furlough. Although intended to affect the 30 two-year New York regiments which were due to be mustered out in the spring of 1864, it, of course, applied to all units in federal service. In May, this provision was broadened to stipulate the conditions under which all volunteer regiments could re-enlist as regiments for three years. In June, the program was improved by giving a $402 federal bounty to each soldier who re-enlisted. In November, it was further announced that whenever three-fourths of a regiment or battery re-upped, the unit would be sent home for a 30-day furlough which began upon their arrival.[39] Any units that re-enlisted or "veteranized" could add the proud word *veteran* to its unit designation; e.g., 11th Indiana Veteran Volunteer Infantry. The implementation of the plan was placed in the hands of regimental officers, who were spurred by the fact that if the unit veteranized, they would stay in service; if it did not, they would be mustered out with the regiment when it completed its term. The governors were given an incentive to support the plan when the War Department announced in June that veteranizing units would be deducted from the states' existing or future quotas. The deadline for action was originally December 1, 1863, but was extended by a War Department general order to January 5, 1864, and subsequently to March 31, 1864, in an effort to extend every opportunity to those who were eligible.

The volunteer infantry regiments had left Indiana in the

73

summer and autumn of 1861 with 1,048 rank and file. By the spring of 1863 few contained more than 400 effectives. Bullets, bacteria, and desertion had reduced some regiments to 250 men. Most regiments had scores of men who were not able to stand the rigors of field soldiering and were detailed to headquarters and depots in the rear. Although still carried on their unit rolls, many of them had not seen their regiments in a year. Every regimental roll contained names beside which were the grim notations "missing in action," or "prisoner of war." To overcome the difference between actual effectives and the number on paper, the War Department was very generous in its definition of the "three-fourths" used as a basis for veteranizing, stipulating that only effectives would be counted and that anyone who had nine months of federal service and had been honorably discharged could enlist and collect the $402 bounty. Veteranization was hotly debated within the Army, but by the final deadline of March 31, 1864, the majority of Indiana regiments and batteries that were eligible had carried out the process. Individuals who did not re-enlist were transferred to non-veteranized units.

In the early spring the veteran regiments began their furloughs. Of course, not all could go at one time. The scheduling was left to departmental or Army commanders. In the Department of the Gulf, General Banks announced that only two regiments from any army corps could be absent at any given time. The 46th Indiana Veteran Volunteer Infantry had voted to veteranize in November, 1863, and immediately began re-enlisting, completing the reorganization on January 2, 1864. In all, 307 men in the 46th veteranized.[40] Before their turn came to return home on furlough, Banks began the Red River campaign, in which he needed every available unit, including the 46th, which marched out of Algiers, Louisiana, on March 6 toward Shreveport, Louisiana. The Red River Campaign was a failure, but for the 46th Indiana it was a disaster. At Sabine Cross Roads on April 8 the regiment was caught unsupported and quickly lost seven killed and 86 captured, who spent the remainder of the war in a prison camp in Tyler, Texas. Before the campaign ended, more than one-third of the regiment's veterans were lost—killed, prisoners, or hospitalized.[41] The 46th finally began its furlough in June and arrived in Logansport where the 30-day rest began. After returning to Indianapolis, the unit was sent to Evansville to participate in the last major Legion expedition of the war. While the 46th was enjoying Indianapolis, Stovepipe Johnson, now a Confederate brigadier general, was back in western Kentucky recruiting volunteers, and attempting to enforce the rebel conscript laws and harass traffic on the Cumberland, Tennessee, and Ohio rivers. By early August, Johnson had assembled a force of 1,870 men who had been armed, equipped, and mounted. He claimed to control eight counties in southwest Kentucky.[42] At this time the Ohio River was at its lowest level in memory and was fordable in numerous places. Citizens in the counties along the river in Indiana and Illinois were concerned. As the 46th entrained for Evansville the federals were assembling a force of 2,000 United States troops at Smithland, Kentucky, at the confluence of the Cumberland and the Ohio. Another 2,000 U.S. troops were coming upriver from Cairo, Illinois.[43]

Alvin P. Hovey, the colonel of the 24th Indiana (and later a governor of the state) was at home on leave in Mt. Vernon and, upon learning of Stovepipe Johnson's activities, informed the commanding general of the Legion, Major General Hughes, that he would like to lead an expedition to Kentucky to break up the guerrilla camps. Governor Morton readily assented and asked the commander of the Military District of Indiana for the use of the 46th and 32d Indiana Infantry. The request was granted. Quarters were not available for the 46th at Evansville, since the Legion had been mustered, and the regiment spent the night on the river in a wharfboat. The next morning was spent in a pleasant grove on the edge of town. At nine o'clock that morning it was rumored that the rebels were crossing at Shawneetown, and the unit hastily embarked on an old mail packet for Mt. Vernon, where it disembarked that evening and bivouaced on the lawn of the Posey County courthouse after being well fed by generous citizens. About midnight a courier from downriver reported that the rebels had captured several boats and were preparing to cross over and take Shawneetown. Soon after, a large railroad ferry arrived from Pittsburgh, going downriver. It was capable of accommodating a thousand men and was soon impressed, loaded, and under way. At 10 o'clock that night Shawneetown came into view but the guerrillas still were several miles downriver. Proceeding slowly because of the low water, the ferry encountered the enemy about two hours later. A small gunboat, the *U.S.S.*

75

Fairplay, had just come upriver and was shelling the rebels. The 46th and some Legion members landed and skirmished with the enemy, who promptly mounted and fled, leaving three steamers that they had captured the day before. All three had been bound upstream with cattle for Sherman's army. The amphibious 46th then returned to Shawneetown where the railroad ferry was returned to her owners and the regiment returned to Mt. Vernon on the *Jennie Hopkins*, one of the liberated river steamers.

At Mt. Vernon, General Hovey was organizing a force consisting of Legion infantry and artillery units, the 32d, and the 46th. The morning that the 46th returned from Shawneetown the Dan Rice circus boat tied up at the landing in Mt. Vernon, with the band playing and the performers in costume. While all those aboard probably looked forward to playing Mt. Vernon, the town turned out to be more than a one-night stand—but a performance that Dan Rice and company would long remember. First, General Hovey impressed the circus horses to pull a Legion artillery battery. The show went on without equestrian acts.[44] While in Indianapolis some of the men of the 46th had obtained some spurious bills. On the face they very closely resembled a five-dollar U.S. bank note, but on the back they advertised a local saloon. The morning after the show Dan Rice presented the regimental commander with a small bundle of the bills and demanded legal tender in exchange, to no avail. The next day Hovey impressed the circus boat because his steamer fleet couldn't handle his growing force. The showmen had recovered enough of their humor by the time the expedition reached Uniontown, Kentucky, that the circus band was playing marches and patriotic airs. As the federals began to disembark, the rebels camped back of the town quickly dispersed, leaving enough horses to enable the artillerymen to return the impressed mounts to the circus, which very promptly left for a more profitable locale. The Hovey task force quickly formed and marched inland to Morganfield, about eight miles from the river. There was almost constant skirmishing along the way, but the rebels declined to stand and fight. After a sharp encounter at White Oak Swamp, two miles below Morganfield, about 20 of Stovepipe Johnson's conscripts were taken prisoner and a large cantonment was burned. Next day, Hovey led a flying column to Giger Lake, nine miles west. Again, the bird had flown.[45]

That morning, General Paine arrived at Uniontown with 2,000 federal troops. Hovey's group then started for Henderson, again skirmishing along the route with rebels who refused to stay and fight. The tired and dusty force arrived in Henderson late on August 20. Most of the Legion and the 46th left the next day for Evansville, where the provisional unit was disbanded. The 46th counted one soldier slightly wounded. Several Legion members suffered minor wounds but no other casualties. From Evansville, the 46th went to Lexington, Kentucky, where it spent the rest of the war doing provost marshal duty.

The last presidential call for troops in 1864 came on December 19, with Indiana's quota set at 22,582. The quota was not filled by volunteers and in March, 1865, 2,082 men were drafted.[45] Now, the entire recruiting effort was in the hands of the federal government, which slowly was attempting to overcome the deficiencies of relying on the militia systems of the various states. Unfortunately, the federal effort came far too late in the war to benefit the armies in the field, for less than a month after the last Hoosier was drafted in March, 1865, General Robert E. Lee surrendered the Army of Northern Virginia, and four weeks later in Texas, the last Confederate remnants gave up the fight.

During the war Indiana furnished 208,367 soldiers and sailors for federal service.[46] If the one-year and two-year enlistments are converted to three-year enlistments, Indiana's contribution is 197,141 men.[47] Indiana has the unique distinction of having raised all of her units on her own soil. After May, 1863, several states, notably New York and Massachusetts, recruited large numbers of black troops in the south in areas under federal control. A few white units and many individual replacements were recruited in the south by other states, but not by Indiana. One black regiment was created from Indiana's small black population, the 28th United States Colored Infantry, in November, 1863.[48] The officers in this regiment were, except for those of field grade, non-commissioned officers from older Indiana regiments who volunteered to accept commissions in the unit. The 28th U.S.C.I. fought in the east with the Army of the Potomac, and had a commendable record.

Indiana troops fought in the first battle of the war, at Philippi, in western Virginia, on June 3, 1861, and in the last battle of the war at Palmetto Ranch, Texas, on May 13, 1865, five weeks after General Lee surrendered. The last Union soldier killed in the war was a Hoosier.

Considering that Indiana's population in the 1860 census was only 1,350,400, the Hoosier contribution is all the more remarkable, for the state had only slightly more than 300,000 men of military age. Of the 197,141 who served, 25,028 died in service—12.6 percent. Two Indiana infantry regiments, the 19th and the 27th, had over 15 percent killed and died of wounds. Thirteen regiments had more than 10 percent killed and died of wounds.[49] Of the 158 regiments and 26 light artillery batteries from Indiana, only three regiments had more killed in action and mortally wounded than they lost from disease—a shocking commentary on health conditions of the era. Understandably, those who returned did not bring back many romantic ideas of their service. These Indiana citizen soldiers, volunteer and conscript, did return with a record that they could be extremely proud of, and one in which future generations could express both pride and gratitude.

---

[1] Theodore Gronert, "The First National Pastime in the Midwest", *Indiana Magazine of History,* Vol. 29, No. 3, pp. 171-86.

[2] *War of the Rebellion,* a compilation of the official records of the Union and Confederate armies, 128 vols. (Washington, 1880-1900).

[3] Lew Wallace, *Autobiography* (New York: Harper, 1906), p. 265.

[4] William H. H. Terrell, *Indiana in the War of The Rebellion* (Indianapolis: Indiana Historical Society, 1960, reprint ed.), p. 11.

[5] Emory Upton, *The Military Policy of the United States* (Washington: Government Printing Office, 1904), p. 264.

[6] Terrell, *Indiana in the Rebellion,* p. 16.

[7] Ibid., p. 22.

[8] Ibid., p. 135.

[9] Ibid., p. 59.

[10] Adam R. Johnson, *The Partisan Rangers* (Louisville: Feller, 1904), p. 104.

[11] Terrell, *Indiana in the Rebellion,* p. 183.

[12] Ibid., p. 186.

[13] Kenneth P. Williams, *Lincoln Finds a General,* 5 vols. (New York: Macmillan, 1951-1959), see Vol. 4, Chapter 3 for a detailed discussion of this campaign.

[14] Thomas L. Livermore, *Numbers and Losses in the Civil War* (Bloomington: Indiana University Press, 1957, reprint ed.), p. 89.

[15] Terrell, *Indiana in the Rebellion,* p. 124.

[16] Williams, *Lincoln Finds a General,* Vol. 4, p. 53.

[17] Livermore, *Numbers and Losses,* p. 95.

[18] Ibid., p. 95.

[19] Williams, *Lincoln Finds a General,* Vol. 4, p. 275.

[20] William F. Fox, *Regimental Losses in the American Civil War* (Albany, N.Y.: Morningside, 1970, reprint ed.), p. 435.

[21] Williams, *Lincoln Finds a General*, Vol. 4, p. 54.

[22] *War of the Rebellion*, Series I, Vol. 23, p. 817.

[23] Terrell, *Indiana in the Rebellion*, p. 204.

[24] Hattie L. Winslow and Joseph R. Moore, *Camp Morton 1861-1865* (Indianapolis: Indiana Historical Society, 1940), p. 379.

[25] Terrell, *Indiana in the Rebellion*, p. 224.

[26] Ibid., p. 226.

[27] Ibid., p. 229.

[28] Ibid., p. 232.

[29] *War of the Rebellion*, Series I, Vol. 23, p. 658.

[30] Terrell, *Indiana in the Rebellion*, p. 237.

[31] Wallace, *Autobiography*, p. 658.

[32] Terrell, *Indiana in the Rebellion*, Vol. 3, pp. 12, 157.

[33] Ibid., Vol. 3, pp. 79, 162.

[34] Ibid., p. 246.

[35] Ibid., p. 56.

[36] Ibid., pp. 58, 60.

[37] Ibid., p. 237.

[38] Ibid., p. 68.

[39] *The Personnel Replacement System in the United States Army* (Washington: Department of the Army, 1954), p. 108.

[40] Thomas Bringhurst, *History of the Forty-Sixth Regiment, Indiana Volunteer Infantry* (Logansport: Wilson, Humphries, 1888).

[41] Ibid., p. 106.

[42] Johnson, *Partisan Rangers*, p. 169.

[43] *Official Records of the Union and Confederate Navies in the War of the Rebellion*, 34 Vols. (Washington, 1894-1927), Series I, Vol. 26, pp. 488, 512.

[44] Bringhurst, *History of the Forty-Sixth*, p. 107.

[45] Terrell, *Indiana in the Rebellion*, p. 59.

[46] Ibid., p. 133.

[47] Frederick Phisterer, *Statistical Record* (New York, 1901), p. 10.

[48] Terrell, *Indiana in the Rebellion*, p. 98.

[49] Fox, *Regimental Losses*, pp. 526-27.

THE ORIGINS OF A MODERN MILITIA

William J. Watt

Interest in the militia slumped temporarily as war-weary Hoosiers came home from the nation's first experience with mass-scale bloodshed and turned to the business of adjusting to life as civilians. While veterans sought a niche in a society that was changing dramatically as railroads and the stimulus of wartime production needs brought industrialization to the Hoosier state, Indiana military authorities were preoccupied with the administrative aftermath of civil war. State military reports lapsed in the latter 1860s as officials labored to settle claims from the recent war. The post-war militia was unorganized and no one seriously suggested that an immediate effort be undertaken to revive it. People needed time to forget the war. Veterans, fatigued by bearing arms, were willing to leave the matter of citizen soldiering to a newer generation of men or, at least, wanted a few years' respite. However, the Indiana militia by this time was an institution with enduring roots and its revival in the 1870s was a logical consequence of that heritage.

The remaining decades of the nineteenth century were unsettled, often turbulent years as the state experienced a transition to industrialization, the growth of cities, and the completion of a rail-transportation network that was especially pervasive in Indiana because of the state's central location. Expanding industry centered on natural resources. Mining, lumbering, and wood-related industries surged in the post-war years, gouging cheap fuel from within the earth of southern and western Indiana, while above ground the thick forest cover was hacked away to provide material for furniture making and construction.[1]

This alteration of the Hoosier landscape and the Hoosier lifestyle eventually was accompanied by economic difficulty as the wartime boom spent itself and went bust in the Panic of 1873. Throughout the remaining years of the 1870s, a lingering depression sapped both economic vitality and the goodwill of labor. Wages were cut, embittering workers, especially those in the minefields and on railroads, where working conditions bred volatile tempers and occasioned violent reactions as employee grievances became more widespread. Strikes erupted with greater frequency, and Indiana earned a national reputation as a focal point for labor trouble. Unrest in the minefields was further inflamed as coal operators brought in black laborers as strikebreakers, adding racial overtones to already troublesome conditions.[2]

A few writers have argued that this era of labor strife was responsible for the re-invigoration of the militia and that militia units found justification for their existence by functioning as a strikebreaking force. This appraisal seems unfair. For one thing, the Indiana militia began to re-emerge in the form of independent companies several years in advance of callups for strike duty. Even though some militia personnel, particularly the officers, may have identified themselves with the interests of the propertied classes, many members were laborers who suffered frustrations akin to those of men they faced during labor disorders. It is difficult to imagine that unpaid volunteer citizen soldiers would have looked forward to strike duty, confronting neighbors or co-workers at mines or industrial centers. It was a thankless chore, turning out at the call of civilian authorities to quell disorders involving workers with whom they sympathized. The reluctance of many Americans to take part in militia service during this era is underscored by the fact that the number of men enrolled in the militia and National Guard through the 1880s remained smaller in proportion to total population than at any other time in the nation's history.[3]

Even though militiamen didn't take up soldiering to intervene in labor disputes, they found themselves called upon with growing frequency to discharge strike duty for the simple reason that no other police force was able to sustain industrial peace. The regular Army was inadequate in terms of its size or its disposition around the country. Local sheriffs and police chiefs had only modest forces at their disposal. Some of them were unwilling to respond to labor trouble, preferring to abandon their duties to the state because of the local political implications of intervening in a strike.

In fact, the involvement of Guardsmen in labor disputes probably set back their evolution as a fighting force. Strike duty detracted from time available to learn tactics and the craft of soldiering, while it put militiamen on the defensive in emotion-packed confrontations that did not enhance their reputation.

The war weariness that had set back militia reorganization began to abate in the early 1870s. In his report for 1870, Adjutant General John G. Greenwalt reported that the state had issued arms to four independent military companies, each comprising 60 men: the Emmett Guards of Indianapolis; Company A, Indianapolis National Guards; Lafayette Scheutzen, and Fort Wayne Light Guards. At that time the state had in its possession a number of surplus arms, including 1,579 Springfield rifled muskets, 500 Enfield rifles, 700 carbines, and an assortment of six-pound cannons. Also in the inventory was a bronze field piece taken as a trophy in the War with Mexico. The artillery pieces were loaned frequently for local celebrations and the firing of salutes.[4]

The state was entitled to an annual payment of $7,120 for arms and equipment, but Greenwalt recommended that it be allowed to accumulate, since the state had no place for the safekeeping of arms and it obviously was premature to attempt a formal reorganization of the militia in Indiana.[5]

By 1872, ten independent military companies had been organized. However, they were not responsible to the state. Greenwalt complained:

> The militia of this state is wholly unorganized, and it has not been deemed expedient to attempt the organization of any part of the militia under the present defective law upon the subject. The most of the states of the Union, as in Indiana, have a militia law, and it is, with one or two exceptions, in all the states inoperative. The principal defect appears to be the want of compulsory measures to enforce service, and next, they all fail in the most essential feature, in that they do not provide for adequate compensation of those upon whom duties are imposed by the law.[6]

In 1873, a detachment of the Emmett Guards responded to a call for assistance arising from a violent encounter between miners and black strikebreakers during a strike at the Western Iron Company and its associated coal mines. Later that year, wage cuts on the Pennsylvania Railroad system brought riots to Logansport. Militiamen again were activated for several days of service. Eleven companies were organized to deal with the National Railway Strike of 1877, which affected many Indiana cities and rail lines. In most of these cases, the presence of militia units had a calming effect and few incidents of violence involving the troops were recorded.

In April, 1878, a more serious clash occurred when blacks who had been employed as strikebreakers at mines in Fountain County interrupted members of a militia company who were drinking at a saloon in Stringtown. Many of the militiamen were miners who had been out of work for a year—displaced by these very strikebreakers. In the melee that followed, three blacks were killed outright and another died later of injuries. Governor Williams called upon other militia units to restore order. The local company, known as the Wabash Guards, was disarmed and several of its members were tried on murder charges, but acquitted. At the adjutant general's direction, 37 members who were miners were discharged in the belief that their continued service offered nothing but the potential for further trouble. In June of that year, following renewed disturbances, the company was disbanded.[7]

In his 1874 report, Adjutant General W. W. Conner called for the enactment of a new militia law, saying that the governor could not authoritatively utilize the militia during emergencies such as the labor trouble of the previous year. He recommended the formation of at least one company in each congressional district and the raising of four units in Indianapolis. Conner also said that many of the guns owned by the state were obsolete and should be disposed of to help finance the purchase of newer models: "I would at least dispose of the damaged guns, as the room they occupy is more valuable to the state than the guns."[8]

For several years, members of the Indiana Legion had called for a statewide encampment. The initial one didn't take place until 1882 and was arranged under circumstances that dramatized the stinginess of state assistance to its military forces. The encampment had much of the atmosphere of a county fair; it was made possible by donations from Indianapolis civic leaders and the willingness of railroads to provide free transportation. Members of Raper Commandery of Knights Templar agreed to pay encampment costs in turn for the right to collect gate fees and to maintain a sutler's concession. Paying spectators were attracted by drill competition and shooting events which included contingents of National Guardsmen from other states. A few regular soldiers were on hand to help lay out the camp area and to function as headquarters guards.

In addition to the competition, the session centered on drill, guard mount, and parades.[9]

At the time of the July 1-6 encampment at the State Fairgrounds, the organized Indiana Legion stood at 29 infantry companies, five artillery batteries, and one cavalry troop. Enrolled strength was 103 officers and 1,491 enlisted men.

Another statewide encampment was conducted at Indianapolis in 1883 as Colonel Eli Lilly headed a citizens' committee that raised prize money for drill competition. Thirteen regular officers were detailed as judges and inspectors during the period, forerunners of today's teams of Army evaluators who assess the Guard's readiness at annual training stints.

Statewide training sessions were not ventured during the following two years, but one was scheduled in 1886 after Lafayette citizens pledged $4,000 to help offset expenses. In addition to the drill and marksmanship competition, sham battles were planned in an effort to bolster gate receipts. A hitch developed when Adjutant General George W. Koontz learned that Barnum's Circus also was due for an engagement in Lafayette at a time that would conflict with the Guard's "field day" of competition. Koontz subsequently agreed with circus promoters to share revenues, giving Barnum's 60 percent of gate receipts and the state collecting 40 percent. The combined affair was preceded by a joint parade of militiamen and circus performers. Indiana soldiers marched in line with gilded chariots, elephants, and other accessories of "the greatest show on earth".[10]

In 1889 the General Assembly adopted a landmark amendment to the state's militia law. It authorized the enrollment of men aged 18 to 45 into as many as 48 companies of 50 privates each, although the governor was empowered to increase the number during emergencies. An annual appropriation of $37,000 provided the first state support for encampments and included a $3.50 uniform allowance for each member. The law authorized a state contribution of $10 per month per company to help pay for armory rentals. Lawmakers stipulated that the uniform would be patterned after that worn by the regulars: dark blue blouses, light blue trousers, and forage caps. Legion members were exempted from jury duty. At that time most of the weaponry in the hands of Indiana Legion members consisted of the now-obsolete 1873 Springfield breechloader and various refinements.[11]

Labor trouble in 1894 resulted in intense involvement of the Legion in quieting disruptive strikes. Forty companies were in the field from eight to 20 days each. The costs of civil disturbance duty exceeded the legislative appropriation and Governor Claude Matthews arranged to finance the overage, confident that the subsequent legislature would reimburse him. It did. The encampment was canceled that year because Adjutant General Irvin Robbins believed that strike duty provided sound training, and because funds were lacking in any case.

On June 2, Governor Matthews ordered a force under General Robbins to Daviess and Sullivan counties in reaction to reports that 500 miners had gathered to prevent the movement of coal on the Baltimore & Ohio Southwestern Railway. Nine companies were detailed. Guardsmen encountered minor derailments and damage to a switch. They remained until the railroad could effect repairs. Most of the men were relieved two days later. On June 3, Brigadier General Will J. McKee arrived in Vincennes with 250 Guardsmen to escort coal trains in the Shelburn area. Track had been sabotaged. A military train moving to Shelburn encountered miners and a brief shooting incident ensued. The miners escaped, but militiamen found dynamite and fusing near the tracks. The force was doubled as trouble continued. Coal trains were burned, and sentries fired shots at miners who were stoning military trains on the nights of June 6 and 7. One gatling gun squad member was injured. The Legion's presence eventually stabilized the situation in southwestern Indiana and officials began phasing out the citizen soldiers on June 11.[12]

In July, a strike at Chicago by members of the American Railway Union generated widespread violence. Federal troops were called in and, in one incident, regular troops guarding a work train in Hammond fired on rioters, wounding three persons and killing a bystander. Hammond and Whiting were placed under martial law as 15 companies of Legion members were ordered to northwestern Indiana. The regulars left as soon as the militiamen arrived on the scene. The Indiana troops safeguarded key installations but avoided clashes with striking railroadmen. As the situation eased, militiamen were released.[13]

The year's labor troubles rekindled official interest in the state of militia affairs and spurred endeavors to modernize the Indiana Legion. That autumn, a committee of militia officers wrote reorganization legislation for presentation to the 1895 session of the General Assembly. In his address to the legislature Governor Matthews praised the Legion's endeavors during the preceding troubled year but noted: "On the whole, the militia is only fairly well equipped, still lacking much that is essential."[14] The reorganization proposal had his support and was enacted by large margins, 75-10 in the House and 32-15 in the Senate, although amendments whittled authorized levels of funding.

Maintaining tradition, the law separated militiamen into two categories. The active militia included able-bodied males between ages 18 and 45 who were enrolled or mustered. The sedentary militia encompassed all males subject to bear arms under the Constitution but who did not belong to the active militia. "The active militia shall be styled the National Guard," it declared. The statute authorized a maximum of 48 infantry companies, three artillery batteries, a signal corps, a hospital corps, and one band for each infantry regiment or artillery battalion. An annual appropriation of $45,000 was voted.[15]

The National Guard Act required units to conduct a mimimum of 24 drills and four public parades annually. During encampments, pay was set at $1 a day. When called out for state duty by the governor, privates were entitled to $1.50 daily, plus subsistence; non-commissioned officers received $2, plus subsistence, and commissioned officers were compensated at a rate equal to corresponding grades in the regular Army. The practice of electing company officers was retained, although non-commissioned officers (five sergeants and four corporals in an infantry outfit) were appointed by regimental commanders upon the unit commander's recommendation. Units were required to maintain a mimimum membership of 40 privates and could recruit to a maximum of 72. Enlistments were for an initial three-year term, with subsequent enrollments optional at two or three years. The law allowed the governor to disband a company if it failed to meet minimum strength standards, flunked inspections, neglected to file required reports, or became "lax in discipline, negligent in drill or other duties or members lose interest in their organization or become insubordinate."[16]

Companies adopted their own constitutions and bylaws to

cover penalties for non-attendance and for the administration of unit funds. A set of regulations, published later in 1895, required that fines for failure to attend an annual encampment would be levied at $5. Penalties ranged downward to a minimum of 50 cents for non-attendance at a parade and ten cents for missing a drill.[17]

The regulations, drawn up by General McKee, the Guard's brigade commander, tried to resolve the problem of incompatibility between one's civilian occupation and part-time military service. In contrast to today's far-reaching policies and laws which safeguard civilian employment rights for Guardsmen, the 1895 regulations only required the consent of employers before militiamen could be enrolled.

An infusion of equipment, including 200 stands of arms from the federal government, began that year. Quartermaster officials issued campaign hats, leggings, mess utensils, meat plates, canteens, haversacks, and knapsacks.[18]

About 3,000 Guardsmen attended the July, 1895, encampment at Fairview Park, north of Indianapolis. A torrential rainstorm on the eve of the seven-day training period soaked the area and about 1,400 Guardsmen were housed in the halls of the state capitol for the night.

General McKee described the training program:

> The daily routine which was observed throughout the week commencing Monday morning, embraced a formal guardmounting in each regiment, 50 minutes of company or squad drill, an hour and a half of regimental drill, and a regimental parade in each regiment, and two schools of an hour each for officers and non-commissioned officers.[19]

The schedule was varied by occasional practice on the rifle range and by a Thursday afternoon review before Governor Matthews. The impact of a better-organized militia, coupled with the operation of summary courts martial during the encampment, substantially reduced the number of men absent without leave. AWOLs had been a common and debilitating feature of the militia system during its more casual era.

In his annual report for 1895, Adjutant General Robbins said that the organization was limited to 46 company-sized maneuver units because the appropriation was insufficient to finance the 51 combat units authorized. "We have been cramped for means as it is; still by the assistance of the National allowance of $13,000, we have succeeded in fairly equipping the

87

present organization," Robbins reported. However, the adjutant general did avow that "the state could with ease place 2,600 drilled men in the field, at ten hours' notice, ready for service. With some inconvenience, this number could be doubled in a very short time. There are at least 6,000 young men in the state who have had experience in modern drill regulations. In case of disturbance, at home or abroad, this would form the nucleus of many thousand more."[20]

In this report for the following year, Robbins said that the successful operation of the militia law vindicated the wisdom of the legislature in adopting it, but he observed that the Guard still was strapped for money. It owed railroads about $4,000 from the previous year's encampment and was compelled to reduce the 1896 summer training period to six days in order to remain within its budget. The Guard declined to accept new companies to replace those which failed to maintain their strength and training "in order to have a smaller force thoroughly equipped, than to have the maximum force allowed by law partially prepared for service."[21]

McKee reported a decline in camp strength that year and attributed it to the funding limitations, more stringent enforcement of regulations, and the onset of a business recession. The 1897 encampment was canceled because over-expenditures of the previous year drained $5,289 from the budget before the new year began. The remaining funds from the $45,000 appropriation were utilized for equipment purchases.

This was the status of the Indiana National Guard on the eve of the war with Spain, cramped for funds but better organized than at any time since the Civil War and, perhaps, in the state's entire history. Professionalism was marginal by modern standards, but the Hoosier Guardsman of the mid-1890s was familiar with close order drill and had at least rudimentary training in marksmanship. Although the rifle he handled was the outdated Springfield, it represented an advance over Civil War-era muzzle-loaders only recently retired from the arms room. Still lacking the full complement of clothing and field gear, the Guardsman—unless he was a raw recruit—possessed enough of a uniform to identify him as a soldier and carried equipment essential to sustain him in the field. In the months to come, the National Guardsman would be one of the nation's key instruments as it rejected a heritage of isolation and emerged as a world power.

Politicians' and newspapers' clamorings for punitive action against Spain for its oppression of Cuba already had spurred momentum for war when the battleship *Maine* exploded in Havana harbor on February 15, 1898. The call for war reached a furious pitch and it now was shouted by militiamen as well, because they believed that their formations were the logical augmentation to a regular Army that had dwindled to little more than a frontier police force and whose 26,000 officers and men represented a smaller share of the population than at any time since the nation's founding. Although Congress initially added two artillery regiments to the regular Army, it amounted to an insignificant expansion for a field force that would have to face 80,000 Spanish troops in Cuba. Regulars argued for a new volunteer force under their direct control as a means of bypassing the state militia units. Congress recognized that it could not ignore the Guard because it was organized for mobilization, if only partially trained. The modest size of the regular force already was constraining the battle plans of President William McKinley and Secretary of War Russell Alger. They feared that it might be months before an invasion force could be marshalled for action in Cuba and Puerto Rico. Meanwhile, the strident cry for immediate assault upon the Spanish possessions was posing a sensitive political problem for an administration unprepared for war.

Late in April, Congress approved a plan to expand the Army. It represented middle ground between the professionals' call for volunteers to be placed under their direct control and the strong lobbying of the National Guard for the principal role of ready reserve. Congress authorized the President to call for volunteers for federal service, but stipulated that militia organizations which volunteered as units would be accepted in that form. Furthermore, the states would be empowered to recruit new militia formations whose officers would be appointed by their governors. These also could be incorporated into the volunteer army. At the same time, the regular Army was authorized to enlarge its manpower to 64,000 officers and men (although that level of strength never was achieved). Certain specialized units were to be organized by the regular Army, bypassing the states and the militia structure.[22]

Although popular enthusiasm for national expansion was far more muted in Indiana than on the Eastern Seaboard, the *Maine* sinking galvanized political support for war and the

89

National Guard's leadership began preparing for it. About April 1, Adjutant General James K. Gore noted the imminence of armed conflict and urged company commanders to recruit their units to a maximum of 84 men. This recruiting in excess of normal strength allotments was designed as a cushion against the winnowing of manpower that would result from examinations for physical disability, the rejection of underage volunteers, and the discharge of those whose personal circumstances would compel them to remain at home.

President McKinley, after authorization by Congress on April 22, issued a call to the states for 125,000 volunteers to serve terms of two years unless discharged sooner. On April 25, Governor James A. Mount received a telegram from Secretary of War Alger, describing Indiana's share as four regiments of infantry and two light batteries of artillery: "It is the wish of the President that the regiments of the National Guard or State Militia be used as far as their numbers will permit, for the reason that they are armed, equipped and drilled."[23]

That night, Guardsmen were ordered to report to the State Fairgrounds for organization and mustering into federal service. They were willing volunteers and without compulsion to serve if they didn't want to do so. A gubernatorial proclamation of April 25 emphasized this fact. "Any member of the National Guard whose business affairs would be jeopardized or whose domestic relations would subject his family to inconvenience and hardship, will be permitted to stand aside honorably and without prejudice," it stated.[24]

The mobilization was a dramatic affair. Guard personnel were notified, "some by the sounding of the riot call, others by the use of the fife and drum corps, some by telephone, and messengers were dispatched for those who lived in the country."[25]

As Guardsmen boarded hastily assembled troop trains for the journey to Indianapolis, they were given rousing sendoffs. Clattering across the night-cloaked Indiana landscape, the trains were met at each stop by crowds of shouting celebrants, lusty bands, and booming cannon. This was to be a war of conquest and glory, or so common folk believed, and for the last time in its history the departure of fathers, brothers, sons, and neighbors was attended by unrestrained jubilation. Almost as if denoting the passing of a century which saw Indiana transformed from a frontier territory to an industrial state, it was a final great outpouring of martially inspired patriotic fervor.

Guardsmen poured into an improvised cantonment at the State Fairgrounds, named Camp Mount in the governor's honor. The fact that Indiana became the first state to fill its quota of volunteers is testimony to the organization of an Indiana National Guard that had emerged since enactment of the revised militia law three years earlier.

The numbering of regiments continued the pattern used during the Mexican War and Civil War; the numerical designations for the War with Spain picked up where Civil War numbering had left off. The four 2,000-man National Guard regiments which reported to Camp Mount were designated the 157th, 158th, 159th, and 160th Volunteer Infantry regiments. A similar numbering system transformed the militia artillery units into the 27th and 28th Artillery batteries.

When mustering into federal service occurred, Guardsmen were enrolled as individuals, rather than as militia units, since it was the obvious intent of the federal government to use them in service abroad. This form of enrollment avoided the Constitutional uncertainties associated with the use of the militia in foreign wars.

Eager for a taste of foreign adventure, the citizen soldiers chafed at delays in receiving equipment, weeding out the physically unfit, arranging the discharge of those with job or domestic conflicts, resolving squabbles over political appointments to command and staff positions, and determining to what extent regular Army officers would be included in Guard formations to provide a professional nucleus of staff expertise. Guardsmen waited impatiently in the warming, humid springtime while the tedious processes of military bureaucracy were carried out. They were fearful that the regular Army would deny them the chance for heroism and for thrilling episodes in what was sure to be the first opportunity to carry the notion of Manifest Destiny to foreign shores. Their impatience intensified as the Hong Kong consulate cabled word to the Navy Department that the Pacific Squadron under Commodore George Dewey had swept the Spanish fleet from the Far East with a fast, furious gunnery duel in Manila Bay. Overnight, Dewey and the Navy became celebrities in a nation unwinding on a patriotic binge; militiamen ached for the opportunity to share in the luster. But they continued to wait, at Camp Mount or other stateside marshalling points, as Cervera's fleet was reduced by Sampson at Santiago. The naval victories guaranteed a short war, one that would end too soon for Hoosier militiamen to smell gunpowder on the battlefield.

On May 10, the 157th and 158th regiments were mustered into federal service. The former left five days later for Chickamauga Park, Georgia, which was becoming a vast gathering point for regulars and volunteers alike. Then traveling 650 miles from Camp Thomas, Georgia, to Port Tampa City, Florida, Guardsmen of the 157th believed that they were bound for Cuba, since Port Tampa City was the staging point for units destined for the Caribbean. An unlikely jumping-off place situated at the end of a single rail line, the port soon was choked with men, horses, and carloads of equipment. At one point the regiment's mounts and gear were loaded on transports while the men waited in stifling heat for the order to board. But news of the Battle of Santiago eliminated the need for the Hoosiers as part of an expeditionary force. They proceeded to Fernandina, Florida, their cantonment for a month, then returned to Indiana where they were mustered out on November 1. The regiment recorded 19 deaths from disease and accident.

The 158th did not get beyond camp life. Departing for Chickamauga Park on May 16, it arrived to face five months of monotony. The grounds became so unsanitary that the regiment was discharged on November 4. Ten of its soldiers died of non-combat causes.

Upon mustering into federal service, Guardsmen of the 159th Volunteer Infantry Regiment found themselves stripped of arms in order to equip properly the predecessor regiments. Eventually, they regained some equipment and were ordered to Camp Alger, at Dunn Loring, Virginia. In August, the regiment moved to nearby Thoroughfare Gap, where it went into camp in an old stubble field that was thoroughly saturated with water. In a few days, the campsite was so muddy that streets were impassible and sanitary conditions were disgraceful. The regiment moved to Camp Meade, Pennsylvania, and then to Indianapolis for discharge in November. The regiment counted 11 fatalities.[26]

The 160th, also initially shunted to Chickamauga Park, was scheduled to join the fighting in Puerto Rico, which had been

92

invaded July 25, but the orders were countermanded when an armistice was announced. The regiment waited at Newport News, Virginia, during the Puerto Rican episode and then was rotated to camps in the south, winding up at Charleston, South Carolina, where it was assigned occupation duty at Matanzas, Cuba, in January, 1899. The 160th remained in Cuba until March 26 and was mustered out at Indianapolis on April 25. Twelve of its soldiers fell victim to fatal disease or injury.

Similar frustration burdened the artillerymen, as the 28th Artillery Battery never got beyond Chickamauga Park. It returned to Indiana, counting one death during tedious months of camp life, and was relieved on October 31. The 27th Artillery Battery, however, came closest to firing a shot of any of the Indiana militia units called to federal service. Landing in Puerto Rico on August 4, the battery joined other militia and regular units in preparing to engage the Spaniards. It was on the firing line and ready for action when a messenger reported news of the peace protocol. More fortunate than the others in other respects too, the battery suffered no fatalities during its active-duty term.

Late in May, 1898, President McKinley issued a second call, this time for 75,000 volunteers; Indiana's quota was made known on June 18, when the state was asked to raise another infantry regiment and two companies of black soldiers.

The new regiment, designated the 161st, was commanded by Colonel Winfield T. Durbin, then serving as a member of Governor Mount's staff and as Republican national committeeman. Mustered into federal service on July 15, the regiment didn't leave Camp Mount until August 11, when it journeyed to Jacksonville, Florida, and then to Savannah, the embarkation point for Cuba, where the regiment was designated as part of the occupation force. At mid-December, the troopship *Mobile* steamed into Havana Harbor, past the ghostly wreckage of the *Maine*—a broken and twisted mass of iron, visible above the surface of the water—while men stood bareheaded, some in tears, as the band played the national anthem.[27]

The regiment debarked for Camp Columbia, at Mariana, Cuba, where it pulled garrison duty until March 29, 1899, and returned home by way of Washington and was discharged on May 3. Twenty Guardsmen died during the course of active duty. Durbin, upon returning home, mounted a successful campaign for the governorship.

The levying of the black companies engendered both confusion and controversy. Although Indiana had had two black militia companies since the 1880s—despite a Constitutional ban on their participation—the War Department opposed their activation because they were commanded by black officers. Governor Mount had sought permission to enroll them in the volunteer forces and finally secured federal acquiescence. For a time it seemed that the venture might falter because of difficulty in raising the troops. The Indianapolis *Journal* reported that attempts to raise the two companies were practically failures. The newspaper quoted Mount as saying that he supported the effort to create the companies largely because of pressure from black leaders, but was frustrated that recruiting was proceeding so poorly. However, newspaper accounts a week later reported that recruiting had improved enough to fill the 212-man complement for the two units. They were mustered into federal service and trained in southern camps, but never were involved in combat or foreign service. Historian William H. Smith, writing in 1903, claimed that the dispute between Indiana and the War Department over the recruiting of the two companies resulted in federal reprisals against the state by denying its volunteer units the opportunity to participate in combat. This assertion has not been confirmed.[28]

With the Guardsmen away from the state for federal duty, only one unit, an artillery battery at Dana, remained available to state officials for use as a civil defense force. After the May, 1898, callup, Hoosier Guard officials acted to organize additional companies, and 15 units were formed. An Indianapolis unit was activated, but not used, during disorders attending a plate glass workers' strike at Alexandria. Eight companies were alerted for duty during confrontations between white and black mine workers in Vanderburgh County. Their assistance was not required. Aside from the Spanish war effort, the closing months of the nineteenth century were quiet ones, militarily, in Indiana, and Guard officials endeavored to increase their inadequate state appropriation, but without success.

What had been for Hoosier militiamen a six-month war of boredom and frustration seemed an unlikely advertisement for the militia system. Any sense of being involved in a drama of historical significance ebbed quickly in the heat of malarial southern camps or in the confinement of troopships that never sailed. Although the brief binge of jingoism transformed the United States into a Pacific power, the impact of the nation's achievement was diluted at the time by scandals involving unpreparedness, "embalmed beef", and widespread epidemics of disease among the troops. For the most part, the militia volunteers were bypassed in the real fighting. Despite its small numbers, the regular Army carried the brunt of the action in Cuba. However, the war with Spain was to have far-reaching consequences for the National Guard.

Although it was a regulars' war, more than 124,000 volunteers were mustered into federal duty during the opening of the war effort, an achievement that could not have taken place at that pace without the existence of already organized and partially equipped state militia units. While Hoosier Guardsmen were unsuccessful in their desire to encounter the enemy, other Guardsmen did so, and with generally creditable results. Although the 71st New York Regiment was excoriated for breaking under fire at the battle of San Juan Hill (while armed with out-of-date Springfields whose blackpowder charges exposed them with every shot to a concealed enemy equipped with smokeless hardware), other Guard units drew praise. In the Philippines, the Guard helped subdue the Spaniards and then was forced to remain for many months as tension between the occupying United States and independence-minded Filipinos erupted into a full-scale guerrilla war. Furthermore, the preparedness of militia units at Puerto Rico, including Indiana's 27th Artillery Battery, made a favorable impression on observers.

Guardsmen of the Spanish-American conflict left an important legacy, because the years that followed were ones in which the United States Army groped, as it never had before, for an ultimate definition of the proper structure of America's military system. As memories of battles between blue and gray receded into the background, Army strategists grappled with new theories invoking modern European concepts of organization for war. For the most part, Army planners would come to argue for a larger professional Army, with the militia relegated to third-line status. Ultimately, that view did not prevail because the War Department could not ignore a National Guard that had built new vitality during the Spanish war and had established itself as a worthwhile backup force to the regulars. Although the theorists' memoranda might argue for other echelons of reserve forces, the War Department and Congress ultimately would strike compromises that preserved the role of the National Guard. In a practical sense, the Guard couldn't be passed over. It was a force in being, while others were only jottings on paper.

[1] Emma Lou Thornbrough, *Indiana in the Civil War Era* (Indianapolis: Indianapolis Historical Bureau, 1965), pp. 404-424.

[2] Ibid., pp. 440-454; Clifton J. Phillips, *Indiana in Transition* (Indianapolis: Indiana Historical Bureau, 1968), pp. 350-355.

[3] Russell F. Weigley, *History of the United States Army* (New York: Macmillan, 1967), p. 282; Jim Dan Hill, *The Minuteman in Peace and War* (Harrisburg: Stackpole, 1964), pp. 121-125.

[4] Indiana Adjutant General, *Report* (Indianapolis, 1870).

[5] Ibid., p. 6.

[6] Indiana Adjutant General, *Report* (Indianapolis, 1872), pp. 3-5.

[7] Thornbrough, *Indiana in the Civil War Era*, pp. 453-454; Indianapolis *News,* April 25, 1878.

[8] Indiana Adjutant General, *Report* (Indianapolis, 1874), pp. 3-5.

[9] *History of the National Guard of Indiana* (Indianapolis: Pratt, 1901), p. 103; Indiana Adjutant General, *Report* (Indianapolis, 1882), pp. 9-17.

[10] Indiana Adjutant General, *Report* (Indianapolis, 1886), p. 8; *History of the National Guard of Indiana,* p. 108.

[11] *Acts of Indiana* (1889) 177.

[12] Indiana Adjutant General, *Report* (Indianapolis, 1894), p. 18, pp. 31-35.

[13] Ibid., pp. 20-21; *History of the National Guard of Indiana,* pp. 124-127.

[14] Governor Claude C. Matthews, "Annual Message to the General Assembly," *Journal,* Indiana House of Representatives (Indianapolis, 1895).

[15] *Acts of Indiana* (1895) 53; William J. Watt, "The Birth of the Indiana National Guard," *Indiana Military History Journal,* January, 1978.

[16] *Acts of Indiana* (1895) 53.

[17] Brigadier General Will J. McKee, *Military Law and Regulations for the Indiana National Guard* (Indianapolis, 1895), pp. 59-60.

[18] Indiana Adjutant General, *Report* (Indianapolis, 1895), p. 6.

[19] Ibid., p. 11.

[20] Ibid., p. 6.

[21] Indiana Adjutant General, *Report* (Indianapolis, 1896), pp. 5-6.

[22] Weigley, *History of the U. S. Army,* pp. 295-298.

[23] Indiana Adjutant General, *Report* (Indianapolis, 1898), p. 6.

[24] Ibid., pp. 6-7.

[25] *History of the National Guard of Indiana,* p. 295.

[26] Ibid., p. 329.

[27] W. E. Biederwolf, *History of the 161st Regiment, Indiana Volunteer Infantry* (Logansport, Ind.: Wilson, Humphries, 1899), p. 111.

[28] Indianapolis *Journal,* July 7, 1899; William Henry Smith, *The History of the State of Indiana,* 2 vols. (Indianapolis: Blair, 1903), Vol. 2,

pp. 469-470; Willard B. Gatewood, Jr., "Indiana Negroes and the Spanish American War," *Indiana Magazine of History*, Vol. 69, No. 2.

THE NATIONAL GUARD IN A NEW CENTURY

William J. Watt

The National Guard revitalized itself quickly after the Spanish war, without even a brief period of stagnation like those occurring after the Mexican War and Civil War. At the beginning of 1900, the Indiana Guard consisted of 11 infantry companies and two artillery batteries, generally reflecting units raised to provide a standing militia for state emergencies while other Guardsmen were away for the war. Their return spurred the enrollment of additional units. Twenty-five infantry companies and a third artillery battery were added to the roster during 1900. Encampment strength that year stood at 1,830, of an enrolled total of 2,118.

The Guard further was stimulated by action of the 1901 General Assembly to authorize drill pay, something that militia leaders had urged for years. Following the legislature's action the Military Department of Indiana required weekly armory drills of not less than 90 minutes of actual instruction, as well as three days of rifle practice each year. Drill pay ranged from 20 cents for privates to 30 cents for sergeants and 50 cents for captains. On range practice days, privates were entitled to $1.00, sergeant $1.10, second lieutenants $1.20, and captains $1.30. Pay was given in semiannual installments on the last day of April and October.[1]

A subsequent order established fines for absence from drills, amounting to a forfeiture of 60 per cent of the pay for a subsequent drill. Officials decided that regimental and battalion bands were not eligible for drill pay.[2]

The rapid reorganization of the Guard in Indiana and other states had an impact upon War Department reorganization planning. By 1903, the Guard nationwide had attracted personnel totaling more than 116,000—a force too large for Congress to ignore, even though regular Army theorists were beginning an unrelenting campaign to eliminate the militia as a ready reserve. In the words of Guard historian General Jim Dan Hill: "they underwrote their perpetuation in the defense scheme of the future by reorganizing at once from the grassroots up."[3]

The reorganization debate resulted in the Militia Act of 1903 (discussed in Chapter I) , which, despite several defects, for the first time set meaningful standards for the performance of Guard formations and for their entitlement to federal assistance.

That year, a regular officer was detailed to inspect the Indiana National Guard to determine if the state's forces were eligible for federal funds under the new law. His report was favorable. It was a significant year in other respects as Hoosier Guardsmen joined with regular Army personnel for joint maneuvers at Camp Young, near West Point, Kentucky. During the Guard's annual encampment—this time at the present site of Ft. Benjamin Harrison—tactical exercises were carried out under the guidance of regular officers led by Colonel Arthur L. Wagner, considered to be one of the leading military educators of the era.

In 1904, Brigadier General Oran Perry, the Guard's quartermaster general, reported: "Since the passage of the 'Dick Bill' very material progress has been made toward placing the Guard of this state on an equality with the troops of the regular establishment as far as equipment is concerned."[4]

Units began to retire black-powder Springfields as shipments of Krag-Jorgenson rifles were provided by the War Department (which was making them available as newer 1903 Springfields were allotted to the regulars) . The state also received 3.2-inch field guns, replacing some of its artillery museum pieces. Nationwide, the Guard remained very infantry-heavy, since federal and state governments were unwilling to provide extra funds for specialized units such as cavalry or artillery. In 1905, money provided under the Dick Act permitted Guard officers to attend Army officer schools, with travel, quarters, and subsistence provided by the War Department.

However, one area of military skill—marksmanship—was suffering badly. The 1900 report of Adjutant General James K. Gore described marksmanship as very deficient. During the 1902 encampment no range practice was conducted, "owing to the only accessible range being unavailable by reason of the growing crops."[5]

General McKee, the brigade commander, called for the establishment of permanent ranges. In 1906, the state received nearly $60,000 in federal aid for arms, equipment, and rifle practice. Extensive regulations and recommendations concerning marksmanship were published that year. By 1907, 21 ranges had been constructed at the Guard's rented armories. Command emphasis on marksmanship brought improvements. That year, Indiana ranked 29th among the states in national team competition. The re-emphasis on marksmanship training was reflected in the annual reports of adjutants general, who reported in tedious detail the rosters of qualified marksmen and team competitors.

In 1905, further legislative amendments to the militia law organized the Indiana Guard as a division and created a major general's slot for its commander. It also grappled with the problem of Guardsmen's civilian employment rights by stipulating that: "a person who deprives or prevents employment by another, or who annoys or obstructs another who employs a guardsman or who dissuades from enlistment by threat"[6] is guilty of a misdemeanor. The law also said that corporations and other associations (unions, for example) could not discriminate against individuals who were in the Guard. The legislation also exempted Guardsmen from the road and poll taxes.

The anti-discrimination provision attempted to deal with opposition to Guard service that had festered during three decades of militia involvement in labor trouble, an involvement that had placed Guardsmen in the uncomfortable and unpopular role of policemen during episodes of violence. If the account by Adjutant General Frank L. Bridges, writing in 1914, can be taken at face value, the employment safeguards didn't work:

> Regardless of the statements of labor leaders, the writer has been informed that unions have refused membership to National Guardsmen and have thereby refused to permit men to provide their families with the necessities of life, until they secured a discharge from the National Guard service. This statement is made on my own experience in two instances and upon the experiences as stated to me by other officers many times. While there is a law in this state prohibiting this action on the part of unions and other organizations and a fine is provided, yet the fact that this statute is on the books has not changed the conditions which secured the enactment of the law, as it is almost impossible to secure evidence for conviction.
>
> This attitude of union labor is no worse, however, in its effect on the discipline of the Indiana National Guard, than the attitude of some employers of labor who not only fail to encourage National Guard enlistments, training, and discipline which might be made so beneficial to them, but who complain about the time

100

spent by their employes in the service and who in some instances have discharged men from their employment on account of it. In such cases, of course, evidence for conviction is also difficult to secure, other reasons being easily found, and the statute now in force which provides a penalty for this action on the part of employers is likewise ineffective.[7]

Another serious shortcoming during this era related to armories. Rent support was inadequate and many of the halls used for weekly drills were cramped, drafty, and cold during the winter months. A State Armory Board was created in 1907 but was not activated. A 1909 report called for a statewide armory building program. Writing in 1914, Adjutant General Bridges described armory conditions:

> The armory situation of the State of Indiana is certainly serious. Indiana has lagged behind all other Central States in the building of armories. Even first-class officers and first-class men cannot possibly be inspired to give first-class service when they meet and drill in small, poorly lighted, poorly arranged and unsanitary armories such as we have over the State. The armories are usually on the second or third floor of an old business building, with dark halls, easily broken into by thieves, poorly lighted and poorly ventilated and in many cases not heated at all or poorly heated by stoves. . . . The armory at Bloomington, for which $600 rent is paid per year, is an old church, poorly heated, barren and dilapidated. One which was in use when I came to office but which has since been discontinued, was an old livery stable, which had been made over into an armory by taking out a few posts and putting in a cement floor. Nearly every armory in the State has at one time or another been broken into, and in my visits to many of these armories I have found usually that breaking into one of them is a very simple matter. . . . This fact has cost the State and the Company Commanders individually thousands of dollars, which might have been saved with good armory buildings. The Company Commanders are under bond and many of them become discouraged and quit the service on account of this property accountability.
> . . . The question of armories is one which enters largely into the question of discipline. The State cannot hope to have a real efficient National Guard unless it is willing to provide armories. It must be remembered that the officers and men performing this service are doing it from a patriotic sense of duty. Their small drill pay is used up in expense incident to the service and, in many cases, especially in the case of the Company Commanders, the officers advance money to the organizations repeatedly.[8]

In Indianapolis, a citizen-sponsored Indianapolis Armory Building Association was formed in 1915 to raise private sector funds for Guard armories, but it was a slow process. Governor Samuel Ralston rated state armory conditions as poor, their inadequacy a deterrent to enlistment and the cause of lower unit ratings by federal inspectors. In some cases, rent allotments from the state were insufficient to cover costs, and men were obliged to pay them out of their state allowances. Terre Haute Guardsmen were assessed contributions for utility services.[9]

Although the earlier years of the period were rather quiet ones on the labor front, Guardsmen were involved on several occasions in helping local law enforcement authorities protect prisoners from lynching attempts. One of these incidents flared into a violent confrontation that resulted in one of the most troublesome situations ever faced by the Indiana Guard.

It began with the fatal shooting of an Evansville policeman by a black resident. State officials first became involved on July 5, 1903, when the Knox County sheriff asked Governor Winfield Durbin for help because he feared that a mob might attempt to remove the prisoner, Lee Brown, from the jail at Vincennes where he had been transported from Evansville for safekeeping. Durbin's instructions to Colonel George W. McCoy, commander of the Guard's First Regiment at Vincennes, were to the point: "Preserve order and save a lynching."[10] The governor also authorized McCoy to swear in as many as 1,000 deputies in order to forestall the outbreak of racial violence.

There was no trouble at Vincennes, but the situation at Evansville, a city of long-smoldering racial problems exacerbated by the recent incident, turned into a nightmare. On the afternoon of July 6, an Evansville Guard company was called out, along with 100 sheriff's deputies, as an angry crowd gathered near the Vanderburgh County jail. The assemblage refused to believe that the prisoner no longer was held there. In any case, authorities feared for the safety of other black inmates.

Tension built throughout the afternoon and evening, as militiamen were subjected to repeated taunts and stonings. As many as 500 men actively were involved in the mob, while onlookers equaled their number. The mob advanced toward the jail, crowding Guardsmen as it moved forward.

Captain Julius F. Blum, the company commander, warned ringleaders against further movement and instructed his troops to stand firm. Shortly after 10 p.m., part of the mob tried to force the jail alleyway; participants pushed a bicycle in front of them to ward off bayonets. The mob again began stoning; one Guardsman fell, struck in the head. Moments later, shooting started. No one is certain who fired the first shot. Captain Blum and Colonel McCoy were inside the jail at the time. In his after-action report the captain said no order to fire ever was given to the Guardsmen.[11]

The Indianapolis *News* reported: "The most generally accepted story is that as the mob moved . . . gradually encroaching on the militiamen, one man stepped forward and fired several shots at a militiaman . . . then there was a spasmodic fusillade from other members of the mob, the bullets pattering against the jail walls and doing no particular damage. Then the militiamen began firing, in which they were joined by the deputy sheriffs."[12]

In the melee that followed, six rioters were killed outright and five died later of injuries, according to the account of the *News*, which placed the total of injured at 23. Blum's version, written a week later, placed the death count at nine and said that four Guardsmen were among the injured, as was one deputy. Other reports place the injured total as high as 35. The deputies, armed with shotguns, had fired from jail windows and many of the wounds, including those inflicted on two of the Guardsmen, were from buckshot.[13]

Reinforcements were rushed to the city, where much of the hostility toward blacks was replaced by hatred toward Guardsmen. As bands of men roamed the streets, blacks fled the city by the hundreds. Some never returned. Although newspapers and most public officials were sympathetic toward the Guard— taking the line that the rioters brought trouble on themselves— there was considerable bitterness among the local populace. At least five members of the militia company were fired by their civilian employers because of their connections with the National Guard. The presence of Guard units in force for several days in Evansville eventually cooled the situation, although feelings ran high for weeks. Most of the militia units were relieved on July 9.[14]

In 1907, Blum's company was called out during a strike of furniture workers at Tell City. A rioter had been killed during a clash between employees and peace officers. The local marshal then resigned. The arrival of Guardsmen restored order.

Later that year in Fontanet, northeast of Terre Haute, a

series of explosions rocked the DuPont Powder Works, culminating in a blast in the main magazine that ignited 65,000 kegs of blasting powder. The town of 1,200 virtually was wiped out, with more than 20 persons killed and hundreds injured. Tremors from the explosion were felt 200 miles away. Guard units were activated to protect against looting, clear debris, and provide temporary housing in tents for the homeless. Medical personnel aided civilian authorities in treating the victims, while other militiamen attempted to control thousands of sightseers who clogged the area. Two Guard companies were on duty for six days.[15]

Riots erupted after Muncie traction workers went on strike in January, 1908, and local police were unable to cope with the situation. A regiment of Guardsmen was activated but phased out after 500 local residents were deputized. The city was under martial law for two weeks. In 1909, a company was sent to Gary because of threatened trouble during an election, but no problems developed. In December, three units were alerted but not used during a stone workers strike in southern Indiana. Two companies were on duty in Porter County for several days in 1912 and again in 1913 as authorities acted to halt gambling activities at a racetrack near Mineral Springs.

On the night of March 23, 1913, a vicious storm system swept across the state, spawning tornadoes in Terre Haute and other western Indiana areas. Heavy rains caused record flooding throughout central Indiana during the following days. The Indianapolis westside was under water. Railroad and highway bridges were knocked out along the White and Wabash rivers. Serious flooding occurred at Fort Wayne, Logansport, Peru, Terre Haute, and Mt. Vernon. Guardsmen were activated to deal with tornado damage at Terre Haute while four companies aided flood victims at Indianapolis. Food, fuel, drinkable water, and clothing were in short supply in the stricken areas and militiamen operated supply stations in affected cities. A field hospital, manned by militiamen, functioned for several days in Indianapolis. Guard units were involved in cleanup activities for eight days. The 1913 adjutant general's report described the flood duty as "very arduous and the most trying that the Guard has ever had to perform in the history of the state . . ."[16]

A traction workers strike at Indianapolis in November, 1913, resulted in numerous injuries and extensive damage to trolley company property. Two thousand Guardsmen, virtually the entire organization, were mobilized for five days and were supported by 1,000 temporary sheriff's deputies.

Although the Guard was receiving more equipment, its members were more professional, and it had played visible roles in domestic emergencies other than strikes, the organization began weakening in Indiana in 1913 and 1914. Legislative opponents of the Guard led an unsuccessful fight to kill it during the 1913 General Assembly. The Guard then became a political issue as well, with Adjutant General Bridges coming under fire for its lapses. In 1914, General McKee, its brigade commander for nearly 20 years, was dumped, further polarizing political factions.

Another blow fell in June, 1915, when the War Department cut federal funding for ten companies because they were short of strength. Federal officials recommended reducing the Indiana Guard's organization from a brigade to two regiments. The inspection report of Brigadier General Albert L. Mills cited "lack of interest, absenteeism from drills and waning militia spirit" as causes for the decline. It also blamed inadequate armories and poorly trained officers:[17]

> With few exceptions, the infantry organizations of your state are in such condition that the Indiana brigade must in its present condition be regarded as inefficient for federal purposes. Twenty-six companies are rated as proficient.[18]

Bridges countered the criticism with observations that entire brigades in other states had lost federal recognition. "It is not a question of these companies being less efficient; it is because the government is more strict in its requirements," he said.[19]

In November the War Department approved a reorganized Indiana Guard that reduced its strength to two regiments. General Mills further reported that only four other states had a smaller percentage of men of militia age enrolled in the Guard. The Guard counted only 2,209 men on its rosters, out of a militia-age male population of 580,557.[20]

Meanwhile, in Washington, the War Department and Congress were embroiled in yet another fight over Army reorganization. Secretary of War Lindley M. Garrison proposed a new reserve force to be known as the "Continental Army," eventually to number 400,000 and to function as the primary backup to the Regulars. While giving the National Guard increased federal support, he would assign it a minor military role.

President Wilson gave the plan his tentative endorsement but the House Military Affairs Committee balked at the idea. Rep. James Hay of Ohio, its chairman, offered a counterproposal that would drop the Continental Army in favor of a strengthened National Guard. The federal government would equip and train Guardsmen, while requiring that Guard officers meet federal standards for retaining commissions.

Garrison refused to give in, but Guard supporters on Capitol Hill made known that they would vote out either the Hay bill or nothing. Wilson then capitulated, voicing support for the Hay plan. Garrison resigned in anger. The bill, which also increased the regular Army's authorized manpower, was being debated at a time when trouble had escalated on the Mexican border as rival political factions dueled for control of Mexico. After the U.S. Navy occupied Vera Cruz, Francisco Villa, one of the contenders for leadership, retaliated with raids on the border, most notably the assault on Columbus, New Mexico, on March 9, 1916. Brigadier General John J. Pershing led an expedition into the Mexican interior, chasing Villa and earning the wrath of other Mexican politicians who were cool to the idea of an American expeditionary force tramping through their countryside. Villa then raided Glen Springs, Texas.

On May 9, National Guard units of Texas, New Mexico, and Arizona were federalized, since Pershing's 5,000-man force was deep in Mexico and the border towns were vulnerable to further raids. Several weeks later Guardsmen in other states also were called to active duty and again were asked to take the oath as individuals to circumvent any problems associated with using them outside the nation's boundaries.

Indiana officials ordered mobilization of the Guard's two regiments at Fort Benjamin Harrison and made plans for raising a third. Commanders were notified by telegram on June 18 to assemble at the fort for induction into federal service. At that time, the Indiana Guard included 170 officers and 2,367 enlisted personnel. Officials said the Guard would be used only to protect the border and would not cross into Mexican territory except in hot pursuit of raiders.[21]

In addition to the three infantry regiments, an artillery battalion and several specialized companies were scheduled for duty on the border. The artillerymen were short of horses, but the 500-member battalion entrained for the Southwest on July 6. The infantry outfits began departing the next day.

The largest post-war armory facility in the nation, located adjacent to Stout Field on the Indianapolis west side, became the headquarters of the 38th Infantry Division and several subordinate units in 1978.

Completed in 1926 with considerable help from private funding sources, this armory at 711 North Pennsylvania Street in Indianapolis was the home of the 38th for a half-century. Now known as Tyndall Armory, it is still in use.

WORLD WAR I IN FRANCE. Artillerymen of the 150th F. A. Regiment fire a projectile toward the German lines (opposite, top). The regiment, which became part of the celebrated Rainbow Division, was the most decorated Indiana Guard unit of the war. One of the earliest tank vehicles (opposite, bottom) passes a column of Hoosier Guardsmen bound for the front. Horse and mule-drawn regimental trains of the 150th await movement orders in a French village (above).

EARLY AIR GUARD AIRCRAFT. Indiana's 113th Observation Squadron initially was issued Curtiss JN4H "Jennies", of World War I vintage (opposite, top). Early in the 1930s Douglas O-38s (center) were provided to the squadron. When activated in 1941 for World War II, the 113th was partially equipped with North American O-47 observation craft (bottom). Before the war, all Air Guard units had been observation elements. Post-war reorganizations reclassified most as combat squadrons and Hoosier airmen were issued P-51 "Mustangs" (above) in time for the Korean callup in 1951.

WAR IN THE PHILIPPINES. Cyclone Division Guardsmen of the 149th Infantry Regiment were among the units involved in the bitter fight to regain the mountain region of Bataan Peninsula. This team is in action at Zig Zag Pass (opposite, top). A crew of the 139th Field Artillery engages Japanese defenders during the so-called "Stotsenburg Operation" on Luzon (above). Military Police of the 38th Infantry Division guard prisoners taken in the fighting on Bataan (opposite, bottom). A soldier of the 151st Infantry Regiment scouts for indications of enemy activity on Caballo Island, located at the mouth of Manila Bay.

PEACETIME TRAINING AND CIVIC ACTION. Tankers of the 38th Division begin maneuvers at Camp Grayling in 1962 (opposite, upper left); an Honest John rocket blazes a fiery path from its launcher (opposite, lower left), and airborne Guardsmen of Company D, 151st Infantry, jump at Camp Atterbury in 1967. In 1962, Guardsmen re-established highway connections to Clinton by installing a Bailey Bridge to replace a span lost in a washout (above).

TRAINING IN THE 1970s. 38th Division infantrymen begin an airmobile exercise while others mount an assault river crossing at Camp Grayling. Training activities such as these became regular features of annual encampments during the 1970s.

The 113th Fighter Squadron retired its last F-100 Super Sabre in 1979, exchanging it for the F-4 Phantom (right). Guardsmen used tanks to drag snowbound trucks off Interstate 65 during 1978's paralyzing blizzard.

A team from Company D, 151st Infantry begins a long range patrol mission in Vietnam in 1969 (below). A Hoosier Guardsman undergoes winter combat training at Camp Ripley, Minnesota, in 1980.

Most Guardsmen eagerly took the oath mustering them into federal service, although a few refused it because they thought that they would be "stuck" as regulars after the emergency was over.[22]

Unlike the Spanish War, immediate hardship discharges weren't permitted. Men who refused to report for duty were subject to court martial because the governor could not accept resignations after the presidential call. After mustering-in, however, hardship discharges could be applied for.[23]

Governor Ralston had designated Captain Charles D. Herron, a regular officer stationed at the Canal Zone, as commander of the Indiana Brigade. Herron was a Crawfordsville native and former instructor-inspector of the Indiana National Guard. However, the War Department rejected the appointment, saying that officers could not be brought from foreign service to command militiamen.[24]

Ultimately, the governor settled on Lieutenant Colonel Edward M. Lewis, another regular, as brigade commander. Colonels Leslie R. Naftzger, Indianapolis; Thomas R. Coulter, Vincennes; and Aubrey D. Kuhlman, Auburn, were named commanders of the First, Second, and Third regiments, respectively.

The Hoosiers detrained at camps in the vicinity of Brownsville, Texas. Although welcomed by Texans who were jittery about the prospects of further border raids, few of the Hoosiers actually found themselves on patrol duty. The militiamen wrote home of their attempts to transform scrub areas infested with snakes and scorpions into livable cantonments. During the remaining months of 1916 the units were involved in extensive training programs which peaked in November as 23,000 Guardsmen took part in 12 days of field maneuvers between Camp Llano Grande and Port Isabel.[25]

Some were released in September, as tension in the border country cooled and as pressure intensified to return the militiamen home. Fifteen thousand Guardsmen were mustered out in September, including all companies of college students in order that they might return to school. This action included a Hoosier artillery battery of Purdue students. The early release of college students brought criticism from the press because "they were the ones least needed at home."[26]

On November 24, the United States and Mexico agreed upon a peace protocol. The Third Regiment returned to Fort Harri-

119

son on December 8, and artillery and signal units began filtering home. By mid-February, virtually all Hoosier Guardsmen had been mustered out.

The Mexican Border mobilization once again underscored the value of having a militia that could be activated for combat on short notice. However, it also disclosed serious deficiencies in logistics and transport because the movement of Guard units to the border was completed far behind schedule. Although the Hoosier citizen soldiers saw no action, their months of training on the border provided a dress rehearsal for the general mobilization for European war that was only a few months away.

---

[1] General Order No. 6, March 28, 1901, Indiana Adjutant General, *Report*, (Indianapolis, 1901), p. 61.

[2] General Order No. 8, April 20, 1901, Indiana Adjutant General, *Report*, (Indianapolis, 1901), p. 63.

[3] Jim Dan Hill, *The Minuteman in Peace and War* (Harrisburg; Stackpole, 1964), p. 185.

[4] Indiana Adjutant General, *Report* (Indianapolis, 1904), p. 176.

[5] Indiana Adjutant General, *Report* (Indianapolis, 1901), p. 75.

[6] *Acts of Indiana*, (1905) 131.

[7] Indiana Adjutant General, *Report* (Indianapolis, 1914), p. 181.

[8] Ibid., pp. 179-180.

[9] Indianapolis *Star*, August 2, 12, 1915.

[10] Indianapolis *News*, July 6, 1903.

[11] Indiana Adjutant General, *Report* (Indianapolis, 1903), pp. 10-12.

[12] Indianapolis *News*, July 7, 1903.

[13] Ibid; Indianapolis *News*, July 8, 1903; Clifton J. Phillips, *Indiana in Transition* (Indianapolis: Indiana Historical Bureau, 1968), p. 377.

[14] Indianapolis *Sentinel*, July 8, 1903; Indiana Adjutant General *Report*, (Indianapolis, 1903), p. 12.

[15] Indianapolis *Star*, October 6, 1907; Indiana Adjutant General, *Report* (Indianapolis, 1903), p. 12.

[16] Indiana Adjutant General, *Report* (Indianapolis, 1913), pp. 5-6; Indianapolis *Star*, March 24, 26, 28, 29, 31, 1913.

[17] Indianapolis *News*, June 3, 1915.

[18] Ibid.

[19] Indianapolis *Star*, June 3, 1915.

[20] Indianapolis *News*, December 20, 1915.

[21] Indianapolis *Star*, June 19, 1916.

[22] Indianapolis *News*, June 28, 1916.

[23] Indianapolis *News*, June 23, 1916.

[24] Indianapolis *News*, June 27, 28, 1916.

[25] *The Hoosier Guard* (Published at Mercedes, Texas, for units at Camp Llano Grande, Texas) December 4, 1916.

[26] Logan Esarey, *A History of Indiana* (Indianapolis: Bowen, 1918), 2 Vols., Vol. 2, p. 1085.

INDIANA GUARDSMEN IN THE GREAT WAR

Richard M. Clutter

"The lamps are going out all over Europe; we shall not see them lit again in our lifetime."[1] Thus observed Sir Edward Grey, foreign secretary of Great Britain, in August 1914, of Europe's entry into war. An obscure fanatic electrified with nationalistic fervor for a country, the location of which was unknown to most Americans, had assassinated Archduke Francis Ferdinand, heir to the Austrian throne. As a result, over 30 nations, including the United States, eventually were sucked in varying degrees into a whirlpool of destruction lasting four years.

When war erupted in Europe, Hoosiers were isolationists. As the conflagration continued, they remained uncertain as to which side they should cast their lot if America intervened, for it was not completely clear which nations were most to blame. The invasion of neutral Belgium did arouse in many Hoosiers a dislike of Germany.[2] In Indiana, as elsewhere, however, there were ethnic groups who resisted the thought of bearing arms on Britain's side against Germany and her allies. Persons of German birth or descent, who made up the largest and most influential non-English minority in the state, generally identified with Germany. They alienated fellow Hoosiers by opposing the Belgian relief drive and by becoming abusive in language.[3] The Irish were the second important "foreign" group in the state. From the beginning of the war until America's entrance into it, most of them sided with the Germans to spite England.

America's entry into the war in April, 1917, united the vast majority of Hoosiers on the side of the entente powers. Overall, Indiana zealously supported the war effort. The state's two United States senators voted for war as did all its 13 congressmen. Germany's unrestricted submarine warfare had helped swing Hoosier sentiment against her. The people of Indiana backed the war effort in many ways. In each of the five issues of federal war bonds, Indiana oversubscribed its quota or came close to doing so. At the request of Governor James P. Goodrich and city mayors, the people of the state planted half a

121

million home gardens in 1917 to grow produce and thus free more food for shipment to the hard-pressed allies. The following year over 600,000 gardens were planted. Colleges and universities gave military courses for soldiers, involved themselves in the Students' Army Training Corps, and encouraged campaigns for food conservation and production and for the raising of war funds.[4]

But victory in war depends on soldiers and battles and not just bond drives, coordination of resources, or loyalty campaigns. The first draft quota for Indiana was 17,510 men who were mobilized in August at Camp Taylor, Kentucky. There, they and later Hoosier draftees were trained and organized into the 84th Division along with men from Kentucky. Generally, they were scattered as replacements among several military organizations in the United States and abroad.[5]

Although the general mustering of the National Guard did not occur until August 5, 1917, a few Indiana units were taken into federal service as early as June of that year. Troop A of the First Cavalry Squadron left its home base of Evansville in that month bound as an advance unit for Camp Shelby in southern Mississippi, some 12 miles south of Hattiesburg. The generosity of Evansville citizens helped clothe the members of the troop, bought them a Model T Ford truck, and placed about $1,000 in their fund. The troop had no horses, and its equipment reportedly consisted of two curry combs and four brushes for the nonexistent steeds. Inasmuch as the Evansville men were the first to arrive at the camp, there were virtually no provisions for them. They even had to journey to Hattiesburg to buy food rations.[6]

When the general muster came in August, the state's National Guard consisted of four regiments of infantry, a battalion of engineers, four troops of cavalry (including Troop A of Evansville), two field hospitals, three ambulance companies, a signal corps battalion, and one artillery regiment.[7] The latter unit, the First Regiment, Indiana Field Artillery, received orders to assemble at Fort Harrison in Indianapolis from which it entrained a month later for New York for early sailing to the war front. It fought as the 150th Field Artillery of the 42nd (Rainbow) Division. The other Hoosier units were ordered to report to Camp Shelby, where they were merged with units from Kentucky and West Virginia to form the 38th Division. The Indiana Guard had enjoyed an enlisted strength

122

of only 3,100 men on March 1, 1917, but since then it had been authorized to increase its size to 10,419 officers and men. The Indianapolis *Star,* on the day of mustering, noted that there were then being mobilized as part of the United States Army more Hoosier soldiers than had been under arms at any one time since the Civil War some half century before.[8]

The trip to Camp Shelby occurred in late September. Troop trains included baggage cars organized as kitchens from which men were fed. The cooking was done on a wood-fired sheet iron field range which rested on a bed of sand or gravel on the baggage car floor. When the Guardsmen arrived, only a partially completed tent camp greeted them. Muddy roads bogged down trucks on the grounds, a cut-over, charred pine forest. Weeks of work were necessary to bring about some resemblance to a true military post as the men labored to clear out the myriad of tree stumps to provide drilling areas.[9]

Brigadier General Lewis, commanding general of the 38th Division and of Camp Shelby, once complimented Colonel Robert L. Moorhead, commander of the 139th Field Artillery, by saying that he and his men had so improved the appearance of the unit's area that it looked as though they had been working there for two months rather than fewer than two weeks. Moorhead's response was that he and his men hoped to be in France in two months.[10] Little did the Guardsmen know that they would remain, at least as a unit, at Shelby virtually a year before departing for the war zones of Europe.

Although the new 38th Division was bolstered by infantry personnel from Kentucky and West Virginia, it consisted mostly of Indiana units. Old state designations gave way to new federal ones. Across the country, Guard regiments were numbered in the hundreds, and the divisions were numbered 26th through 42nd. The redesignations of the 38th were as follows:

State Designations	Federal Designations
Headquarters, First Brigade	76th Infantry Brigade Headquarters
Sanitary Troops	
1st, 2nd, 3rd Ambulance Cos.	113th Sanitary Train
1st, 2nd Field Hospital Cos.	113th Sanitary Train
1st Sep. Squadron, Indiana Cavalry	
Troop A	Headquarters Co., 151st Infantry
Troop B	Battery F, 139th Field Artillery
Troop C	Company C, 152nd Infantry
Troop D	Company M, 152nd Infantry
1st Sep. Battalion Indiana Engineers	113th Engineers

State designations	Federal Designations
Indiana Signal Corps	
Company A (Radio)	113th Field Signal Battalion
Company B (Wire)	113th Field Signal Battalion
1st Regiment, Indiana Infantry	151st Infantry
2nd Regiment, Indiana Infantry	152nd Infantry
3rd Regiment, Indiana Infantry	137th Field Artillery (75 mm)
4th Regiment, Indiana Infantry (excl. L, M and MG)	139th Field Artillery (155 mm)
Companies L, M and MG of the 4th Regiment	139th Machine Gun Battalion
2nd Regiment, Kentucky Infantry	149th Infantry
2nd Regiment, West Virginia Infantry	150th Infantry[11]

Serious training began the first week of October, 1917, but it had to be done with makeshift equipment. The artillery troops, for example, drilled with dummy guns having logs as barrels. The camp mechanics improvised them from axles and wheels procured from blacksmith shops in Hattiesburg.[12]

Shelby's being a tent city bode ill for its inhabitants during the winter of 1917-18 when the temperature fell as low as 15 degrees below zero. The cold prompted the men to close their tents too tightly at night, which shut off ventilation from the crowded interiors. The pine-burning tent stoves tended to clog up their screen-smoke arrestors; when the men removed them to reduce the amount of smoke, several tents caught fire. The discomfort of the soldiers was compounded by the fact that many of the requisitioned overcoats and wool uniforms and much of the heavy underwear arrived late.[13]

Presumably the hardships of camp were rendered more endurable by the patriotic zeal of the soldiers. The characteristic attitude seems to have been a willingness to be in the armed services coupled with an impatience to begin fighting the enemy. By that time, it was March, 1918, and the soldiers had been at Shelby for six months. It was understandable that they were puzzled as to why they were not being sent abroad. This was especially so in that the British and French were experiencing great difficulties with the Germans. Because of an armistice agreed to by the Russians and Germans in December, 1917, the latter had been able to concentrate their fury against the British and French by swinging over forces into the western theater. There followed at least five German offensives from mid-March to mid-July, 1918.

The first attack was that of the Somme, launched on March

124

21. The German objective was to break through British forces between the Scarpe and Oise Rivers northeast of Paris, pushing a bulge in the stubborn trench lines toward the vital metropolis. Seventy-one Teuton divisions confronted 26 of the British and 2,500 heavy guns faced 976. An artillery specialist brought over from the Russian front by the Germans engineered a shattering bombardment which began on March 21 and lasted five hours. It included gas shells. The Germans experienced great success at first as they overran the forward lines of the enemy. After four days, they had advanced 14 tortuous miles and were bombarding Paris with guns of 70-mile range.[14]

Owing to the desperateness of the situation, the British acquiesced to French General Ferdinand Foch becoming general-in-chief of the allied armies in France. The French directed more divisions to the support of the British. When a German attempt to take Amiens straight north of Paris was thwarted, the offensive ended on April 5. The result of the fighting was the capture of 90,000 prisoners by the Germans and 163,000 casualties for the British and 77,000 for the French. The casualties of Germany were as great in number as those of her enemies.[15]

While war ravaged Europe, the Indiana Guard remained at Camp Shelby through the spring and summer of 1918. After the conflagration, the adjutant general of Indiana, Harry B. Smith, complained in his official report of 1919 that ". . . no explanation has ever been offered as to why a splendid division of troops, thoroughly trained, was kept in camp in the United States when there were repeated calls for troops to resist and check the forward movement of the German Army."[16]

The Shelby warriors were treated to a visit by Governor Goodrich on March 30, 1918, and officers of the 152nd Infantry gave him a luncheon. In addition to praising the troops, the governor said, "I am delighted with what I have seen in Hattiesburg and at Camp Shelby. The site of the camp is an excellent one, and I frankly confess to a pleasant surprise."[17]

Although the extent of the development of the camp at the time of the governor's visit is not clear, when the troops moved out in September, 1918, there reportedly were 900 buildings. Sixty-nine were in the hospital range alone. The camp also could boast of three theaters, and the number of men training there had reached 25,000.[18]

Even though the 38th Division was not shipped abroad as a unit until the fall of 1918, it was called upon to provide replacements for the fighting overseas. In May, after orders for preparation for embarkation were canceled, a requisition came for 6,000 troops. The 139th Field Artillery alone was called upon for 500 while the 151st Infantry lost 200 of its 365 men. Obviously these removals left gaping holes. They were filled with fresh recruits from Camp Taylor who had to be trained.[19]

The War Department often broke up state units to organize a true national army. The Indiana elements of the 38th Division were separated for assignment to other units even after the entire division's arrival in France. This made it very difficult for historians to trace many Indiana components, except for those such as the 150th Field Artillery Regiment which remained intact and the actions of which are described below. So it was with the 6,000 replacements. After landing in France, they were scattered from Brest at the tip of the Brittany peninsula on the Atlantic coast to the city of LeMans, some 150 miles inland.[20]

A significant event in the history of the 38th occurred when Major General Robert L. Howze arrived at the camp on August 30, 1918, to assume command of the division. The troops apparently were pleased with the appointment and hoped that his arrival signaled their imminent embarkation for Europe. He replaced Brigadier General Frank H. Caldwell. Howze had graduated from West Point Military Academy and had distinguished himself while a captain of cavalry in the battle of Santiago during the Spanish-American War. He also had fought in the Indian wars in the United States and in the Philippine Insurrection. As a commander with General John J. Pershing during the punitive expedition into Mexico in 1916 to chase down Francisco "Pancho" Villa, he had gone to the farthest point south with the expedition.[21]

A few days after Howze took command, he announced that the division would be known in the future as the Cyclone Division because of the cyclone which had hit the camp in April. Thus, the unit acquired its famous First World War nickname. Its shoulder patch is a shield bearing the interlocked letters "C" and "Y." Howze praised the division as one of the best of the Army. He said the artillery crews were good, the machine gunners had been splendidly trained, and the

126

riflemen were unsurpassed. He further claimed that every officer and man was anxious to get at the "despicable Hun."[22]

The growing impatience of the men no doubt was intensified by the knowledge of the vast numbers of Americans were pouring into the battlefields and European training camps. The Hattiesburg *American* reported at the end of August that one and a half million Americans were by then on foreign soil.[23]

Even at Camp Shelby, the long-awaited time of adieu finally arrived. By late September, 1918, all units had left for east coast sailing points; oceanic crossings to France followed in October. Infantry units were dispatched to inland LeMans while artillery personnel went to camps of the Brest coastal region. By that time the war was in its last few days and some ten newly arrived divisions were being broken up for use as replacements. One of these was the 38th. On fronts where limited ground gains exacted extremely heavy manpower tolls due to artillery shell explosions, deadly machine gun fire, and hand-to-hand combat with hand grenades and bayonets, there was a constant need for infantry reinforcements, both men and officers. Such replacements sometimes had to reach their new posts the best way they could on their own or in small groups by walking, riding trains, or hitch-hiking.[24]

The war ended on November 11, 1918, without the 38th having seen action as a unit. Although it did not fight intact, 301 officers and men who at some time or another had been connected with the division lost their lives. The number who died in battle was 105 (including 50 in the 150th Field Artillery, which had been separated from the 38th upon induction). Those who succumbed to wounds numbered 47, those taken out by accidents were 25, and pneumonia and influenza claimed 81 of the remaining 124. Forty-eight died of accident or disease before the division left Camp Shelby.[25]

The 38th was officially demobilized at Camp Taylor, Kentucky, on March 8, 1919, some two months after the demobilization of the 137th and 139th Field Artillery regiments of the division, which were the first Indiana Guard units to return to the States. It might be instructive to examine briefly the career of the 139th before tracing some of the battle exploits of the 150th.

As early as July, 1917, Adjutant General Smith had asked Lieutenant Colonel Robert L. Moorhead to organize the Fourth Regiment for draft into federal service by the date of Guard mobilization, August 5. Moorhead had served under Smith in the Second Infantry, I.N.G., for 17 years, including service in the Spanish-American War. Most of the men of the Fourth bought their uniforms at their own expense. After receiving training, minus rifles, at Fort Harrison in Indianapolis, they left for Camp Shelby on September 25 with the understanding that they were to train there for four months. Upon arrival, they were surprised to learn that they were to be redesignated as artillery and were to be known as the 139th Field Artillery.[56]

During mid-September, 1918, the 139th entrained for Camp Mills on Long Island; and, on October 6, it sailed on the White Star *S.S. Cedric* for Liverpool. For protection from German submarines, the ship was part of a convoy of 11 British ships, all camouflaged and escorted by a second-class cruiser and, for a time, by several American destroyers. Many men aboard the *Cedric* came down with influenza or pneumonia. The crowded conditions left little space for drilling or exercising, and the sea was turbulent most of the way across. Some of the personnel suffered sea sickness the entire voyage.

The war was dramatically brought home to the soldiers about a mile off the coast of England when the ship sustained two torpedo hits. But it was able to steam into Liverpool; from there the men traveled by train to Southampton, where they boarded vessels which conveyed them across the English Channel to Cherbourg, France. Departing Cherbourg, they passed by train near Paris and stopped for a few days at Ploermel before advancing to Camp de Meucon which long had served as a French artillery training ground. In the days that followed, the batteries drilled with new Schneider 155mm howitzers, while the officers attended classes taught by French and American officers who had served at the front. When word came that the Germans were asking for armistice terms, the regiment's sentiment was that the war should not be terminated until the German fatherland, which had not yet been invaded, had suffered some of the same horrors of war that had been inflicted upon France.[28] They were disappointed, for news soon came of the acceptance of the armistice. Although they hoped to be in the army of occupation, they were told that they would soon return to the United States. They were ordered back to Brest, where they were asked to serve as the guard of honor to receive President Wilson and his entourage, arriving for the peace conference. On that proud occasion, the regiment wore the cyclone insignia for the first time.[29]

On December 15, 1918, the 139th and part of the 137th Field Artillery embarked for home on the *George Washington* which had just brought over President Wilson. They pulled into New York harbor on December 23, where they were met by welcoming airplanes performing aerobatics overhead and by many New Yorkers. By January 10 they were marching in a triumphal homecoming procession in Indianapolis with the 137th. They were the first Hoosier troops to return home from France, and the spectators lined the streets to pour out their welcome to them.[30] On January 20 they were demobilized.

The most heralded of all Indiana Guard organizations during the war was the 150th Field Artillery, commanded by Colonel Robert H. Tyndall, who had been in the military since enlisting as a private in a volunteer infantry battery during the Spanish-American War. After that conflict, he had re-enlisted in Battery A of the National Guard and had served on the Mexican border with the rank of major.

Although there is no indication that other units would have functioned with less valor than the 150th had they been placed in like circumstances, it nevertheless was the 150th that went overseas first, returned late, and was often in the thick of the fighting. Indeed, it spent more days actually on the front than any other howitzer regiment with the American Army. Upon being mustered into federal service, the 150th was incorporated into the 42nd (Rainbow) Division, which was one of the first three divisions sent abroad and was made up of National Guard organizations from 26 states and the District of Columbia. The regiment was a horse-drawn heavy artillery (155mm) organization consisting of three battalions of two batteries each.

The men left Fort Harrison in Indianapolis for Camp Mills, Long Island, on September 7, 1917, only two days after having been mustered. About 200 persons, mostly women and children, braved mud and downpouring rain to say their goodbyes to the excited passengers of the train.

The regiment left the United States on October 19, 1917, on the *President Lincoln* as part of a convoy carrying 56,000 men. They arrived at the port of St. Nazaire in France on October 30, from which, after several days delay, they were transported via trains to Camp Coctquidon for three months of training. Cannoneers learned to operate their pieces, horse drivers drilled in harnessing their teams and maneuvering them, and signal men practiced with telephones and wireless sets. They became accustomed to the deafening roar of the six-inch guns. By the latter part of February, they were judged ready for battle and were ordered to the Lorraine front.[31]

The regiment did not actually fire its first shot in battle until March 1, 1918; but, after that, its service included participation in a furious attack the first three days of May which featured intense cannonading of enemy positions with a total of 92 guns, counting those of the 17 French batteries aiding the 150th.[32] Elmer Sherwood of Linton, Indiana, and a soldier of the 150th wrote of the battle as follows:

> Aeroplanes fly above us, an observation balloon is up to our right and our guns are booming and jarring the earth. . . . The gun crews are sweating, their energies, minds, muscles, applied to the work of ramming shells into the breach of cannon, pulling the lanyard, which releases the firing pin, whereupon the projectile goes hurling toward Germany. In the front lines the doughboys are anxiously awaiting the zero hour when they will go over the top.[33]

Leaving the Lorraine front in mid-June, 1918, the Rainbow Guardsmen joined General Foch's army of maneuver and hiked to meet the Germans near the Marne River. By then, United States troops were landing on French shores at the rate of 50,000 per week. Three-quarters of a million American men were in the nation, and five divisions were on the front.[34]

The manpower scales were tipping against Germany, and she was getting desperate. On July 14, at midnight, the great battle of the Champagne front, one of the turning points of the war, began.

After helping break the German drive at Champagne, the Rainbow Division headed southward to the region of Chateau-Thierry, a strongly American front.

Over 5,000 Rainbow soldiers were killed or wounded in the two weeks of fierce fighting on the Chateau-Thierry salient. After pursuing the Germans across the Ourcq River, the 42nd, by forced hikes, made its way to the offensive against the St. Miliel salient. Once the troops hiked continuously for about 18½ miles.

The St. Mihiel operation, which lasted from September 12 to 24, was the first all-American undertaking and a great victory. General John J. Pershing had continuously been called upon to disperse his American troops as replacements to plug breaches and raise morale among Allied forces. Although Pershing realized this was necessary, he also demanded the right to establish an all-American army and throw it against the enemy. His chance came with the St. Mihiel battle when American forces at the front numbered 17 divisions.[35]

The month of September witnessed a succession of German disasters; St. Mihiel was one. The American attack came just as the enemy had begun to evacuate their positions. The result was the seizure of a large number of prisoners and weapons.[36] That paved the way for a Franco-American assault northward on Sedan in the Meuse-Argonne drive. It was a story of tortuous advance against stubborn enemy resistance. Air activity was so great that, at times, the sky was black with planes. Sherwood once counted 82 aircraft overhead at once.[37] Sedan was taken, and the Hindenburg Line was broken. As a result, the Germans agreed to an armistice. When it came on November 11, 1918, the Rainbow Division, including the 150th Field Artillery, had reached the northernmost point attained by the First American Army.

Following the battles, the officers and men of the 42nd Division received a letter of congratulations from General Pershing:

> After leaving the region of Chateau Thierry you had scarcely been assembled in your new area when you were ordered to advance by hard night marches to participate in the attack of the St. Mihiel salient. In this first great operation of the American army you were instructed to attack in the center of the 4th army corps and to deliver the main blow in the direction of the heights overlooking the Madine river. In the battle that followed you took every objective in accordance with the plan of the army commander. You advanced fourteen kilometers in twenty-eight hours. . . . You took more than 1,000 prisoners from nine enemy divisions. You captured seven villages and forty-two square kilometers of territory. You seized large supplies of food, clothing, ammunition, guns and engineering material. . . .
>
> Since September 12th you have taken over 1,200 prisoners; you have freed twenty-five French villages; you have recovered over 150 square kilometers of French territory and you have captured great supplies of enemy munitions and material.
>
> Whatever may come in the future, the men of this division will have the proud consciousness that they have thus far fought wherever the American flag has flown most gloriously in this war. In the determining battle before Chalons, in the bloody drive from Chateau Thierry to the Vesle, in the blotting out of

the St. Mihiel salient and in the advance to Sedan you have played a spendid and leading part. . . .[38]

The citation to the division was signed by Brigadier General Douglas MacArthur and Colonel William N. Hughs, Jr. It read, in part, as follows:

> . . . Out of the 224 days of the great war which have elapsed since it first entered the line the division has been engaged with the enemy 180 days and the balance of the time has been spent in moving from front to front or in reserve close behind the front.
>
> The division was marched by road, traveled by camion and moved by train; it has held a wide sector front in Lorraine; it has been in battle in Champagne, in the Woevre, at St. Mihiel and in the Argonne. It was the only American division to assist in the disastrous defeat of the great German offensive of July 15th on the battlefield in Champagne. From that time on it has taken part in every large American operation.[39]

Following the armistice, the 150th became a part of the army of occupation. With the rest of the Rainbow Division, it marched into Belgium and through Luxembourg and, on December 3, crossed the German border at Echternach. Passing through several German towns, the men reached Bad-Neuenahr where they enjoyed a victorious Christmas dinner. After spending about four months in the Rhineland, the 150th entrained for Brest, France, in April for the long trip home. Sailing on the *Great Leviathan,* the regiment arrived at Hoboken, New Jersey, on April 25, 1919. On May 7, the troops marched through the streets of Indianapolis before thousands of shouting onlookers on Welcome Home Day, which the mayor had proclaimed as a holiday. At their head marched their commanding officer, Colonel "Bob" Tyndall, as they, along with personnel of the newly returned Base Hospital 32, passed through the flower-strewn victory arch on Monument Circle. A thousand flags lined the way and laurel swung from great white columns. Airplanes circled and dipped overhead.[40] The boys finally were home.

Of the one and a half million American men who saw battle in the First World War, about 440,000 were Guardsmen. Approximately 40 percent of the 5,000 American soldiers who died in 200 days of battle, and the 206,000 who were wounded, were of the Guard.[41] According to one report, the Rainbow Division, which included Indiana's 150th, "spent more consecutive days in touch with the enemy and a greater total of time engaged with the enemy than any other division of the American Expeditionary Forces."[42] The 150th earned battle streamers for Champagne, Marne, Aisne-Marne, St. Mihiel, Meuse-Argonne, Champagne, and Lorraine. Colonel Tyndall received the Distinguished Service Medal, the Croix de Guerre with two palms, and, on July 11, 1923, was declared a commander of the French Legion of Honor by presidential decree.

Although Indiana's 38th Division was not privileged to fight as a unit, it did supply badly needed and well-trained replacement troops for units in Europe. The division's men spent their days at Camp Shelby impatiently awaiting orders to depart for the front lines. The fact that the orders were slow in coming was not their fault. Certainly, direct fighting on the front, though the surest route to glory, was not the only way to aid the war effort. For example, the 113th Engineers assigned to the 38th erected the largest such project in the country. It built the Headquarters Detachment and train at Latrecey and a huge veterinary hospital at Lux, as well as numerous barracks, warehouses, and camps. It also helped construct the regulating yards at Liffol-de-Grand and completed a large remount station.[43]

Base Hospital 32 originated with the desire of a group of physicians, surgeons, and nurses to serve in the war in the event the United States became involved. The hospital personnel arrived at Contrexeville, France, as early as December, 1917, where they established a military hospital on a rail line approximately 50 miles behind the front lines. By the first of September, 1918, the hospital reportedly had admitted 2,682 American and 884 French patients. The number of British treated numbered 177 while 12 enemy prisoners had been patients. Of the total number admitted, 2,810 had been returned to duty; 11 had died. The remainder had been sent to other hospitals or were still being treated by "32." The biggest month for the hospital was September, 1918, when 2,319 patients were admitted. The number of admittees in October, the month preceding the armistice, was 2,301.[44]

Unfortunately, the scarcity of records and the scattering of the troops will forever prevent the full story of the Indiana National Guard in the First World War from being told. Most of the countless acts of sacrifice and heroism which

133

formed the strands of the tapestry of victory will remain unknown to the present and future generations.

---

[1] Grey apparently made this statement as he watched lamplighters on August 4, 1914, the day England declared war on Germany, turn off the lights in St. James Park, London.

[2] Clifton J. Phillips, *Indiana in Transition: The Emergence of an Industrial Commonwealth*, 1880-1920 (Indianapolis: Indiana Historical Bureau, 1968), pp. 586-588; Cedric C. Cummins, *Indiana Public Opinion and the World War*, 1914-1917 (Indianapolis: Indiana Historical Bureau, 1945), p. 1316.

[3] Cummins, *Indiana Public Opinion*, pp. 45-53.

[4] George C. Cottman, *Centennial History and Handbook of Indiana* (Indianapolis: Hyman, 1915). See in this volume the supplement "Highlights of Indiana in the World War," ed. Edith Margaret Evans and Freeman T. Felt, pp. 9-11.

[5] Phillips, *Indiana in Transition*, p. 607.

[6] Leonard E. Webster, "A Military History of the Indiana National Guard, 1816-1966," typescript, p. 25.

[7] Phillips, *Indiana in Transition*, pp. 608-609.

[8] Indianapolis *Star*, August, 5, 1917.

[9] Webster, "History of the Indiana Guard," pp. 26-28.

[10] Robert L. Moorhead, *The Story of the 139th Field Artillery: American Expeditionary Forces* (Indianapolis: Bobbs-Merrill, 1920), p. 32.

[11] Ibid., p. 24; Webster, "History of the Indiana Guard,", p. 27.

[12] Moorhead, *Story of the 139th*, p. 31.

[13] Ibid., pp. 46-48.

[14] Cyril Falls, *The Great War* (New York: Putnam, 1959), pp. 331-334.

[15] Ibid., pp. 334-337.

[16] *Indiana Year Book*, 1919, pp. 746-749.

[17] Indianapolis *Star*, March 31, 1918.

[18] Hattiesburg *News*. (No date is given. Indications are that it was September, 1918).

[19] Webster, "History of the Indiana Guard," p. 43.

[20] William J. Watt, "The Story of the 38th Infantry 'Cyclone' Division, Indiana National Guard," typescript, 1967.

[21] *Camp Shelby American*, August 31, 1918; Moorhead, *Story of the 139th*, p. 67.

[22] *Camp Shelby American*, September 10, 1918.

[23] Hattiesburg *American*, August 31, 1918.

[24] Webster, "History of the Indiana Guard," p. 32.

[25] Ibid., pp. 32-33.

[26] Moorhead, *Story of the 139th*, p. 3, p. 11, p. 24.

[27] Ibid., p. 36.

[28] Ibid., pp. 75-79.

[29] Ibid., pp. 127-130.

[30] Ibid., p. 145.

[31] Elmer W. Sherwood, *Rainbow Hoosier* (Indianapolis: Printing Arts Co., n.d.), pp. 40-41.

[32] Ibid., p. 57.

[33] Ibid., pp. 57-59.

[34] R. R. Sellman, *The First World War* (New York: Criterion, 1962), p. 133.

[35] Falls, *The Great War,* pp. 355-356.

[36] Sellman, *The First World War,* p. 136.

[37] Sherwood, *Rainbow Hoosier,* p. 82.

[38] Quoted in Ibid., pp. 139-142.

[39] Quoted in Ibid., pp. 44-46.

[40] Indianapolis *Star,* May 8, 1919; Indianapolis *Star* (Extra), May 8, 1919.

[41] R. Ernest Dupuy, *The National Guard: A Compact History* (New York: Hawthorn, 1971), p. 106.

[42] Sherwood, *Rainbow Hoosier,* pp. 177-178, quoting an order issued on February 15, 1919.

[43] *One Hundred Thirteenth Engineers* in France (n.p., n.d.), p. 10.

[44] Benjamin D. Hitz, *A History of Base Hospital 32: Including Unit R* (Indianapolis, 1922), pp. 94-96.

SURVIVING A MILITARY RECESSION

Ralph E. Dimmett

Having just fought the "war to end all wars," it was unlikely that America would sustain a strong peacetime military establishment. Woodrow Wilson's all-consuming passion was the creation of a peace-oriented League of Nations, not the preservation of the nation's ability to wage war. In the words of historian Samuel Eliot Morison, what had been the most popular war in our history while it lasted became the most hated after it was over. Post-war literature, plays, and films took on a decidedly anti-war tone. In sharp contrast to earlier wars, no general officer was elevated to high political office. Wilson's failure to secure American participation in the League, coupled with the conservatism of his successor, Warren G. Harding, foretold a return to isolationism and relegated military preparedness to a level of insignificance.[1]

These policies were guaranteed of continuation in the administration of Calvin Coolidge, an apostle of thrift in both words and money, who was hostile to expenditures on behalf of the nation's armed forces because he was at a loss to see who we might fight and because such expenditures contravened his cherished economy programs. To Coolidge, the business of America was business; and dollars saved from government were assets to the private sector.

General John J. Pershing, the wartime commander of the American Expeditionary Force, disagreed, as did the outgoing chief of staff, General Peyton March. March and the general staff had proposed that the Army be expanded to 500,000 from the 130,000 it had been reduced to in 1920. The ambitious plan also called for universal military training, and therefore promptly was rejected by Congress.

Pershing, with the help of Colonel John MacAuley Palmer, proposed a smaller regular Army and a greater reliance upon citizen soldiers. This philosophy was adopted in the National Defense Act of 1920 (see Chapter I), which increased the authorized strength of the Army to 280,000, backed up by the citizen soldiers of the National Guard and a new Organized Reserve. Implementing plans called for the dropping of the territorial organization of forces and the grouping of the Army into nine corps areas, each including one regular, two Guard, and three Reserve divisions. The National Guard was to have more control over its own affairs. While the regulars were to train the citizen soldiers, it was with the understanding that the Guard was increasingly to train and to lead its own formations. However, peacetime monetary stringencies and the continuing spate of anti-war sentiment sapped this program of much of its vigor. The 1920 law did provide a firm foundation for the modern National Guard.[2]

In Indiana, the civil defense functions normally carried out by the Guard had been placed with the wartime Indiana State Militia, which was mustered out in 1920. Adjutant General Harry B. Smith was compelled to wait until the adoption of the 1920 federal legislation before he could reorganize the Guard; the state was without a militia for about six months. Fortunately, there were no emergencies of consequence during this interval. Early in 1921, two companies were created and the Guard was being beefed up as part of a five-year reorganization program.

The Guard reorganized on a steady schedule and nearly 4,000 of its members marched in the November 4, 1921, review in Indianapolis in honor of Marshal Foch, the wartime allied commander in France. Participants were volunteers and many paraded without uniforms or arms because the new units had not received any equipment.[3]

Unlike other states, which had experienced setbacks after attempting premature and large-scale reorganizations, Smith paced the re-creation of the Guard in Indiana. The Indiana Guard was designated as part of the 38th Infantry Division, which also included units in Kentucky and West Virginia. However, the majority of forces, including most of the leadership, was allocated to the Hoosier state. The division commanding general and the brigadiers to command the division's artillery brigade and one infantry brigade were to be drawn from the ranks of the Indiana Guard.[4]

Named to command the 38th in 1923 was Robert H. Tyndall, an Indianapolis businessman who had commanded the 150th Field Artillery in France and who had been elected national treasurer of the American Legion. In 1924 he became the youngest major general in the United States. At the outset, Tyndall's troops were led by experienced officers and non-commissioned officers, most of them veterans of the recent war. During 1921, 97 per cent of the commissions granted were to veterans with overseas experience.[5]

During the 1920s and 1930s attrition cut deeply into the ranks of junior officers, in part because of the usual reasons of job conflicts and changing personal interests, but also because Army officer training programs generally were closed to Guardsmen. However, the Officers Reserve Corps proved to be a source of new leaders, as did the Indiana Guard's own NCOs, who were able to qualify through the completion of correspondence study or on the recommendation of boards of officers. A number of direct commissions were given to outsiders, based upon their civilian credentials.

Officers wore Sam Browne belts reflecting British influence on our military services. Sabres were carried in formations and ceremonies. Boots were highly polished and spurs were attached. The choker collar was retired shortly after World War I and replaced with a uniform blouse with lapels. Formal evening wear, for those who could afford such expenditures, included a mess jacket (white in summer), a dress shirt with wing collar, and black tie. The standard side arm was a Smith & Wesson .45 caliber revolver worn on the right hip with butt forward. Young men joining the Guard's enlisted ranks could be assured that they would wear the uniform of the U. S. Army. The pre-war Guard had had some problems in this respect; frequently there were not enough uniforms and equipment to go around. The huge stockpile of surplus material on hand eliminated this problem. The surplus, however, did not include cotton uniforms. An all-purpose enlisted uniform consisting of wool breeches, wool blouses with choker collar, wool shirts, and wool leggings was bad enough in the warm Hoosier summers, but Guardsmen were forced to endure its discomfort farther south at Camp Knox, Kentucky. The uniform was not overly martial in appearance, either. The one saving aspect of the hot, scratchy, ill-fitting uniform was the jaunty campaign hat provided to all personnel. This was first issued to the regular Army in 1912 and caught the public's fancy—as well as the military's—in a manner as yet unabated as a result of news photos of Pershing wearing such a head piece during his punitive expedition against Pancho Villa in 1916.

Guardsmen in the 1920s and '30s became familiar with the

1903 Springfield rifle, a welcomed weapon because individual marksmanship was highly prized during this period, and the Springfield was a marksman's delight.

Other new equipment, however, was slow in coming when it came at all. Tight budgets scaled down the artillery and automatic weapons of infantry divisions; the 38th's howitzer companies were not issued their authorized 81mm mortars and .50 caliber machine guns. As late as 1938, the year of Munich, howitzer units were armed with three-inch Stokes mortars—inferior weapons even during World War I—and horse-drawn, wooden-wheeled howitzers. There were no horses, and the guns were dragged by Guardsmen.[6]

Unit spirit was promoted by the sponsorship of athletic competition, which was mandated by Guard officials to promote physical fitness. Statewide tournaments were conducted annually in all major sports.

With but one exception, Camp Knox, Kentucky, was the site of summer training for the division every year until it was mobilized for World War II. Many of its barracks and facilities were of World War I vintage. The camp had a surfeit of rough terrain and frequently a deficit of water, which compelled water conservation measures when the division was in bivouac. Movement of the division's personnel to summer camp was a complex military operation in itself. Troop trains were used for most of the personnel and they spent long hours in transit, frequently traveling over 200 miles from points of departure, while enduring numerous layovers on railroad sidings. Such trucks as existed in the division's inventory made the overland journey with difficulty. Staff cars were non-existent; regimental commanders had to drive their own cars or arrange to rent them. Fifteen days were allotted for field training, and the 38th was the first of the Guard divisions to train as a complete unit in peacetime. When the division had its end-of-camp reviews, hundreds of spectators, many of them from Indiana, were in attendance.

While the United States provided Camp Knox, it was up to Indiana to provide home armories. At first encouraged by the promises of the War Department, adjutants general became discouraged when funds for badly needed armories failed to materialize from any source. During the early 1920s, however, units managed to keep together, train, and protect their issued property in spite of inadequate buildings. They often drilled in makeshift facilities. The division headquarters was located in a private residence, while many units trained in old homes, abandoned warehouses, or vacant basements. Close order drill was conducted in public streets.[7]

Through private funding, Madison provided unusually fine armory facilities only a few months after its artillery battery was federally recognized on April 1, 1921, but many other units were not so fortunate.

The 1923 report of the adjutant general was optimistic: "The armory question for the ING has greatly improved over the last year. Although still handicapped by lack of suitable armories, the units are gradually adjusting to what has been furnished them."[8]

Two years later, the account was less favorable:

> Attention has been called to the large amount of rentals paid by the state for armories, due to the fact that only one of the armories now used by the Guard is owned by the State. One other armory is being purchased on the installment plan and the armory in Indianapolis is being erected by outside capital. Where real estate is being purchased on the installment plan, it is an expensive proposition and in view of the large savings that could be made in rentals by state-owned armories it would be real constructive economy for the state to buy or build sufficient armories to house permanent units of the Guard.
>
> During the fiscal year October 1, 1924, to September 30, 1925, $90,808 was spent by the state for armory rentals. The greater part of this money was wasted, when taken into consideration that the state is no better off now than they were a year ago, insofar as savings of rental is concerned. . . .
>
> It is the duty of the state to provide suitable armories. In time of need the state does not hesitate to call every Guardsman away from his work and his home, no matter how great the sacrifice or loss. The state and federal government requires these men to drill one night of every week at the armory and they are subject to call at any time. In most cases at present the so-called armories are storerooms, or rooms over storerooms, badly lighted, badly ventilated, badly heated, badly arranged. They are absolutely unsuited for purposes of drill or the safekeeping of property, to say nothing of the unattractiveness of the place, . . .[9]

By 1928 the situation had changed substantially. The state acquired a large amount of real estate on which modern facilities were built. In January, 1925, the State Armory Board had been activated to manage the real estate assigned to the Guard and to acquire additional holdings. It made rapid strides and in a short time could report that it managed property for the Guard valued at $2,259,000.

If the nation's military forces had difficulty during the prosperous 1920s, the depression area brought no relief. At one point the White House decided to cut the War Department budget by $80 million, a huge sum for those times. Funds for the regular Army were to be cut by 51 per cent and the National Guard also was affected.

Despite the overall economic situation, the Indiana Guard flourished during the depression with regard to manpower. Adjutant General Paul Tombaugh reported in 1931:

> The strength of the National Guard and Naval Militia on September 30, 1931, was greater than ever before. Although this can be attributed partially to present economic conditions, nevertheless there is evidence of growing interest in the National Guard and the Naval Militia which is reflected in enlistments and applications for commission. Practically all units have the full strength authorized by law and most organizations now have a waiting list for people desiring to enlist.[10]

This continued despite a decrease in pay. The National Guard Bureau announced that, for fiscal 1934, paid armory drills would be reduced from 48 to 12. Almost all the Indiana organizations agreed to perform the other 36 drills without compensation. The Adjutants General Association and the National Guard Association strongly protested this severe cut and the federal government relented to the extent that it finally agreed to pay for 36 drills. Every organization in the Indiana Guard agreed to take part in the full 48.

The concept of a seagoing militia goes back to the 1880s, and 15 states had created naval units as part of their militia structures by the time of the Spanish-American war. In 1914 the units were given federal recognition by Congress, and many naval militiamen were activated for service during World War I.

Indiana did not form a naval unit until the adoption of authorizing state legislation in 1927. It included an annual appropriation of $20,000. Initially, Hoosiers took part in training cruises with militia units from other Great Lakes states. Eventually, two training ships, the U. S. S. Hawk and the YP-26, were assigned to the state and were based at the new naval armory at Michigan City. A naval armory also was constructed at Indianapolis. Organized as a battalion, the militia maintained three fleet divisions and a communications reserve at Indianapolis, and a fourth fleet division and a communications detachment at Michigan City. Communications reserve units also were established at Evansville, Richmond, Marion, Gary, and South Bend.

During the 1930s, the organization became known as the Indiana Naval Force and participated in the flood relief effort in 1937. Selected officers and petty officers were attached to Navy vessels for annual training periods. However, the growth of the Naval Reserve resulted in the decline of the naval militia units nationwide. Although the Military Department of Indiana still owns the two armories, they are leased to Naval Reserve units.[11]

Guardsmen were used extensively during the 1920s and 1930s to deal with natural disasters and civil disorders. On March 18, 1925, tornadoes severely damaged the city of Princeton and virtually destroyed the town of Griffin. More than 60 fatalities were recorded and several hundred persons were injured. Within an hour a battery of the 139th Field Artillery was providing assistance in Princeton by rescuing the injured and recovering the dead. Another unit of the 139th took charge of disaster relief activities in Griffin. The artillerymen and selected companies of nearby infantry regiments were on duty in the storm-swept region for a week.[12]

Flooding on the lower Wabash and White Rivers prompted a January 15, 1930, call-up of Battery D of the 139th Field Artillery in the vicinity of Hazelton, where citizen soldiers aided civil authorities in patrolling and providing assistance to civilians. A devastating cyclone ravaged the town of Vernon in July, 1932, and units of the 150th Field Artillery performed police duty and provided tentage and other emergency equipment.

The most dramatic involvement of Indiana citizen soldiers came during the great floods of January and February, 1937. Adjutant General Elmer F. Straub began receiving numerous calls for assistance from civil authorities throughout southern Indiana on January 21, 1937, as the Ohio River and its southern Indiana tributaries were rising rapidly. Immediately, units in New Albany and Evansville were ordered to active duty, while several other companies were placed on alert. By the next day, much of southern Indiana was under water and the Guard was coping with a steady stream of requests for emergency equipment such as blankets, cots, tents, stoves, and drinkable water. The Guard secured the release of equipment from regular Army and Civilian Conservation Corps warehouses and became the lead civil agency coping with the relief effort. On January 23, martial law was proclaimed in southern Indiana and the entire Guard was called up: 321 officers and 3,395 enlisted personnel, and 28 officers and 303 enlisted men of the Naval Militia. General Tyndall set up headquarters at French Lick, and most of the units were on duty for more than two weeks. Guardsmen evacuated stranded people, made provision for transportation of supplies and refugees via truck and rail, arranged emergency housing for those who had been forced to leave their homes, organized and transported a hospital train to Louisville, and provided additional transportation services for civil authorities working in the flooded area. The Naval Militia and State Police organized a radio network that became the primary communications network for the disaster relief effort. Guardsmen compelled evacuation of reluctant homeowners and General Straub later claimed that this action was partially responsible for avoiding any loss of life.[13] Guardsmen also patrolled against looting. In Tell City, which was under 12 feet of water and covered with a massive oil slick, 150 men patrolled the city enforcing "no smoking" orders in an effort to prevent fires. First Sergeant Harry Grube, member of a South Bend company ordered to active duty at Tell City, recalled that Guardsmen took in pets that had been abandoned in the flooding and fed scores of dogs and cats each day.

The Guard also was used to assist authorities whenever a president visited the state. A small contingent was activated during a visit to Indianapolis by President Hoover, and more than 1,000 were on duty when President Franklin D. Roosevelt came to Vincennes to dedicate the George Rogers Clark Memorial.

President Hoover's 1929 visit to Ohio River cities resulted in tragedy when Battery E, 150th Field Artillery, of Madison, fired a salute as he passed downriver. During the series of firings a burning wad from one of the guns ignited a powder bag, which then exploded. Seven Guardsmen were injured. One soldier later died and, as late as 1979, the Indiana legislature still was making a biennial appropriation to compensate one Guardsman, William Stephanus, who was seriously injured in the incident.

Citizen soldiers also were called upon to provide assistance to those made most destitute as a result of the impact of the Great Depression. In 1931 a Guard unit helped to dispose of surplus Indiana National Guard property to local charitable organizations to enable them to provide relief to their constituents. Considerable quantities of old clothing and other items were made available to groups throughout the state.

The Guard was activated in August, 1930, to deal with a lynching episode in Grant County. Three black youths had been apprehended and charged with rape and murder, and a mob took the law into their own hands, lynching two of the prisoners. Blacks in Marion were outraged because the victims had not been given due process of law, and black leaders warned of possible retaliation. Martial law was declared and two National Guard companies, then in annual training at Camp Knox, were ordered to Marion under the command of Colonel George H. Healey. Guardsmen patrolled the city's black districts carrying loaded Springfield rifles with fixed bayonets. Their presence stabilized the situation, and no further outbreaks of disorder were recorded.[14]

Indiana's mining regions—historic trouble spots throughout the state's post-Civil War history—were the scene of renewed labor strife during the 1920s and 1930s. In 1926 union factions clashed during attempts to organize miners in Vanderburgh and Warrick counties. Several miners were injured in the course of a series of demonstrations. A small contingent of Guardsmen was detailed to Warrick County for a month-long period as a precautionary measure. Disorders erupted at the Hoosier Mine in Sullivan County in July, 1932, and Governor Harry G. Leslie, acting upon requests from local authorities, dispatched three infantry companies to the scene. The units were based at Shakamak State Park, and the Guardsmen's presence cooled the situation. However, a few weeks later, mass picketing began at the Dixie Bee Mine in Vigo County where 6,000 demonstrators had effectively imprisoned a number of miners. Governor Leslie proclaimed martial law on August 3, and 250 Guardsmen were moved by bus from Terre Haute that night. They dispersed the pickets and freed 78 trapped miners, four of whom had been wounded by gunfire before the militia arrived. Again, Shakamak was turned into an operating base and Guardsmen maintained a vigil at the mine using patrols and aerial observation. Violence ebbed, and some of the men were released in October. However, because of the tense situation in the area, a small force was retained at Shakamak for nearly two years. In 1936, 66 officers and more than a thousand enlisted personnel again were called to Vigo County, when a general strike was called in Terre Haute and isolated outbreaks of violence occurred.

Although equipment shortages might have caused some to wonder about the potential effectiveness of the Guard, its formations were made up of dedicated volunteers who attended weekly night-time drills and periodic weekend training periods for rifle and pistol practice. Officers and non-commissioned officers attended extra sessions without pay.

The illusion of peace died hard, despite the aggressive actions of Germany and Japan in the 1930s. In 1933, Congress enacted legislation that would insure that Guard outfits would serve as units in the event of mobilization, ending a controversy over the use of militiamen in foreign wars that had proved troublesome since the War of 1812. However, the dedication of Guardsmen, more than acts of Congress, was responsible for the preservation of the militia system during the bleak decades between the wars. In retrospect, they performed admirably with what little they had on hand in terms of equipment and financial support.

Later, General Palmer would observe: "When the present war started in 1939 we had no effective Army ready for an emergency . . . Through its system of armory instruction the National Guard had attained a degree of efficiency that was amazing."[15] However, if the full intent of the 1920 Defense Act had been carried out, America would have entered the war with 55 Guard and Reserve divisions, their members would have had a minimum of four months of intensive training, officers and non-coms would have been far better prepared, and the system would have provided ten million graduates from the Organized Reserve.

---

[1] Samuel Eliot Morison, *The Oxford History of the American People* (New York: Oxford University Press, 1945), p. 188, pp. 219-220.

[2] Russell F. Weigley, *History of the United States Army* (New York: Macmillan, 1967), pp. 396-400.

[3] *Indiana Year Book* (Indianapolis, 1921), p. 1067.

[4] *Indiana Year Book* (Indianapolis, 1920), pp. 321-233.

[5] *Indiana Year Book* (Indianapolis, 1921), p. 1045, p. 1063.

[6] William J. Watt, "The Story of the 38th Division," typescript, 1967, pp. 19-20.

[7] Leonard Webster, "A Military History of the Indiana National Guard, 1816-1906," typescript, 1967, p. 35; Watt, "Story of the 38th," p. 18.

[8] *Indiana Year Book* (Indianapolis, 1923), p. 551.

[9] *Indiana Year Book* (Indianapolis, 1925), p. 51.

[10] *Indiana Year Book* (Indianapolis, 1931), p. 740.

[11] Jim Dan Hill, *The Minutemen in Peace and War* (Harrisburg: Stackpole, 1964), pp. 139-150; *Historical Annual of the Indiana National Guard* (Indianapolis, 1938), pp. 302-303.

[12] *Indiana Year Book* (Indianapolis, 1925), p. 49.

[13] *Indiana Year Book* (Indianapolis, 1937), pp. 90-91.

[14] Indianapolis *Star,* August 10, 1930.

[15] General John MacAuley Palmer, *America in Arms* (New Haven: Yale University Press, 1941), pp. 191-193.

INDIANA'S AIR GUARDSMEN IN PEACE AND WAR

James A. Caldwell and William J. Watt

The armistice that ended the World War left the United States with an inventory of military aircraft and a throng of enthusiastic pilots who desired to keep on flying them. Some of the wood-and-canvas craft went on the auction block and were acquired by barnstormers who became stunt men in the skies at air shows and county fairs across America. Pioneer airmen began to make plans for the first air mail companies, while many veterans sought positions in a skeletonized Army Air Corps. It was only natural that other flyers looked to the National Guard, either through a belief in air power as a growing force in the nation's defense or because the creation of aviation units within the Guard would provide them the chance to sustain what otherwise could have been a prohibitively expensive avocation. This was still the scarf-and-goggle era of American aviation, new, daring, and dangerous.

Indiana's aviation units were among the earliest in the National Guard. In 1921 Wilbur F. Fagley, a wartime aviator and founder of the Curtis Aviation Corporation at Kokomo, persuaded militia officials to convert a battery of coastal artillery to an artillery air observation unit that could support ground elements of the 38th Infantry Division. Headquarters Battery, 81st Field Artillery, was federally recognized in August, 1921, becoming the third National Guard air unit in the country. Organized at Kokomo with a handful of Curtiss "Jennies," the unit was placed under Fagley's command. Commissioned a major, he was killed only a few months later in the crash of a private airplane.[1] Among the initial volunteers to join the air unit were five men—Lawrence Aratz, Matt Carpenter, Elsworth Caldwell, Joseph Meyer, and Ralph Gardon—who became full-time Air Guardsmen and the forerunners of later generations of aviation technicians who have contributed so much to the readiness of Guard aviation outfits.

In August, 1922, the unit was reorganized as the 137th Observation Squadron. A subsequent redesignation as the 113th Observation Squadron occurred almost immediately

147

thereafter; and the renamed unit was federally recognized on January 3, 1923, as an element of the 38th Infantry Division Air Service. The squadron soon included a photo detachment, air intelligence section, and medical detachment.

Upon organization, Air Guard units were provided with World War I surplus equipment, normally eight JN4H or JN6H trainers and supplies of spare parts. Indiana's unit also acquired French Nieuport 28s. There were few navigation aids, and pilots relied on geography books and commercial atlases to provide them with a means of navigating by reference to railroad lines. Weather information was obtained by personal observation. Early airmen advertised their skills, and the Guard, by touring the nation to compete in state-sponsored air shows and flying circuses.[2]

By the end of 1922 the Hoosier air complement included 24 officers and 111 enlisted personnel. At that time, the nation-wide strength of the aviation elements in the Guard amounted to only 136 officers and 643 enlisted men. Despite the interest of early barnstormers, it was difficult to acquire properly qualified officer pilots because the War Department had stipulated that a National Guardsman could not secure a pilot's rating except through a one-year active duty training period.[3]

In 1923 the 113th Observation Squadron established a four-month aviator training program for Guardsmen under 30 years of age. Pilots averaged one hour of flying time each week, plus 15 hours during annual training encampments. Although facilities, aircraft, and support equipment were out of date and in short supply, the squadron did manage to participate in field training in the early 1920s at Wright Field, Dayton, Ohio, and was involved in strike duty at Evansville in 1926.

War Department planners had envisioned 19 National Guard air squadrons, and 14 of them were organized by 1925. However, the Militia Bureau complained: "The equipment in use at present is obsolete and unsuitable . . . It is deteriorating rapidly and in a very short time will be unsafe for flying purposes."[4] One year later the bureau recommended replacement of the wooden Jenny trainers because of their age and because they were not suited for the installation of radios, photo equipment, or machine guns.

Similar problems had plagued the Army's air service, and a trend toward modernization began only with the adoption of the Air Commerce Act of 1926 and the enactment of five-

148

year development programs for the Army and Navy. The former spurred the development of civil aviation by placing the government in charge of navigation aids, airways, and airworthiness certification. The establishment of commercial air mail companies then proceeded rapidly; some of their pilots also became aviators for the National Guard. The five-year programs stimulated the expansion of the Army Air Corps, which had never reached authorized strength levels. In 1926, the corps counted only 919 officers and 8,275 enlisted personnel, about half the number intended by the War Department. Useful aircraft assets included only 169 observation planes and 60 pursuit aircraft. All of the bombers and attack planes were rated as obsolete.[5]

The new interest in Washington began to be felt in the Guard. In 1928 the tables of equipment called for the addition of three standard observation planes, either the Douglas PT-1 or the Consolidated O-17, and a phasing out of the Jennies. That year Indiana's squadron consisted of seven aircraft. Pilots averaged 91 hours of flying time per year and statistics showed that, nationally, there was one fatal accident for every 2,312 hours flown.[6] The PT-1 was suitable only as a training aircraft and the Militia Bureau sought a balance in each squadron between observation aircraft and training planes.

The placing of the 113th at Kokomo had been considered an interim measure because the airstrip, known as Fagley Field, was too small and because the community couldn't provide a sufficient pool of pilots from which to enroll a full complement of flying officers. Fort Harrison's Schoen Field (now the location of the Army Finance Center) was utilized temporarily in 1927 until land was acquired on the Indianapolis southwest side. Weekly training assemblies were conducted at North Armory in Indianapolis.[7]

The state of Indiana acquired the new site outright in 1928 and intended that it be used for the National Guard. This was considered a significant advancement because Guard aviation units typically had been located at municipal airfields or at regular military installations. However, the growth of commercial aviation encroached upon the Hoosier Guardsmen. The Curtiss-Wright Corporation constructed hangars at the new facility, which had been named Stout Field in honor of Lieutenant Richard Stout, who had been killed in a flying accident in 1926. Soon after their completion, Transcontinental Air Transport, the predecessor company of Trans World Airlines, established the first transcontinental airway, utilizing Stout Field as one stopover. (The original T. A. T. passenger terminal now is used by the state Recruiting and Retention Office and the 120th Public Affairs Detachment.) Embry-Riddle, the passenger subsidiary of what then was called American Airways, also inaugurated Indianapolis service from Stout Field. Private pilots and aero clubs then began to locate there.[8]

In 1927 Charles Lindbergh brought the *Spirit of St. Louis* to Stout Field and visited members of the 113th. Although the unit continued field training exercises at Wright Field, it began to increase its support of the 38th Infantry Division. In 1928, when the division conducted field exercises at Camp Knox, Kentucky, the 113th operated out of Louisville's Bowman Field and the aviators undertook artillery spotting, observation flights for infantry units, and aerial photography missions. During this era unit training assemblies were conducted on Monday nights for the short period of one hour. However, oldtimers recall that a considerable amount of effective training was completed in that limited span of time. In those days, there was no basic training school for Air Guardsmen; unit leaders were required to teach the principles of soldiering as well as the specialized techniques of aviation operations. The influx of new aircraft fully materialized in 1931 and 1932. The issue of BT-1 and O-17 training aircraft was completed and 13 squadrons (including the 113th) were equipped with New Douglas O-38s, while the remaining six were outfitted with Douglas O-2Hs.[9] About this time the Guard acquired the Curtiss-Wright hangar facilities, enabling the squadron to transfer its headquarters to Stout Field.

Air Guardsmen were utilized frequently during the 1920s and 1930s for domestic emergency and civil disturbance duties. Most notable was the Wabash River flooding in January, 1930, which placed certain members of the squadron on state active duty for as long as ten days. The airmen located marooned citizens and provided limited supply service to isolated regions. The entire squadron was utilized during the great floods of January, 1937, which inundated much of the southern part of the state. The air observers informed other Guardsmen as to highway routes that remained available for utilization and

150

provided radio communication, because many telephone circuits had failed as a result of the storms.[10]

As air mail companies proliferated and began to carry passengers, controversy arose over the awarding of government mail contracts, which provided the life blood of the fledgling carriers. Postmaster General Walter F. Brown favored companies which had the strongest financial backing and tried to use the awarding of contracts as leverage to compel smaller operators to merge or to go out of business. Resentment on the part of the small carriers led to a congressional investigation, a national scandal, and an order by President Roosevelt in February, 1934, that canceled all air mail contracts. The Army Air Corps was instructed to carry the mail, although the limited size of the air service compelled it to limit its routes to about half those which had been operated by the airlines. Fifty-three National Guard airplanes were turned over to the regulars to create a fleet of 148 aircraft to haul the mail, and a few Guardsmen were involved in the operation.

A combination of over-age equipment and one of the most severe winters in history resulted in numerous accidents, several of them causing fatalities. The inability of the Air Corps to supplant the commercial carriers soon became a bigger scandal than the postal contract awards, and a series of fatal wrecks prompted Secretary of War George H. Dern to suspend operations in March. Meanwhile, a presidential panel began looking into the corps' preparedness. Its subsequent report proposed a number of reforms and set the stage for more autonomy for the air arm.[11]

Meanwhile in Indiana, the Guard was attracting public attention with a massive air show sponsored by the 113th, the Indianapolis Aero Club, the Aircraft Owners Association, and the Kroger Company. About 30,000 spectators turned out for an air show at the Indianapolis municipal field to see formation flying, parachute jumps, and races, which culminated with a victory in the ten-mile race by Lieutenant Howard H. Maxwell, a veteran commercial and Guard pilot.[12]

In the mid-1930s newer O-46s began to filter into Guard aviation units and new officer positions were created for non-pilot observers who helped man the planes. Previously, only the lieutenants commanding the photographic and medical detachments were exempted from rated aviator status. Squadron tables of organization called for one major, five captains,

11 first lieutenants, and 14 second lieutenants—each of whom was required to be a rated pilot.[13] More modern two-way radios were installed in all airplanes by 1936 and extensive cross-country flying was allowed, although aerial gunnery training fell off substantially due to shortages of ammunition.[14]

Pilot shortages began to emerge in the late 1930s and the 113th suffered along with its sister squadrons. In 1939 the squadron had filled only 17 of its 31 officer pilot positions; the unit was operating nine observation aircraft. Adjutant General Elmer F. Straub stated that the Guard would seek out airline pilots or send recruits to regular Army flight training courses. In prior years the second option had proved to be a questionable one because many new pilots abandoned the military for the commercial airline companies as soon as they won their wings. However, after 1939 War Department policy required them to agree to return to their Guard units after commissioning.[15]

As Europe plunged into war, the Army Air Corps began an ambitious expansion program which spilled over into the National Guard. Ten new observation squadrons were authorized, in addition to the 19 already in operation. Two were to start up in 1940 and the remaining eight in 1941. The aircraft strength of each squadron was to be increased to 14, including ten observation craft, one combat plane, and three short range liaison aircraft. Virtually all of the observation planes were to be of the O-47 series. By this time, pilots were accumulating 150 hours of flying time annually.[16] Stout Field was identified for a large-scale construction program, and $1.3 million was spent in 1941 on the development of new runways and hangars, and an administration building and control tower.

On January 17, 1941, the 113th Observation Squadron and its photographic and medical detachments were called to active duty for one year. Mobilization of the airmen followed that of the 38th Infantry Division by one day. Major Oliver H. Stout then commanded the squadron, which included about 150 officers and enlisted men, all from Indiana. The division's air officer was Captain Harvey Weir Cook, who in the late 1920s had served as a full-time instructor for the air squadron. Soon after mobilization he was named to command a P-39 fighter group and was killed in 1942 while on a training flight in the Pacific Theater. Stout, too, soon was transferred to command the 67th Tactical Reconnaissance Group and later the Army Air Base at Greenville, South Carolina.

A few weeks later, the 113th was transported to Key Field, at Meridian, Mississippi, an installation possessing a few runways but lacking hangars, parking ramps, or barracks. The squadron was assigned a support mission to the 38th Division, which was training at Camp Shelby, Mississippi, about 100 miles from Key Field.

As the Hoosiers entered federal service, a massive buildup of the Army Air Corps was under way. An air service that had operated from only 17 bases in 1939 was expanding to 114 by the end of 1941. Pilot training was increased from 300 airmen per year in 1939 to 7,000 a year by June, 1940, as the corps built toward a strength of 84 combat groups.[17]

The value of the National Guard formations was proved during this unprecedented expansion because experienced Guard pilots often became the nucleii of new regular Army observation units. Exceptions were the airline company flyers who were permitted to separate, as were other highly technical personnel who held essential positions in industry. The 1941 report of the National Guard Bureau said that the Guard's squadrons "were so far superior to the average regular Army air unit in pilot experience that they were deprived of many of their seasoned flyers in order to permit the aviation development of the Army as a whole to make progress."[18]

Eventually, the War Department prescribed that at least two experienced pilots were to be retained in each Guard observation squadron in order to avoid entirely denuding them of experienced leadership. Of the 21 pilots mobilized with the 113th, 16 were reassigned within a year. National Guard Bureau officials sought permission to create Guard pursuit squadrons, but a combination of airplane and pilot shortages prevented it. The regulars concluded that the pace was too frantic to permit the development of a parallel system of combat squadron development.

Technically, the one-year active duty period was due to end in January, 1942, but the Japanese attack on Pearl Harbor erased any lingering thoughts about returning home. The 113th then was assigned its initial wartime mission, that of anti-submarine patrol along the Gulf of Mexico. The threat of such attacks was real—or at least seemed so at the time. At one point, the squadron did spot an enemy submarine in the

Gulf; the vessel was promptly destroyed and the 113th earned a battle star to its American Campaign Medal, one of the few Guard observation units to do so. On November 30, 1943, the 113th Observation Squadron was deactivated, after virtually all of its personnel had been used to bolster new Air Corps units. Major William H. Shome, who had been a pilot with the unit, eventually was awarded the Medal of Honor for action in the Pacific.

In April, 1942, Stout Field was placed under federal control and became the operating base of the Ninth Troop Carrier Command which operated C-46 "Commandos" throughout the remainder of the war.

The post-war role of the National Guard's aviation units proved to be a vastly expanded one, growing from a pre-war strength of 29 squadrons to 84 squadrons and their higher and supporting echelons. When the Air Force became a separate entity, the Air National Guard achieved its identity.

Indiana's Air National Guard was reorganized as the 113th Fighter Squadron and was federally recognized at Stout Field, April 14, 1947, with Captain John E. Fesenfield as commander. Many of the officers and enlisted personnel from the old 113th Observation Squadron returned to the unit and worked hard to recruit new men, most of whom had World War II experience. Recruiting proceeded swiftly, in part because of the natural enthusiasm and esprit d'corps possessed by airmen. On December 9, 1947, a sister squadron, designated as the 163rd Fighter Squadron, was organized at Baer Field, Fort Wayne, with Major William R. Sefton as commander. In October, 1950, the 122nd Fighter Wing was formed at Stout Field, with Colonel Allison Maxwell as commander. The 113th and 163rd Fighter Squadrons were equipped with P-51 "Mustang" fighter aircraft. From time to time, the name has been altered to conform to the mission (fighter, fighter-interceptor, fighter bomber, tactical fighter, etc.). One squadron was based at Stout Field and the other at Baer Field.

On February 1, 1951, the Indiana Air National Guard was once again mobilized for active duty, this time for the Korean conflict. Stout Field and Baer Field were named as the immediate active duty training sites. In early 1951 the 122nd Fighter-Bomber Wing Headquarters was transferred to Baer Field, but returned to Stout Field in 1952, where it remained until

1954. The unit then was relocated at Baer Field when the other units were transferred to Hulman Field at Terre Haute.

During the 21 months the Indiana Air Guard was on active duty, no unit was sent overseas. However, the 113th Fighter Squadron was transferred to Scott Field, Illinois; and the 163rd Fighter Squadron was repositioned at Sioux City, Iowa, where it was assigned to the Air Defense Command. Approximately 70 per cent of the officers and airmen ultimately saw foreign service after transfer to other units, and nine Indiana Air Guard pilots actually flew combat missions in Korea. The 122nd Fighter Wing was returned to state control on November 1, 1952. Stout Field and Baer Field again were named home bases for its units.

In early 1954, after a fight with local authorities over safety issues associated with the continued use of Stout Field because of its nearness to the nearby commercial facility at Weir Cook Airport, officials concluded that Stout Field could not be expanded to handle jet aircraft. The 113th Fighter Squadron was relocated at Hulman Field, Terre Haute, where new hangars, runways, and supporting facilities were constructed.

During the following years the 122nd's squadrons were equipped with F-80, F-86, and F-84 aircraft. Each conversion was accomplished by the men of the wing.

They also began to use Camp Atterbury as a target range for training missions. Almost daily, from four to a dozen jet fighter planes converge over southern Indiana, dart toward the ground while firing machine guns, cannons, or rockets, or dropping bombs. Their target is the Air Guard's air-to-ground gunnery-bombing range at the Atterbury site. The Hoosier facility is the first of its kind in Indiana. Since opening in July, 1958, aircraft from Indiana, Ohio, Illinois, and Missouri have used the air-to-ground range. It is also one of the few gunnery-bombing ranges open year around.

As the cold war escalated during the Berlin Wall episode of 1961, the government decided to show the muscle of the North Atlantic Treaty Organization and mobilized about 25,000 officers and men of the Air National Guard, who then were deployed at various bases overseas. The Indiana Air National Guard was activated on October 1, 1961, and was designated the 122nd Tactical Fighter Wing. While the 181st Air Base Group and the 113th Tactical Fighter Squadron remained in training status at Hulman Field, the 163rd Tactical Fighter Squadron was called to Chambley Air Force Base in France. Although few of the pilots had much experience with lengthy over-the-water flights, there were no incidents and the group arrived at Chambley later in October and became part of the 17th Air Force. Although the airmen were on frequent duty with their F-84 jets, the crisis ebbed several months later and the 122nd Tactical Fighter Wing was released from federal active duty on August 20, 1962.[19]

Prior to the Vietnam buildup, it had been normal for regular Air Force units to support regular Army divisions in training. However, diversion of regular air assets to Vietnam made it necessary to call on the Air National Guard for assistance. Although not on a full-mobilization basis, squadrons of the 122nd were placed on active duty in 1965 to train with an Army division in Hawaii and in 1966 to work with regular Army units in Alaska. As individuals, some Air Guardsmen were on duty for as long as 30 days, others for only 15 days. Pilots were rotated when personal affairs demanded it.

In 1971 the squadrons of the 122nd Tactical Fighter Wing were equipped with F-100 aircraft, and again the transition was speedy and effective.

In 1974 Brigadier General William R. Sefton was selected by the National Guard Bureau to command Exercise "Western Tactical Air Control System Number II" (WESTACS II). Approximately 3,000 Air Guardsmen from Indiana, Michigan, Utah, Idaho, Washington, California, Nevada, and Oregon participated, with headquarters at Fairchild Air Force Base, Spokane, Washington. During this exercise over 1,100 sorties and 2,110 hours were flown, with no weather aborts, serious in-flight emergencies, or lost time to ground incidents experienced.

In April, 1976, the Indiana Air Guard, then under the command of Brigadier General Richard Petercheff, accomplished its first overseas summer field training. Eighteen F-100s were deployed to Lakenheath, England, refueling along the way from Strategic Air Command tankers. The 122nd Tactical Fighter Wing, Baer Field, and the 181st Tactical Fighter Group, Hulman Field, each provided half the aircraft and personnel. A second air-to-ground gunnery range in Indiana was opened at Jefferson Proving Ground that year. General Petercheff had initiated action to obtain authority to build this range early in 1974. In 1979 the 113th Fighter Squadron retired the last F-100 Super Sabre in the Air Force inventory. The 122nd Tactical Fighter Wing, commanded by Brigadier General Frank Hettlinger, began receiving the F-4 Phantom. The conversion was being completed in 1980.

[1] Jim Dan Hill, *The Minuteman in Peace and War* (Harrisburg: Stackpole, 1964), p. 527; Leonard E. Webster, "A Military History of the Indiana National Guard," typescript, 1967, p. 104.

[2] Hill, *The Minuteman in Peace and War*, pp. 523-531.

[3] *Report of the Chief of the Militia Bureau* (Washington: Government Printing Office, 1925), p. 39.

[4] *Report of the Chief of the Militia Bureau* (Washington: Government Printing Office, 1925), p. 39.

[5] Carroll V. Glines, Jr., *The Compact History of the U.S. Air Force* (New York: Hawthorn, 1973), p. 39.

[6] *Report of the Chief of the Militia Bureau* (Washington: Government Printing Office, 1928), p. 38, p. 74.

[7] Webster, "History of the Indiana Guard," pp. 104-105.

[8] Indianapolis *Times,* August 17, 1931.

[9] *Report of the Chief of the Militia Bureau* (Washington: Government Printing Office, 1932), p. 37.

[10] Webster, "History of the Indiana Guard," p. 106.

[11] Glines, *History of the Air Force,* pp. 128-132; *Report of the Chief of the National Guard Bureau* (Washington: Government Printing Office, 1934), p. 13.

[12] Indianapolis *Star,* May 7, 1934.

[13] Hill, *The Minuteman in Peace and War,* p. 531.

[14] *Report of the Chief of the National Guard Bureau* (Washington: Government Printing Office, 1936), p. 13.

[15] Indianapolis *Star,* October 3, 1959.

[16] *Report of the Chief of the National Guard Bureau* (Washington: Government Printing Office, 1939), p. 9.

[17] Glines, *History of the Air Force,* p. 150.

[18] *Report of the Chief of the National Guard Bureau* (Washington: Government Printing Office, 1941), p. 55, p. 64.

[19] Webster, "History of the Indiana Guard," pp. 108-109.

THE ARMY GUARD IN WORLD WAR II

Robert T. Fischer

In January, 1941, the Indiana National Guard was called into active federal service for one year. Few in our country or state realized at the time that it was to be for a much longer period and that these citizen soldiers were to fight in the costliest and bloodiest war in world history. The mobilization did not just "happen." It was part of large-scale national preparations under way at the time for an eventuality that could require us to defend our country against world powers bent on expansion by military force.

The stage was being set for the mobilization in late 1939. In September of that year Germany invaded Poland, utilizing its newly acquired tactic of blitzkrieg warfare. Poland lasted barely a month before surrendering. In April, 1940, the Germans invaded Norway and conquered it in two months. France capitulated in June, 1940. The air battle of Britain was conducted during the period of August through October of that year and narrowly missed bringing a German triumph over England. In that same October the Italians invaded Greece, and over the holidays in late 1940 and early 1941 the British were fighting in North Africa. To the isolationists in this country, all of these things were happening an ocean away and need not concern us too greatly. To the realists and those capable of thinking beyond our own immediate continent in terms of time and distance, the events in Europe and elsewhere were prophecies come true, and it was a matter of time before we would be forced to participate in order to protect our own national interests.

Hitler's rise to power in Germany in the mid-1930s and his clearly defined intentions, outlined for the world in *Mein Kampf*, combined with the Japanese conquest in Manchuria and the impotence of the League of Nations, were all sober predictions of coming events. The possibility of another national emergency was approaching, and the Protective Mobilization Plan being developed and refined in 1938 by Secretary of War William H. Woodring visualized a 400,000-man force of regular Army and National Guard troops to counter any

158

possible aggression.[1] Woodring was adamant about taking advantage of peacetime to prepare for the eventuality of war. Although our military planning at the time was a good deal more sophisticated than before World War I, it was not any more successful with Congress. When war would come for us late in 1941, we again would not be prepared; and it would be almost three more years before we could lend any significant weight to the outcome of the conflict.

However, Congress at last was awakening to the realities of world events and to the danger that could lie ahead for this country. On August 27, 1940, Public Resolution 96 of the 76th Congress authorized the entire National Guard to be called into active federal service for one year.[2] This was three days before the completion of the first three-week annual field training period ever conducted by the Indiana National Guard. The Army had ordered the Indiana Guard to participate in Second Army maneuvers at the Camp McCoy-Camp Williams training areas in Wisconsin from August 11 to 31. The War Department ordered a general increase in the frequency and intensity of training exercises throughout the country in preparation for the mobilization. In effect, the Indiana National Guard mobilization started with that three-week training period. Less than a month following the August maneuvers, selected officers and enlisted men of the Indiana State Administrative Staff Corps were placed on orders for active duty.[3] Lieutenant Colonel Robinson Hitchcock, the assistant adjutant general, was ordered to active duty that September and appointed Director of Selective Service for Indiana. On September 16 Congress enacted the first national peacetime compulsory service legislation after continuous pressure from President Roosevelt.[4] Draftees were called into service for one year. The regular Army was happy to have the draft and was concerned that it came none too soon for national safety.

The mood and temper of the Indiana Guardsmen was one of wholehearted support for the country. Attendance at drills increased; there were some reorganizations and changes of station for Indiana National Guard units to facilitate training and to take advantage of qualified officers and enlisted men in certain localities, and training and administrative preparation for mobilization became the order of the day.

On January 6, 1941, President Roosevelt broadcast the

159

seventeenth of his famous fireside chats to over 500 radio stations throughout the country.[5] Among the spectators in the small, hot, and humid Oval Office was actor Clark Gable and his wife, Carole Lombard. The President said that Germany, Italy, and Japan were the enemy; and that they eventually would unite against the United States if their program for world control was not checked. "If Great Britain goes down," he said, "all of us in the Americas would be living at the point of a gun. The vast resources and wealth of this hemisphere constitute the most tempting loot in the world." What was to be done? Roosevelt's answer was to arm, more and faster, and become the great arsenal of democracy.

Eleven days after his speech, on January 17, 1941, the Indiana National Guard was mobilized and entered into active federal service. Almost 9,000 men from Indiana, Kentucky, and West Virginia were mobilized as the 38th Infantry Division. Presidential Executive Order 8618 was the instrument that made the division a part of the active military establishment.[6] Of the total division strength, 4,988 officers, warrant officers, and enlisted men came from the Indiana National Guard—well over half of the entire division strength.[7]

It was a great and happy time for the men of the Indiana Guard. They were caught up in patriotic fervor and eager to serve their country, knowing that they would be home in a year. Little did they recognize that they were to play a major combat role in the liberation of the Philippine Islands from the Japanese four years later and that some of them would not return.

Indiana officials began wrestling with the need to create a substitute militia as soon as it became apparent that the Guard would be activated. In November, 1940, Governor Clifford M. Townsend authorized the creation of a civil defense force, and the 1941 legislative session gave the Indiana State Guard a statutory basis. Five regiments were created and the new organization achieved its peak strength in 1942, with 216 officers and 1,988 enlisted men. On a few occasions, the State Guard was used in connection with tornado and flood incidents.

Inductions into the regular forces caused recurring manpower problems, but the I.S.G. was able to acquire weapons and uniforms from the federal government. At war's end, about 100 trucks manned by State Guardsmen delivered nearly 7,000 returning servicemen on the last leg of their homeward journey in time for Christmas. Many soldiers had been thwarted in attempts to get home because public transportation facilities were choked with holiday crowds and military returnees. Without aid from the militiamen, they would have faced another Christmas away from their families. The Indiana State Guard was disbanded in 1947, although the concept of a backup force was re-employed in the 1950s.[8]

Camp Shelby, Mississippi, was the 38th Division's destination. It had been the home of the 38th in World War I. Major General Robert H. Tyndall took the division south by organic military vehicles and by military troop trains and commanded it there until he retired in April, 1941. Major General Daniel I. Sultan assumed command during the period of buildup and reorganization into a full-strength division.

When the division arrived at Camp Shelby, construction was still under way. There were gaps in the officer ranks occasioned by departures for professional military branch schools. Most of the officers would re-join the division later. Fifth Army Corps, the 38th and 37th (Ohio National Guard) Divisions, and the 73d Field Artillery Brigade were scheduled for Shelby.[9] Several thousand draftees, primarily from the states of Indiana, Kentucky, and West Virginia, also were coming to train and to join their home state units. The wartime strength of approximately 18,000 was reached by the 38th in short order, and an intensified training program began for all soldiers from combat infantrymen, to cooks, and unit clerks. A period of basic training followed by continuous unit training was welding the 38th Division into a close, effective military force.

Congress had let the military lapse into a state of unpreparedness with respect to provision of weapons and equipment necessary to conduct training and combat operations. In 1941 the greatest automotive industry in the world still produced cars and prepared for its 1942 models while the Army remained desperately short of tanks and other equipment. Division troops in the Louisiana maneuvers frequently used tree limbs and broomsticks to simulate weapons. Americans were shocked by photographs of mock-up weapons in the Louisiana maneuvers of September, 1941, while department stores were full for the Christmas season.[10] We were ill-prepared to mobilize and to fight, even on the eve of the war.

In August and September, 1941, the division (as a part of

161

the Third Army) participated in what has been called the First Louisiana Maneuver. The actual maneuver area was about 300 miles from Camp Shelby along the western border of Louisiana and extending into eastern Texas. It ran generally in a north-south direction along U.S. Highway 171. The region largely consisted of cut timber land, the road network was poor, and in many areas the ground was soft and spongy. To the average soldier, it was "set up and tear down" and swap trucks and equipment back and forth in order to move.

The War Department saw a long and protracted mobilization, and officers and men were screened with regard to their probable longevity in military service. After the Louisiana maneuver, and to many individuals' dismay, age-in-grade criteria imposed by the Army resulted in many officers and enlisted men being forced off of active duty.

Following the Japanese attack on Pearl Harbor and our immediate entry into war with Japan, enemy submarines were sighted off the coast in the Gulf of Mexico. There was serious talk of an invasion from that quarter. Training was interrupted for the 38th and for several months it was dispersed along the Gulf to guard against such an invasion. A task force of the division was placed under the Southern Defense Command until February, 1942, for this purpose.

In April, 1942, Major General Henry L. Jones took command of the division from General Sultan and was to keep it for almost three years thereafter.

In September, 1942, almost a full year after the division had been reorganized into the "triangular" fighting concept from the old World War I "square" organizational structure, the 38th left again for a smaller scale maneuver in Louisiana, this time near the city of Pelican. Upon termination of that exercise, which was of shorter duration than the first, the division was ordered to Camp Carabelle, Florida, (in the vicinity of Tallahassee) for amphibious training and to return a cadre to Camp Shelby to begin training new draftees. Maneuvers at Camp Carabelle consisted of waterborne assault training, physical conditioning, and exercises in village fighting (supervised by British officers who had fought in that environment).

In January, 1943, the division moved to Camp Livingston, Louisiana, for additional training in fighting against pillboxes, wire entanglements, and fortified bunkers. In January, 1944, the 38th moved to New Orleans, loaded onto convoy ships, and sailed through the Panama Canal for Hawaii.

Even today there are misunderstandings about why the 38th was not deployed overseas until three years after mobilization. A close examination of the chain of events during the period tells us why. As noted earlier, there were not enough weapons and equipment to fully provision the division until many months after callup. The age-in-grade elimination of a large number of the officers and enlisted men took its toll on readiness, and the influx of draftees required time for organization and training. On several occasions the division was denuded of senior officers and enlisted men in order to provide training cadres for selectees and to form the nucleii of other units. More than 4,000 enlisted men volunteered for officer candidate schools during the period. The reorganization from the square to the triangular concept required time to realign units and people. These and other factors kept the division from being stabilized until late in 1943. The division actually was a good barometer of the country with respect to its ability to throw substantial weight into the war, because it was not until this period of the war that the United States, as a nation, was really ready to conduct worldwide combat operations with the necessary manpower and resources to sustain it.

During this training phase, an Indiana National Guard element of the 38th Division was redesignated and assigned to another command for subsequent combat duty in the European theater. It deserves attention because of the many Indiana Guardsmen who went with it, stayed with it, and fought with it. In May, 1942, the Second Battalion, 150th Field Artillery, was separated from the division and joined the 208th Field Artillery as its Second Battalion at Camp Forrest, Tennessee. It later reorganized as the 989th Field Artillery Battalion, deployed to Europe in March, 1944, and distinguished itself in combat from August, 1944, through the end of the war in May, 1945. Many of its Indiana Guard veterans returned after the war to form a key constituent of the post-war 38th Infantry Division Artillery.[11]

The largest flotilla ever to pass through the Panama Canal up to that time moved with relative ease to Hawaii for an additional intensified training period of six months. The division was integrated into the defense of the island of Oahu, and its three infantry regiments were rotated from jungle training into north and south positions for the island's defense. Everyone participated in survival training and learned to live off the land. Night compass marches became quite dangerous because of the terrain and its deep ravines. In July, 1944, the division departed on several ships for an 11-day voyage to an unknown destination, which turned out to be Oro Bay, New Guinea. This was to be their new home for another four months. More training. More training. And more training. Many of the division troops became extremely familiar with the ways of headhunters, some of whom periodically brought in the heads of dead Japanese for bounty. Some of our soldiers also were witnesses to the local laws for the tribesmen and the death sentences carried out against their own members for collaborating with the Japanese.

It was now November, 1944, and the division was in fact a well-trained combat unit. Orders were received for the next convoy move. The officers and men of the 38th were ready to do what they had been trained to do.

It is important to understand the overall strategy on both the Allied as well as the Axis sides in order to fix the 38th Infantry Division in its time and place in the history of the war. The grand strategy on both sides actually had its beginning in the Pacific Ocean insofar as the United States and direct involvement in the war is concerned.

In July, 1941, after a ten-year period of Japanese expansion at the serious expense of American and British interests in Eastern Asia and China, President Roosevelt demanded a withdrawal of Japanese troops from Indo-China, ordered the freezing of their assets in this country, and placed an embargo on their oil supply. Japanese encroachment had become too critical for our national interests to tolerate any longer. The Japanese had the options of going to war to protect what they had already acquired and to further their expansionist policies, collapse economically, or soften their policies and cease their expansion. They chose the former and attacked Pearl Harbor. Their overall plan was to gain control of the Philippine Islands early, solidify their positions throughout the Pacific, and form a defensive chain against attack from the west by securing the Dutch East Indies and a line of key points extending northwest into Burma. The Indies were to be their prime source of oil, rubber, and other strategic materials.

The Japanese drove American forces on Luzon to the south into the Bataan peninsula, and the Luzon Force was compelled to surrender in April, 1942, and to endure the infamous death march north to Camp O'Donnell.[12]

Australia was spared direct attack and was used later in the Pacific campaign as the initial base for re-conquest of the region. In August, 1942, General MacArthur started the long road to reoccupy the Pacific Ocean and eventually to conquer Japan itself. In late 1943 the Allied strategy was changed. Rather than fight for every island and piece of land, a by-pass method was initiated whereby only certain territories were attacked and secured to serve as logistical bases for gaining control of other key islands.[13] This in effect isolated many Japanese and left them in no position to fight. The method shortened the distance and military effort necessary for the planned invasion of Japan itself.

The island of Leyte was key to this strategic approach to Japan. The next step, however, was a subject of considerable discussion. It centered on whether to attack Formosa directly and bypass Luzon, or whether to secure Luzon as a stepping stone for Formosa. The Joint Chiefs of Staff, as well as Admiral Nimitz, wanted to attack Formosa directly. General MacArthur contended that to seize and liberate Luzon was not only a political as well as a moral obligation for the United States but also was a military necessity if we were to successfully attack Formosa.[14] This was of such concern that President Roosevelt met with MacArthur and Nimitz at Pearl Harbor in July, 1944, to address the question.[15] MacArthur won out, and on October 3, the Joint Chiefs of Staff directed him to invade Luzon.

The first taste of combat for the division in World War II came on December 6, 1944, when troops of the 38th landed under fire in Leyte Gulf. Enroute to the gulf, the 149th Infantry lost 122 men as a result of a Japanese suicide plane dive onto the deck of the SS Marcus Daly.[16] Enemy paratroopers had taken the nearby Buri airstrip, and enemy planes flying low strafed the landing areas. It was rainy; soldiers were waist deep in mud, jeeps bogged down, bivouac areas were under water, and fox holes were swimming holes. The airstrip was re-taken and fighting continued for five days, with the exception of minor mopping-up operations for two weeks thereafter. Although this was a brief operation, it was an

165

opportune time and place for a taste of combat that sharpened the division for the next fight. In one month, the 38th would land on the island of Luzon and ultimately avenge the loss of the Bataan Peninsula some 32 months earlier.

On Christmas Day, 1944, the division staff was briefed at Eighth Army headquarters and was provided Operation Plan M-3, which directed landings on Luzon by the 38th Infantry Division (reinforced) as a separate task force. On January 19, 1945, plans were changed. Now the division was to participate as a part of the XI Corps and was issued Operation Plan M-7.[17] The new mission required changes in command and staff planning at all levels and added to the confusion already caused by lack of adequate telegraph and telephone communications, scattered locations of all units involved, inaccurate plans and drawings of ships that were to be loaded, and difficulties of coordination with other units to be landed on Luzon with the division. The final shipping assignments were not made until January 21, just five days before final outloading. From January 26 to 29, all supplies, equipment, and troops were loaded; the move was made to Luzon, and the landings were accomplished.

Eleventh Corps Field Order 3 specified the division's role in the M-7 operation. It consisted generally of landings in the southern Zambales Province, securing the airfield near San Marcelino and the naval base on Subic Bay, and the seizure and occupation of an east-west line from the South China Sea to Manila Bay which would seal off the Bataan Peninsula from the north. On January 30 the mission would be modified to include participation in amphibious operations south and east of the Bataan Peninsula.[18]

During the five months the division was engaged in combat operations on Luzon, there were several significant actions in which it was involved in separate locations; some of which were conducted simultaneously. Although the Luzon campaign was not "phased" in the military sense of the word, the author will use the term in this narrative merely to group the more important geographical and sequential combat operations in order to make them more readable and understandable.

Phase I—The initial landings on Luzon on January 29, 1945, through the fight for Zig Zag Pass which terminated on February 14.

Phase II—The action in the southern portion of the Bataan Peninsula, including the fight to gain control of two significant roads, beginning on February 11 through four amphibious landings ending on April 17.

Phase III—The move beginning on March 7 west of Fort Stotsenburg to cut off Japanese escape routes to the north. It terminated on April 30.

Phase IV—Operations from April 30 through June 30 to secure the area east of Manila.

Phase V—All combat actions on Luzon after June 30.

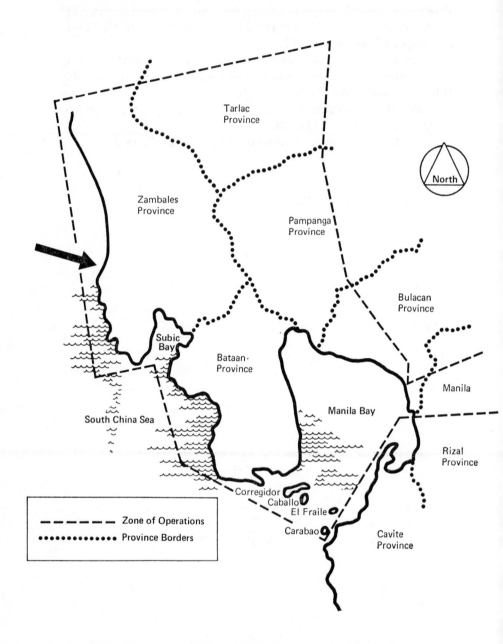

Initial landing site and zone of operations of the 38th Infantry Division
during Operation M-7 from January 29 to June 30, 1945. (not to scale).

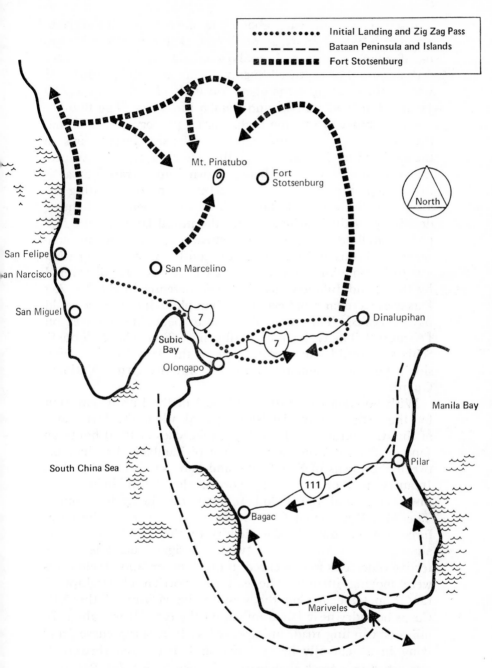

Phases I, II, and III in Operation M-7 for the 38th Infantry Division. (not to scale).

Intelligence gathering about the enemy on Luzon commanded a major effort at all levels. Prior intelligence was based almost solely on friendly guerrilla reports since there was a scarcity of captured enemy documents and prisoners of war. Estimates before the operation itself placed about 12,800 Japanese in the Zambales and Bataan provinces. The number was later proved to be too high. Aerial photographs indicated that they were not occupying their defensive installations in the specified landing areas. Intelligence even began to suspect that the Americans were being drawn into a trap, but as it turned out, the enemy had in reality been consolidating for a fight to the east and the north at the expense of fighting decisively on the beaches.[19] After the initial landings, the first photo intelligence of any consequence revealed enemy concealed positions and activity to the south and east along what was to become known as Zig Zag Pass. It was later discovered by the 152nd Infantry that Japanese defenses in the Zig Zag Pass area were far more elaborate than photo intelligence could have revealed. They were the first to penetrate the area on February 2. The regimental intelligence officer, Major Noble F. Schlatter, would later become one of the 38th Infantry Division's postwar commanders in the Indiana Army National Guard.

With no enemy opposition, Phase I of the Luzon campaign for the 38th Infantry Division opened when the first waves of the division assault force hit the beaches at 0830 hours on January 29, 1945, on the west coast of Zambales Province between the towns of San Felipe and San Narciso. The 151st Infantry was on the left (north), the 149th Infantry in the center, and the 152nd Infantry on the right (south). The 34th Regimental Combat Team, as a part of the corps force, landed south in the vicinity of the San Miguel. The airstrip at San Marcelino as well as assigned beachhead protective objectives were secured in quick order, and all elements were moving inland. The east-west portion of Highway 7 ran from Olongapo on the west to the vicinity of the XIV Corps boundry near Dinalupihan on the east. It was about 20 miles of winding road, unimproved surface, sharp curves, and lying in a generally heavy forest and dense underbrush. It was a tortuous track that became known as Zig Zag Pass.

The 34th Regimental Combat Team secured Highway 7 south to Olongapo, at which juncture the 152nd Infantry relieved it and attacked east along the same road. After two miles of open terrain and another five miles of a narrow mountain valley approach, the entrance to the pass was found to be blocked by Japanese Colonel Sanehira Nagayoshi's 39th Infantry Regiment of the 10th Infantry Division, the core of the "Bataan Garrison."[20]

Eleventh Corps estimated that the pass could be taken in a week. In effect it took a full 13 days of fighting against some of the most fierce and determined resistance encountered in the entire southwest Pacific to that time. Initially, the 149th Infantry was moving east along the north side of the pass, the 152nd Infantry was stopped, and the 34th Regimental Combat Team was ordered to pass through the 152nd on February 3. The 34th passed as ordered but soon became bogged down and could not continue. Both elements became entangled, and the 151st Infantry was ordered to continue the attack in the same zone. Confusion reigned.

On February 6 Major General Jones was relieved and ordered to report to XI Corps Headquarters. Brigadier General Roy W. Easley, the assistant division commander, took temporary command of the division in place. The following day Major General (then Brigadier General) William C. Chase arrived and assumed command of the 38th Division.[21]

On the same day that Major General Chase assumed command, the Third Battalion of the 152nd Infantry was continuing a methodical advance in its zone in the vicinity of what was to become known as Bloody Ridge. It was, indeed. About noon that day, the Japanese had directed intense mortar fire on the battalion aid station. One doctor was dead and another wounded. Some soldiers had been wounded a second time while on litters awaiting treatment. The situation was chaotic. It was then that the battalion executive officer, Major Kenneth W. Brewer, earned the Silver Star for his courageous action under enemy fire in organizing men and vehicles and directing evacuation of the area. He is officially credited with saving approximately 60 wounded.[22] Major Brewer would later be reassigned to the Second Battalion of the 152nd Infantry as its commander in combat, and several years after the war he would command the 38th Division.

Fighting in the pass was so close and the situation changed so rapidly at times that infantry and field artillery units were constantly changing missions in order to mutually assist sister units at critical times. In one such instance on February 9, elements of the 152nd Infantry were ordered north of Highway 7 to assist the 151st Infantry, which could not be disengaged. Both regiments were intermingled in the same fight, and Lieutenant Colonel Jesse E. McIntosh, executive officer of the 152nd Infantry, was placed in control of all units north of the highway. He would later command the 152nd Infantry on Luzon and would become one of the division's post-war commanders in Indiana.

On February 14, Highway 7 and Zig Zag Pass were secured. The Japanese had defended on extremely rugged and unassailable terrain with a maze of entrenchments, caves, connecting tunnels, pillboxes, and gun emplacements. They could not be located until division troops were within Japanese fields of fire. Not an inch was given, nor were there any withdrawals. The ferocity of the Zig Zag Pass fight can be attested to by the fact that almost 2,400 of the enemy were killed and only 25 prisoners were taken.[23]

Phase II of the campaign began during the final days of the Zig Zag Pass fight. On February 11 the 151st Infantry began organizing what was known as the South Force to conduct a series of amphibious landings in the southern tip of Bataan. An East Force from the 149th Infantry began preparations for a move south along the east coast of the peninsula. The Fifth Air Force soon was conducting relentless bombing and strafing raids along Highway 111, which ran from Bagac on the west coast to Pilar on the east. The Highway 111 terrain was similar to that of Highway 7 at Zig Zag Pass, but was not defended in depth or to the extent that the pass was. In fact a great number of the Japanese had infiltrated north out of the Bataan Peninsula itself.

The East Force moved down the peninsula without heavy resistance. On February 15 the 151st Infantry landed on the beaches of Mariveles with relative ease. It was on this same day that a motor column sighted moving rapidly south along the Manila Bay coast was spared being fired upon because of an order to closely look and identify before firing. It turned out to be General MacArthur and part of his staff.[24] By February 24 the southern Bataan Peninsula had been secured. On the same day the 151st Infantry provided a force that landed on Corregidor to assist in the final phases of that operation.

Troops of the 151st Infantry landed on Caballo Island on

the morning of March 17, following field artillery preparation fires and a concentration of bombs being dropped. The 163rd Field Artillery Battalion supported the operation with fragmentation and smoke rounds. The 151st made steady progress until it encountered two large concrete mortar pits in the center of the island, which could not be taken because of the protection afforded by them and the surrounding terrain. Tanks were brought up, but to no avail. Finally, with the help of the Navy, division engineers constructed what they called their "Rube Goldberg." It was a ship fitted with pumps and gas pipeline strung onto shore and up the hill to the mortar pits. Diesel oil and gasoline were pumped from the ship, up the hill, and into the pits. With the addition of two bombs being lowered into the ventilator shafts, the oil was lighted and the resulting internal fire and explosions caused complete destruction inside. On April 13, the regimental troops entered the pits after they had cooled. Two hundred seventy-nine dead Japanese were found inside.

In the entrance to Manila Bay was El Fraile Island, and upon it sat a massive structure known as Fort Drum. The fort was a concrete structure about 350 feet long, about 150 feet wide in the middle, rising over 50 feet above the ground, and built in the general shape of a large ship. It had two large gun turrets mounted on top. The sides and top were of reinforced concrete 15 to 30 feet thick in places. When the Americans left the island in 1942, the guns had been rendered inoperative, and the only firepower from the island was in the form of small arms fire from within. The "Rube Goldberg" used in the Caballo operations was immediately thought of to destroy the inside of the fort, and a "Trojan horse" was designed, using another Navy ship with a gangplank so troops could get on top of the structure. Elements of the 151st Infantry and the 113th Engineers undertook the assault mission on April 13, and the resulting oil, gas, and bombs produced such violent fires and explosions that it was five days before division troops could even descend below the first deck. On April 18, 60 burned and suffocated Japanese were counted.

On April 16 elements of the 151st Infantry assaulted Carabao Island. The operation was supported by a large preparation of field artillery fires from the mainland by the 139th Field Artillery and followed several days of bombing and strafing by the Air Force. Napalm was dropped and tunnel entrances were closed by great land slides. The assault went as planned without opposition. Detailed investigation of emplacements, caves, and tunnels the next day disclosed the fact that the island had not been occupied for several days.

Thus, on April 17 was the whole of the south Bataan Peninsula and all of the island approaches to Manila Bay securely in the hands of United States forces.

The action resulting in division victories in the Zig Zag Pass area and in the extreme southern tip of Bataan had a disintegrating effect on organized enemy forces, and individual Japanese soldiers as well as small units had been infiltrating north. Generally west of Clark Field and Fort Stotsenburg, and north of Zig Zag Pass, lay a series of natural escape routes to the north in the vicinity of the junction of the Zambales, Tarlac, and Pampanga Provinces. On March 7 the 38th Infantry Division was ordered to relieve the 43d Division in the sector with the mission of cutting off Japanese escape routes to the north and destroying all enemy forces in the area. Thus began Phase III of the campaign.

Some elements of the 43d Division remained in place and were attached to the 38th Division. Because of the number of 38th Division units to be involved in the operation, the 43d Division elements now included, and the complexity of a multiple attack from different directions, a separate task force was formed to control the operation. On March 10 at Fort Stotsenburg, 38th Division Advance (Task Force) opened its command post with the division artillery commander in charge.[25] This was also the day that all division units to be included in the operation moved into the area. The terrain was unlike any thus far encountered in the M-7 Operation. Small streams ran between high ridges, individual hills were covered with grass, bamboo thickets abounded, scrubby trees covered numerous paths and enemy caves, and chalk cliffs with caves and tunnels overlooked many of the paths. Thickets like those found in southern parts of the peninsula were present in certain areas but were scattered. Our primary forces consisted of elements of the 149th Infantry, 152nd Infantry, 169th Infantry (from the 43d Division) and four artillery battalions.

The general plan was to attack in several directions from around the perimeter of the area towards the center near Mount Pinatubo, where the Japanese had been concentrating their forces for a defensive action that would allow them a natural

174

terrain escape route to the north if the defense did not hold. From the standpoint of fields of fire and natural cover, the terrain favored the defense throughout the assigned sector. Japanese forces in the area consisted of some combat elements, some support troops, and naval units from the Subic Bay area.

Enemy resistance in the area ranged all the way from light in many places to stubborn last-ditch defense in others. The Japanese were determined to stand on every foot of ground, and where a sizable force was encountered it became a fight to the death involving maneuvering and firepower. As their unit organizations fell apart from relentless attack by division elements, it became a battle of attrition of the individual soldier. There were significant battles on and around terrain features known as the "Motor Pool," "Sawtooth Ridge," and others. In many instances, every strongpoint became a separate battle by itself.

On March 22, in the vicinity of what came to be known as Spence Ridge, some individual officers and men of the 149th Infantry had captured an enemy 37mm Antitank Gun and were personally manning the weapon in direct fire against the Japanese. Acting as assistant gunner on the crew was Lieutenant Colonel Carl O. DeBard, commander of the 139th Field Artillery Battalion, who would after hostilities become a commander of the post-war 38th Division.[26]

By April 11 the division mission of destroying all Japanese forces in the area was virtually accomplished. The Division Advance (Task Force) was dissolved, staff augmentation from division headquarters was released, and the division artillery headquarters assumed tactical control for three days, after which division headquarters assumed responsibility.[27] Mopping up operations had in effect begun in mid-April and were in progress when the 6th Division relieved the 38th Division on April 30.

Phase IV of the campaign consisted of operations to the east of Manila to destroy or disperse all enemy forces in the immediate area. It was a switch of roles for the 38th and 6th divisions, because the 38th was to relieve the 6th east of Manila. By prior arrangement between the divisions, the relief was effected by regiments, and at 1800 hours on April 30 command passed between the two divisions.

The next two months consisted of a series of combat actions not unlike the previous fight in the Stotsenburg area. Patrolling and reconnaissances in force characterized initial regimental and battalion tactics in most instances. Once a Japanese strongpoint was discovered, it was attacked in force. As opposed to the Stotsenburg phase, there were enemy combat units intact, and in their prepared defensive positions it often would take a full week or more to destroy them.

Toward the end of June, the major divisional elements were moving into positions near Bayanbayanan in preparation for taking over new sectors in south Luzon. Manila had been secured from the Japanese to the east and the north. At 2400 hours on June 30, the 38th Infantry Division passed from control of the XI Corps to the XIV Corps. Operation Plan M-7 had been completed. To that time, the division alone had accounted for 20,547 Japanese killed and 645 prisoners of war taken.[28]

Phase V of the Luzon campaign is identified in this history only to serve as a separation from the M-7 Operation with respect to combat operations. For several weeks after transfer to XIV Corps control, the division was engaged in mopping-up operations. Practically all of the organized Japanese resistance had ceased by this time. Elements of the 38th were employed in various parts of southern Luzon to hunt down and neutralize small bands of the enemy, to search out individual Japanese soldiers and kill or capture them, and in general to make a finite sweep of the assigned areas to insure complete elimination of all resistance. Although the pace of fighting was nothing like the previous five months, it was no less intense and bitter in many isolated actions throughout the area. It was still a war, and it was conducted on both sides that way. In between firefights, men of the division had a chance during this phase of operations to learn something about Filipino life and customs, by virtue of rest camps set up near towns and villages.

A "flash" precedent message was received on August 11 that the Japanese had sued for peace. The War in Europe had been over since May when Germany surrendered. But no official cease-fire order accompanied the "flash" message about Japan. Was it really so? What really happened was that the Japanese had offered on August 10 to accept the Potsdam surrender terms, with four minor reservations, but it was not until August 14 that the terms were accepted formally by the Japanese. The next day the official cease-fire was transmitted to the division.[29]

On August 1, Major General Frederick A. Irving had assumed command of the division, and it was he who accepted the formal surrender of enemy commanders in the immediate area. But it was not without great difficulty that small groups of Japanese soldiers and individual holdouts were notified of the surrender and were convinced to stop fighting. Some held out for years before they surrendered.

Some of the division's soldiers had already begun leaving for home on the point system in July. When in September it was announced that the 38th would not be retained in the islands for occupation duty, it was a time for rejoicing, celebration, and preparation for going home. Major General Irving and some of his staff departed by air early, and the remainder of the division started by convoy for the United States on October 12. The division's separation center was designated as Camp Anza, California, and the 38th Infantry Division was deactivated at that location on November 9, 1945.

During the fighting on Luzon, the division suffered 37 officers and 527 men killed in action; and 109 officers and 1,957 men wounded in action. One man was reported missing in action. The 38th accounted for almost 24,000 enemy killed. Fewer than 700 prisoners of war were taken. The tenacity, leadership, spirit, and professionalism of the soldiers of the division were clearly demonstrated when comparisons of both sides are made in terms of combat effectiveness. Perhaps the most significant aspect of the myriad of detailed analyses of the 38th Division's combat record in World War II is the fact that for every soldier of the division who gave his life in combat, there were almost 40 Japanese soldiers killed by the division. This is amazing when considering the minute number of enemy soldiers who chose to surrender rather than fight and die in place.

Officially recorded Indiana elements of the division that fought in the war from which the current organization of the Indiana Army National Guard takes its lineage are the 151st and 152nd Infantry regiments, 139th, 150th, and 163rd Field Artillery battalions, 38th Signal Company, 738th Ordinance Company, 38th Quartermaster Company, 38th Reconnaissance Troop, 113th Engineer Battalion, and the 113th Medical Battalion.[30]

The term, "Avengers of Bataan," was first coined by General MacArthur with reference to the 38th Infantry Division. The entire Luzon campaign entailed the employment of several regular Army as well as National Guard divisions, and some individuals within the Army took exception to the term being applied solely to the 38th. As a result, it was not officially given to the division, but reference to it and common usage throughout the many World War II chronicles, unit histories, and War Department documents leave no doubt that the 38th Infantry Division units were, indeed, the Avengers of Bataan.

[1] Walter F. Millis, ed., *American Military Thought* (Indianapolis: Bobbs-Merrill, 1966), p. 418-420.

[2] R. Ernest Dupuy, *The National Guard, A Compact History* (New York: Hawthorn, 1971), p. 117.

[3] *Indiana Year Book* (Indianapolis, 1941), p. 108.

[4] Russell, F. Weigley, *History of the United States Army* (New York: Macmillan, 1967), p. 427.

[5] Henry R. Luce, ed., *Time Capsule: History of the War Years 1939-1945* (New York: Bonanza, 1972), pp. 9-10, Year 1941.

[6] *Indiana Year Book* (Indianapolis, 1941), p. 107.

[7] Ibid., p. 108.

[8] William J. Watt, "The Indiana State Guard," *Indiana Military History Journal,* January, 1976.

[9] Leonard E. Webster, "A Military History of the Indiana National Guard, 1916-1966," typescript, 1967, p. 43.

[10] Weigley, *History of the U. S. Army,* p. 432.

[11] *Unit History, 989th Field Artillery Battalion,* January 17, 1941—May 9, 1945 (n.p., n.d.).

[12] Brig. General Vincent J. Esposito, ed., *The West Point Atlas of American Wars,* 2 vols. (New York: Praeger, 1959) Vol. 2, p. 125.

[13] Captain Sir Basil H. Liddell-Hart, *Strategy,* 2nd ed. (New York: Praeger, 1967), p. 273.

[14] Esposito, *West Point Atlas,* Vol. 2, p. 150.

[15] Russell F. Weigley, *The American Way of War* (New York: Macmillan, 1973), p. 291.

[16] Webster, "History of the Indiana Guard," p. 62.

[17] "38th Infantry Division M-7 Operation Historical Report," (reproduced by the 670th Topographical Company, 1945), p. 11, 166.

[18] Ibid., p. 8.

[19] John Toland, *The Rising Sun* (New York: Random House, 1970), p. 630.

[20] "M-7 Historical Report," p. 116.

[21] Ibid., p. 1.

[22] Letter dated March 17, 1945, from General Chase to Mrs. Dolores M. Brewer and accompanying citation for bravery and award of the Silver Star to Major Brewer, dated February 7, 1945.

[23] "M-7 Historical Report," p. 116.

[24] Ibid., p. 40.

[25] Ibid., p. 66.

[26] Ibid., p. 77.

[27] Ibid., 89.

[28] Ibid., p. 142.

29 Gordon R. Young, ed., *The Army Almanac,* 2nd ed. (Harrisburg: Stackpole, 1959, p. 613).
30 Ibid., p. 636.

CITIZEN SOLDIERS IN AN UNSETTLED WORLD

William J. Watt

The Guard thrived in the post-war years despite occasional manpower slumps. Although few citizen soldiers saw active duty for combat, their frequent utilization in response to natural disasters and civil disorders underscored the continuing value of the organized militia. During the years after World War II the need for a vigorous National Guard was affirmed, both as a civil defense force for state service and as a reserve contingent for the regular Army.

Although Department of Defense planners skirmished frequently with Guardsmen over the organization and employment of citizen soldiers, talk of relegating the Guard to third-line status softened to whispers. As the size of the regular Army establishment dwindled during peacetime, the role of Guardsmen as an integral part of the nation's defense force gradually became more apparent to the Pentagon.

Only a few months after Indiana's citizen soldiers returned from worldwide wartime duty, military planners began the process of reorganizing the Guard. The Indiana State Guard had functioned as the state's civil defense force while the Guard was away at war. In March, 1946, Adjutant General Ben H. Watt announced plans to shift back to an organized National Guard with a proposed quota—Army and Air—of 17,324. On March 24, five newly named regimental commanders met at Tyndall Armory to begin the transition.[1]

In June that year, the 38th Infantry Division became an all-Indiana outfit, losing units formerly located in Kentucky and West Virginia. Too few units were organized to justify field training until 1948 when annual encampments resumed at Camp Atterbury. Camp strength that year was about 4,300.

Although President Harry S. Truman had begun the process of integrating the active services, a proposal to raise a black company under the command of black officers was written in 1948. Before accepting their commissions, the black officer designates referred the matter to the Indianapolis chapter of the National Association for the Advancement of Colored People. The organization, in a letter from its president, Wil-

180

liam T. Ray, objected strongly.[2] Although the officers then backed away from the plan, a black unit, the 915th Motor Ambulance Company, later was created. It was the only Indiana Army Guard outfit to be activated for the Korean War but did not re-enter the Indiana Guard structure after the conflict ended. Gradually, Indiana units were integrated, although there were few black officers until the mid-1960s, when special efforts were undertaken to secure their enrollment.

The eruption of war in Korea prompted speculation that the Indiana Guard, largely made up of veterans of World War II, might be activated. During the late summer of 1950, eight National Guard divisions were called to federal service, but the 38th was not among them.

Questions then were raised about the combat readiness of the Indiana division, but Adjutant General Robinson Hitchcock termed the Cyclone Division "as ready for federal service as any other division." However, he doubted that it would be called upon, noting that the 38th represented virtually the entire strength of the state's organized militia and that Indiana would be left without a National Guard.[3] Despite Hitchcock's pronouncements, many officers doubted that the 38th was yet developed to a point that would have enabled it to serve effectively on active duty.

The first significant post-war use of Guardsmen for domestic emergency duty occurred in October, 1952, when two artillery battalions were activated to deal with a serious outbreak of forest fires in Morgan-Monroe State Forest and nearby woodlands. Five other companies joined them for several days of fire fighting duty.

Next year, with the Korean conflict still boiling, the Department of Defense proposed that younger men (aged 17 and 18) who enlisted in the National Guard no longer be considered exempt from draft into the active Army. Defense planners reasoned that there were enough World War II veterans to sustain the Guard's strength. However, Adjutant General Harold A. Doherty said the plan "would wipe out the Indiana Guard," because about 60 percent of its members were under deferrment for age reasons. At that time, Indiana units still were building and had filled only 50 percent of their authorized positions. Fortunately, the federal plan was not implemented.

Armory building programs began gaining momentum in the

1950s and, for the first time in the militia's history, units trained in adequate facilities. The steady progress, largely the result of federal assistance that defrayed three-fourths of the construction costs, culminated in the 1970s with the opening of the Indianapolis Armory, adjacent to Stout Field in the city's west side. The 101,366 square foot building represented the largest National Guard armory erected in the nation during the post-war period.

By 1954 the Indiana Guard was well on its way to the fulfillment of strength levels called for in post-war plans. Lieutenant General W. B. Kean, commanding general of the Fifth U. S. Army, rated the 38th Division's units at annual training that year, citing 44 company-sized units as superior, 49 excellent, and 19 satisfactory. There were no unsatisfactory designations. Furthermore, 97 percent of the men enrolled in these units actually were on hand at Camp Grayling for the annual training encampment.[5]

Although the Indiana State Guard had disbanded after the war, officials believed that a backup state force was justified in the event that the Guard was activated for federal duty. The new force was designated the Indiana Internal Security Corps. Every community with a National Guard armory was to have an I.S.C. unit, and the corps' structure was to be equivalent to that of an infantry division. During the first year, 500 officers and 1,200 men enrolled in the new organization. Initially, training focused on large-scale civil defense exercises. Later, weekend training sessions of two hours' duration emphasized traffic control, first aid, guard duty, and limited practice with firearms. Internal Security Corps members were used in 1956 during floods at Spencer and at Plymouth. However, the corps was plagued constantly by personnel turnovers at a level that threatened to turn it into a revolving door operation.

The 1955 report of the adjutant general commented that "it has been extremely difficult to sell the idea of the Internal Security Corps to the citizens of Indiana because of the lack of uniforms, equipment, and pay."[6]

In October, 1954, the 113th Engineer Battalion was activated for three days in connection with a strike by State Prison guards at Michigan City. A week later Guardsmen of the 113th again were in uniform, this time combating floods along the Little Calumet River. A number of units were called up throughout the state that month to deal with the aftermath of autumn floods.

Next year, these same citizen soldiers were activated in the aftermath of a fierce explosion that heavily damaged the Standard Oil Company refinery at Whiting. The blast hurled large chunks of metal into neighborhoods surrounding the refinery complex. Fortunately, there were no fatalities. Men of the 113th Engineers were on duty for six days.

A smouldering controversy over union representation at the New Castle, Richmond, and Hagerstown manufacturing plants of the Perfect Circle Corporation stimulated contingency planning by law enforcement officials in August, 1955. Governor George N. Craig called officials of the company and the union to his office and told them that he would not tolerate violence. Several Guard officers were on hand and Craig advised the group that he had given the Guard instructions to be ready to move into New Castle in the event of trouble.

On October 5, bloody rioting occurred as a mob numbering more than 1,000 persons stormed the New Castle installation. Eleven persons were wounded, some of them non-strikers in the plant injured by rioters. Other demonstrators outside the building were injured as city police fired upon them from within the factory.

When the outbreak occurred Craig was vacationing in the Bahamas, Adjutant General Doherty was hospitalized, and Assistant Adjutant General John McConnell was out of the state. Captain William A. Scott was acting as adjutant general. Staff officers already had prepared plans to respond, but did not execute them because of the governor's absence. Horace Coats, Craig's assistant, directed the Guard to move into position, but the Guard leadership hesitated when it learned that Lieutenant Governor Harold W. Handley disapproved of its employment in the labor dispute. Subsequently, Coats told the Guard officers assembled at the Statehouse that he had been in contact with Craig by telephone and the governor had made it plain that he would replace the Guard leadership if it did not respond—Handley's objection notwithstanding. Guard officers went into seclusion to avoid Handley and advised Major General Carl O. DeBard, the division commander, to carry out Craig's wishes and leave to the courts the determination of who is in command when the governor leaves the state. DeBard agreed. Brigadier General Wendell C. Phillippi, the assistant division commander, was delegated the overall command of the operation, while Colonel Howard S. Wilcox exercised tactical command of the 600-man task force that moved into the three cities, although the most extensive deployment occurred at New Castle.

Armored vehicles and sandbagged machine gun emplacements were situated at plant gates, while roving patrols and roadblocks were utilized to preserve the peace. When Craig returned, he declared martial law in Henry County, Hagerstown, and the area surrounding Perfect Circle installations in Richmond. There were few incidents of trouble but the Guardsmen weren't released until mid-November.

The governor's declaration created problems in that full martial law requires the military to assume the responsibility for operating local governments, utilities, and other civil functions. In one instance, a local judge abandoned his court, indicating that it now was the responsibility of the military to run it. Consequently, every gubernatorial proclamation of this type involving the Guard since the Perfect Circle dispute has limited the provisions of martial law and has been careful to delineate the geographical zones of responsibility for the military.[8]

A landmark undertaking to stimulate officer procurement and training began in February, 1956, with the establishment of the Indiana Military Academy at Tyndall Armory. Created as a state officer candidate school to prepare Guardsmen for commissioning as second lieutenants, the academy initially enrolled 42 candidates for a six-month course of instruction involving seven weekends and two full weeks of field training. Major Jack K. Elrod was the first I.M.A. commandant. Two years later the course of instruction was broadened to ten weekends and was coupled with three weeks of field training at Camp McCoy, Wisconsin. In 1965 the academy was moved to Camp Atterbury, where it flourishes today.

High water and ice jams on the Wabash River brought a clamor for National Guard assistance in February, 1959, and the flood emergency proved to be more extensive than any since the great flood of 1937. More than 1,200 Guardsmen were activated for duty in cities along the river as the crest moved downstream.

The post-war 38th Division, which encompassed virtually the entire manpower of the Indiana Army Guard, had been organized along wartime lines since its reactivation in 1946. However, several restructurings since have occurred. In 1959, for example, the "triangular" division that had prevailed in World War II and Korea was abandoned in favor of the so-called "pentamic" division. The 38th was the first Reserve Components formation to be revised under this approach, which was built upon five battle groups, each one self-sustaining in terms of supply and administration. Only four years later the division was converted under the "ROAD division" concept (for Reorganization Objectives Army Division), which tended to restore the triangular foundation of three infantry brigades, tailored to fit particular assignments by attaching support elements found in several organic support battalions. Neither reorganization materially altered the division's strength levels.

As the 1950s ended, the Indiana Guard enjoyed prosperity in terms of its size and reputation. Callups for domestic emergencies had not resulted in public hostility of the type that had been associated with Guard utilization during labor troubles in earlier years. Strength stood at record levels, in part because federal selective service legislation provided for a six-year military obligation, all or most of which could be discharged in the Reserve Components. Hoosier citizen soldiers were frequently in the public eye in their role of community assistance, and the National Guard "jeep" was a frequent signpost on Indiana highways during holiday weekend periods, when the Guard joined forces with the Indiana State Police in efforts to curb traffic fatalities.

The 1960s, however, proved to be an exceptionally demanding decade. The routine challenges of disaster duty prevailed at a brisk pace at a time when the Vietnam buildup—and the Guard's potential role in that conflict—was placing acute demands upon officers and full-time technicians. Meanwhile, flaring racial troubles posed difficult missions for the Guard because of the tense and confusing nature of racial outbreaks, coupled with the occasionally troublesome aspects of dealing with local officials during such occurrences.

The 1960s also saw the passing of the one-night-a-week training assembly. It was supplanted by daylong or weekend periods—known as MUTAs, for Multiple Unit Training Assembly. The new system was more efficient, because the former night sessions required almost as much administrative time as an entire weekend. Multiple assemblies also made possible weekend field training at Camp Atterbury.

The more traditional role of community assistance was underscored in October, 1961, when a contingent of the 113th Engineer Battalion erected what was believed to be the longest "Bailey bridge" in the country, 200 feet of bridgework across the Wabash River at Clinton, where a washout had left the town isolated. Actual construction time was 37 hours. When the span was completed, the town mayor and Governor Matthew E. Welsh were the first persons to cross it. Two months later, Guardsmen dismantled the Bailey bridge after highway officials restored an alternate route across the river.[9]

The Internal Security Corps gave way in 1962 to the Indiana Guard Reserve, which prevails into the 1980s as the state's organized militia when National Guard forces are away from the state. The I.G.R. was organized as a tactical brigade, encompassing eight battalions and 53 company-sized maneuver and support units. The initial complement was 230 officers and six warrant officers, many of them retired Guardsmen or World War II veterans. Over a period of time, I.G.R. members acquired uniforms and conducted occasional training assemblies. Maintaining enlisted strength always proved troublesome, but the organization did succeed in stabilizing officer participation to an extent that would permit it to undertake a limited militia role, as well as the supervision of armories, in the event that National Guard units were called to federal service.[10]

In 1962 the 38th Infantry Division became the first Reserve Components division to train with the nuclear-capable Honest John rocket. Honest John firings by the Third Battalion, 139th Field Artillery, were among the highlights of annual training exercises at Camp Grayling until 1977, when the weapon was retired from the Army inventory.

An indication of the extent to which the 38th had beefed up its effectiveness during the latter 1950s and early 1960s came during the Cuban missile crisis of 1962. The division, then under the command of Major General Phillippi, was alerted for possible mobilization, and Phillippi and his staff were called to Washington to await activation orders. Several officers believed that the 38th would have been called up if it had not been for a mistake by Pentagon officials, who announced that the 36th Infantry Division of Wisconsin would

186

be ordered to federal service. When the error was called to their attention, the Army leadership decided to let the mistake stand, rather than suffer the embarrassment and the inconvenience that correcting it would have caused.

The worst weather disaster in the state's history, in terms of loss of life, occurred on Palm Sunday, April 12, 1965, when three bands of tornado funnels ripped through communities in 20 counties. The towns of Russiaville, Alto, Greentown, and Dunlap were obliterated. The final death toll reached 137; hundreds were injured. Governor Roger Branigin activated the Guard that evening and more than 1,200 citizen soldiers answered the call. Guard personnel provided emergency power to Marion and Berne, and undertook search and rescue efforts, security against looting, and the delivery of water and food. Units also conducted a detailed damage survey throughout the stricken area. More than 400 Guardsmen remained on duty the following weekend.[11]

The Vietnam buildup brought radical changes to the Indiana Guard when, in November, 1965, the 38th Infantry Division was one of three Reserve Component divisions to be designated part of the Selected Reserve Force. These units were given priority for federalization. S.R.F. meant filling the division's personnel and equipment inventories to their fully authorized levels and achieving a state of readiness that would permit a seven-day alert status. For Guardsmen in units so designated, it also meant a 50 percent increase in armory drills. Not all 38th Division units were tagged for S.R.F. assignment. Indiana would have provided the artillery elements, an infantry brigade, support battalions, and the division headquarters and administrative sections. Selected Illinois and Michigan units— amounting to an infantry brigade, an artillery battalion, and several company-sized units from each state—would have augmented the 38th upon activation. It was a perplexing time for enlisted personnel, many of whom had joined the Guard in hopes of avoiding extended active duty during a time in which they were beginning careers and marriages. Activation rumors rippled through armories every drill weekend. There was widespread speculation that, if called up, the division would be assigned to garrison duty in the Canal Zone, which would enable it to train for tropical warfare—and everyone knew where that would lead. In 1967 there were reports that activation orders had been written at the Pentagon, then rescinded at the last minute. The 38th stood down from S.R.F. status in May, 1968, but the experience had durable implications. By then, Indiana Guardsmen were among the best trained and equipped in the nation, especially with respect to vehicles, as World War II equipment finally was retired. Later that year, the division was reorganized in a three-state configuration. Headquarters elements, the division artillery, the 76th Brigade, and numerous support units were provided by Indiana. Michigan and Ohio each contributed an infantry brigade—the 46th and 73rd, respectively—plus support and specialized units (such as Michigan's 1st Battalion, 246th Armor). Non-divisional units— about a brigade in size—became part of what was known as Separate Command.

In retrospect, S.R.F. was a fortunate occurrence, since it no doubt played a role in the survival of the 38th as one of only eight National Guard divisions to remain in being after the 1968 reorganization. Fifteen other Guard divisions were eliminated in the shakeup.

A massive end-of-January storm in 1967 dumped two feet of snow on northern and central Indiana. Thousands of autos were stranded as 15-foot drifts accumulated on highways. Meanwhile, central Indiana was glazed with ice. Adjutant General John S. Anderson ordered Guard units in affected areas to place themselves at the disposal of local authorities. Twenty-five armories were opened to receive stranded travelers and local residents whose homes were without power or heat. Helicopters rescued storm victims and delivered food, medicine, and blankets. Guard engineers opened U. S. 41 from Kentland to Gary. After the emergency ended, State Police Superintendent Robert O'Neal commented: "The force of the blizzard had just about brought our efforts to a standstill . . . when the National Guard stepped in. Without their help, the storm toll might have been much worse."[12]

The Department of Defense activated more than 24,000 Reserve Components personnel to contribute to the escalating Vietnam war effort in April, 1968. Among them were the 214 members of Company D, 151st Infantry, which operated in Greenfield and Evansville. The company, designated as a long range patrol unit, had just received high ratings for jungle warfare training in Panama and its personnel also were airborne qualified. Under the command of Captain Kenneth W. Himsel, the unit received several months of intensive training

188

at Fort Benning, Georgia, and then was assigned as a part of the Second Field Force in Vietnam. Himsel was transferred temporarily to other assignments, but his brother, Ronald, the company's executive officer, succeeded him. Kenneth Himsel eventually returned to command the unit in Vietnam as a major.

The unit's mission centered on reconnaissance and intelligence gathering, often behind enemy lines. Although its orders generally were to avoid direct confrontations with enemy forces, Company D occasionally was involved in battles and in operations to rescue pilots downed in enemy territory. Two of its members, Sergeant Robert T. Smith and Specialist Four Charles K. Larkins, were killed in action against enemy troops, and First Lieutenant George L. Kleiber died in a helicopter crash. Company D was one of the most decorated American units in Vietnam as its members earned 19 Silver Stars, 175 Bronze Stars, and 110 Purple Hearts. It was welcomed home with an exuberant ceremony in November, 1969.

Smouldering racial tensions erupted into sporadic violence during the latter 1960s, much of it centered in northern Indiana's industrial cities. It was a period of anxiety, false alarms, and rumors of impending violence, real and imagined. The Guard first became involved in August, 1964, when Gary Mayor A. Martin Katz alerted the state to possible disturbances surrounding the planned transfer of black students to a white-only school in his city. The Guard's involvement in this episode was limited to contingency planning, although the after-action report noted that it represented an entirely new situation from those usually faced by the Military Department of Indiana. Lieutenant Colonel Alfred F. Ahner, then acting chief of staff, recommended that the Guard develop procedures for emergencies involving racial trouble. The resulting policy stressed that the Guard would be used only after a total commitment of local and state police, and that the Guard would only be utilized to protect life and property. When Guardsmen were activated for riot control duty, they would be accompanied by local police officers who would be in a better position to make lawful arrests of demonstrators.

Mayor Katz sounded another alarm on July 15, 1966, when he voiced fears of violence in connection with a rock music concert expected to draw several thousand spectators, among them gangs of black juveniles that had been causing trouble

189

in the city. Several units were placed on alert, including the 113th Engineer Battalion which already had a training assembly scheduled that weekend. General Anderson stated that, in the event of a riot, Governor Roger Branigin's guidance was to "treat as insurrection and put down by any means." In addition, the adjutant general's policy stated that Guardsmen could return fire if fired upon, but only after state police or city police have fired, "and then it will be directed fire rather than firing indiscriminately." Bayonets were to be fixed at the time troops were committed to action.[13] The predicted outbreak did not materialize and units were taken off alert status late on the night of the concert.

Violence erupted in South Bend on July 25, 1967, as 36 fire-bombings were reported. A disturbance at a neighborhood center had resulted in a rockthrowing and shooting incident in which seven black youths were wounded by shotgun fire from South Bend police. The atmosphere was worsened by rumors that one of the shooting victims was near death. State Police reported that groups of blacks and whites were milling in the central and western portions of the city. Rocks were thrown at passing vehicles and firebombs heavily damaged a furniture store, tavern, and gas station. Intelligence sources hinted that some rioters possessed automatic weapons. Three hundred Guardsmen were activated in South Bend; another 700 were placed on alert. Military officials desired to maintain a low profile, and for the most part, activated units were held at the South Bend armory in readiness for street duty if the situation got out of hand. Meanwhile, rumors of threatened disturbances spread throughout the state and resulted in requests for Guard forces from mayors at Richmond, Gary, East Chicago, Indianapolis, and Fort Wayne. Although racial outbreaks did not occur, Guard officials were forced to undertake the tedious processes of contingency planning to deal with the potential for multiple emergencies.

Later that year national attention was focused on Gary, where Richard G. Hatcher had upset the local Democratic political organization in a bitter primary election and appeared likely to become the first black mayor in the state's history. The intraparty struggle continued after the primary. Racial tensions surged as many blacks feared that the Lake County Democratic machine, under the control of County Clerk John G. Krupa, might try to throw the election to the Republican nominee, Joseph Radigan, rather than accept Hatcher's ascendancy to political power in a city whose population was 55 percent black.

Tempers were frayed as the autumn campaign began and Krupa infuriated Hatcher by purging 5,200 black voters from the registration lists. Hatcher supporters went to federal court in an effort to postpone an election they feared would be stolen from them. A district judge ruled that the election would proceed, but under guidelines set forth by the court and under the supervision of federal marshals. Racial unrest intensified. In a routine civil defense planning conference with Lieutenant Colonel Clyde C. Wright, outgoing Mayor Katz called for the activation of 9,000 Guardsmen to supervise the election. On October 4, Krupa wrote Governor Branigin that "black power agitators" were converging on the city and called for the alerting of National Guard units in northwestern Indiana. At the same time, word was spread that a riot would occur if Hatcher lost. Meanwhile, State Police intelligence units advised the governor of potential racial trouble. General Anderson issued a warning order on October 31, instructing units to drill in armories on election night, November 7, but not to assemble until after the polls closed.

With feelings running high, the governor, General Anderson, State Police Superintendent O'Neal, and Attorney General John J. Dillon (who also served as a legal officer for the Guard) met to determine what action to take. Branigin ordered the Guard to place a sufficient force on duty during the election, but not within Lake County.

Two days later, a Morgan Superior Court judge prohibited the governor and adjutant general from using the Guard in connection with the Gary election, citing provisions of an 1895 law that forbade a muster of Guardsmen within five days of an election in any county. The old law had been intended to insure that the militia could not be used to intimidate voters.

At Dillon's request, the Indiana Supreme Court met in emergency session to hear the state administration's appeal. The attorney general argued that the prohibition against mustering applied only to unit officers and did not limit the governor and adjutant general, that other language in the same statute allowed mustering if imminent danger was present, and that the plaintiff in the case had no personal standing in the

191

matter. The Supreme Court agreed and struck down the lower court's action.

Three thousand Guardsmen stood by at armories in northwestern Indiana as the balloting commenced. The outcome remained in doubt for several hours after the voting ended; meanwhile, hundreds of blacks gathered in front of Hatcher's campaign headquarters. Rumors continued to fly as the crowd swelled to more than 3,000. When Guard officials heard a report that bands of armed men were entering Gary, several units began a convoy movement to an assembly area within the city. Moments later Hatcher's victory was announced, the reports of armed intervention were discounted, and the crowd began to subside. The movement order was countermanded and Guardsmen reversed their course. However, personnel remained on alert at nearby armories until mid-morning Wednesday.

Units were alerted again on July 26, 1968, after a series of fires and sniping and looting incidents in Gary left six persons injured. The mayor ordered a curfew and Guardsmen were on duty for four days. In June, 1970, 140 Guardsmen were employed at Michigan City, where two nights of racial incidents resulted in fires, rockthrowing, and sniping. Guardsmen operated roadblocks and roving patrols to seal off sectors of the city.

In April, 1970, tension had shifted to college campuses after President Nixon expanded the Vietnam war with the announcement of a Cambodia invasion. However, at Indiana State University in Terre Haute, the trouble was racial, as black students invaded a dormitory and smashed windows on the campus. Disorders continued for several days, and the State Police riot squad and several national Guard companies were alerted for possible deployment. National anti-war demonstrations spread to Indiana and Purdue universities in May. R.O.T.C. installations were targets of protesters. At Purdue, students battled with campus police. After the tragic confrontation between rioting students and Ohio Guardsmen at Kent State University, in which four students were killed, National Guard armories became focal points of protests. Demonstrators marched on several armories in northwest Indiana and State Police received reports of planned attempts to burn them, as well as the R.O.T.C. building at Notre Dame University. During the tense three-week period, Guard officials acted to secure armory property and weapons, while avoiding confrontations with

192

students. There were numerous alerts and key Guard officials pulled exhausting duty as they managed the delicate situation. There were no serious occurrences.

After the Kent State incident, Adjutant General John N. Owens was quoted as saying that, in the event of campus disturbance, Guardsmen would employ the same emergency procedures followed by the regular Army. Guardsmen would disembark from their trucks, fix bayonets, and receive two clips (16 rounds) of ammunition, which would be placed in ammunition pouches. They would load only on a platoon leader's order and would fire only on his order.[14]

A month later, the controversy over utilizing Guardsmen in civil disorders was fueled by Dr. Phillip S. Kronenberg, a political science professor at Indiana University, who released a report assessing the readiness of Guard units. He described it as the least prepared of public agencies to face civil disorder. The report, prepared under a Justice Department grant, said, in part:

> It is the fault of the structure of the Guard and not of the individual Guard leaders . . . The Guard primarily has a war mission and lacks a sensitivity toward a threat of rhetoric—which we probably saw at Kent State. The Guard, especially in Indiana, is relatively untested in major civil disturbances . . . Related to this lack of experience is the fact that a large part of the Indiana Guard membership has not experienced hostile gunfire or other physical threats—that such green troops might be trigger-happy is a real possibility.[15]

Adjutant General Owens retorted: "We are a group of men the governor can call on to meet any emergency, manmade or natural." He observed that more than 25 percent of the Guardsmen were active Army veterans and pointed to the Guard's effectiveness during incidents such as the Perfect Circle strike.[16]

The winding down of the Vietnam war, coupled with the growing unpopularity of military institutions, began to sap the Guard's manpower in the early 1970s. By 1971, unit waiting lists had evaporated because the threat of draft callup had been removed from many young Americans. For the first time in years, recruiting efforts had to be pursued. The retention rate in Indiana units had plummeted to only five percent. However, ambitious recruitment and retention programs turned the situation around and, by 1974, Hoosier units were full again and remained so for nearly two years, when the full impact of the ending of the draft again spurred the process

193

of erosion. In 1973 women were recruited for the first time, 34 during the initial year. They were not permitted to be members of combat units, but, as the years passed, hundreds joined headquarters and support units and were integrated into the system quite smoothly, despite occasional grumbling from old-line NCOs.

The enrollment of women was made possible by a state constitutional amendment that eliminated the reference to the militia as comprising only *male* citizens. The original state constitutional definition of the militia also had excluded blacks, but that restriction had been lifted in 1936—at least a half century after blacks had begun to serve in the militia and Guard.

The 1970s also saw the passing of the M-1 rifle, hated for its weight, its tendency to eject hot brass into the firer's face, and an eight-round clip that never seated properly on the first try. It was replaced by the automatic M-16, delightfully light in weight but looking like something out of a toy catalogue. Officers still weighted their hips with the regulation .45.

Annual training at Camp Grayling in 1973 proved to be an exceptional event as the entire 38th Infantry Division, 14,000 personnel from three states, trained together for the first time since the Cyclone Division was organized in its tri-state format. The joint exercises were supervised by Major General Robert G. Moorhead, the 38th's commanding general, and required the erection of temporary base camps for the larger-than-normal complement. However, training at Camp Grayling was scrapped during the following year because of the Arab oil embargo. Most units trained at Camp Atterbury in an effort to conserve fuel normally consumed during the convoy movement to northern Michigan.

In 1973 the Indiana National Guard honored one of its most distinguished alumni, General Lewis B. Hershey, by dedicating the drill hall at the Angola armory in his name. Hershey had enlisted as a private in the Indiana National Guard in 1911 and eventually received a lieutenant's commission. After callup for World War I service, he decided to remain in uniform and joined the regular Army in 1920. As the nation's selective service director during World War II and much of the postwar period, his became one of the most familiar names in America.

Sporadic violence associated with a strike by independent

truck drivers throughout eastern states prompted a gubernatorial callup of Indiana Guardsmen in February, 1974. Forty helicopter pilots were activated to patrol the state's major highway arteries, while 60 other Guard personnel maintained vigils on overpasses, where there had been numerous incidents of sniper fire. Non-striking truckers were urged to travel in convoys during daylight hours.

Turbulent spring weather spawned multiple tornadoes— perhaps 30 in number—on April 3, 1974. Funnels of death hacked a path across northern Indiana from west of Monticello to Angola. Downstate, another band of twisters cut a swath from Tell City to Madison. Meanwhile, in east-central Indiana the storms skipped across rural areas. The hamlet of Kennard was all but wiped out. Heaviest damage was at Monticello, Madison, and near Rochester. The following morning, Governor Bowen asked President Nixon to declare 30 counties as disaster areas, citing preliminary damage estimates in excess of $70 million, a known death toll of 41, and an injury list of 769.[17]

Guardsmen were on the scene within minutes after the storms hit, assisting in the rescue effort, providing security, and opening armories to storm victims. At Monticello, the National Guard armory became a temporary county courthouse, since most of the downtown was devastated. Federal-state disaster relief centers were opened in seven cities; armories were utilized for that purpose in Monticello, Angola, New Castle, New Albany, and Tell City.

January, 1977, brought both fuel and weather crises. Not once during the month did thermometers top out above 32 degrees. Four days of bitter cold, with morning readings of minus-15 or colder, triggered natural gas curtailments and shortages of kerosene. In the early hours of January 28, a cold front blasted across the state, dropping temperatures 20 degrees in one hour. Winds gusting to 50 m.p.h. created 12-foot drifts in north-central Indiana. Governor Bowen called out the National Guard. The new assault of cold weather compelled several natural gas utilities to cut service to larger industrial and commercial customers to an extent that forced them to shut down. In Indianapolis, 150 business firms stopped work. Helicopters could not fly and conditions in northern Indiana were so severe that rescue teams could not reach stranded motorists. Passengers aboard buses stalled in White County were evacuated, one at a time, by snowmobiles. Most of the state's armories became refuges for stranded travelers. On Saturday, January 29, adverse weather prevented road-clearing or helicopter activity. On the following Monday, Guardsmen used heavy trucks and tanks to open Interstate 65. A snarl of semitrailer trucks impeded the work and tanks dragged the trucks off the roadway. Finally, on Tuesday morning, the important highway was reopened.

The governor's final request for federal disaster assistance described the National Guard's involvement:

> The Indiana Military Department responded by placing 60 National Guard armories on 24-hour alert to provide manpower and equipment as needed and to provide food and shelter to stranded motorists and local citizens. Through January 30th, the National Guard had contributed 1,300 mandays of storm disaster assistance, expended $72,000 in active duty and over-time pay, activated two heavy equipment task forces to assist the Indiana Highway Department in opening I-65 and I-69, and provided helicopters and other equipment in transporting emergency supplies, food, medicines and citizens. On Friday night, January 28, 1,195 people were sheltered in National Guard facilities. During this period, the Indiana National Guard answered 6,000 calls for assistance.[19]

In 1977 a further reorganization ended Ohio's affiliation with the 38th Infantry Division. Its 73rd Brigade was replaced by a new Second Brigade, made up of Indiana units. The manpower for the expansion within Indiana largely was provided by units formerly associated with M.D.I.'s Separate Command. The reorganization, however, did force conversion of several units to other combat arms.

Late Wednesday, January 25, 1978, the most intense blizzard on record lashed the state, bringing quick paralysis to the transportation system and forcing people to shelter. Fortunately, the Weather Service had given several hours' warning, and thousands who otherwise might have been stranded reached home before the storm's onslaught. The weathermen's ominous forecast alerted key Guardsmen and other civil defense officials to gather at their duty stations. An official activation order was issued late that night, and 24 armories were opened to receive stranded motorists.

Packing 50 mile-an-hour winds, the storm pushed drifts to eight feet deep Wednesday night as temperatures slumped 30 degrees within a few hours. The rapid temperature drop avoided the icing normally associated with such storms. Gusty winds against ice-laden lines could have wreaked havoc with electric power and telecommunications systems, as it did later in Ohio, where half a million homes lost power. Early Thursday morning, Governor Bowen declared that a major disaster had occurred and called on federal officials for assistance.[20]

Brisk winds continued Thursday, piling drifts even higher and closing all roads in the state, except for streets in urban areas of Lake and Vanderburgh counties. Wind chill readings were in the −50 range, and rural electric cooperatives in central and southern counties reported widespread outages. Hundreds of motorists were rescued by Guardsmen and State Police. Guardsmen who could make it to armories used six-wheel-drive trucks to blast through deep snow in efforts to rescue imperiled motorists. In many cases, only tracked vehicles could buck the drifts; unheated armored personnel carriers were used as ambulances.

The wind didn't ebb until noon Friday. Twenty inches of snow had fallen, and waves of drifts were stacked to the tops of overpasses on north-central interstate highways. Even the Guard's six-wheel-drive vehicles were succumbing to the snow. On Friday afternoon, helicopters were able to undertake the most critical emergency runs, including numerous incidents in which pregnant women, panicked by isolation, went into false labor. On Friday, motorists still were being plucked from buried cars—two days after the storm had commenced. Curfews were ordered in Indianapolis and several other cities because of interference with snow-clearing operations and the threat of looting. More than 700 Guardsmen were on duty; many others were stranded at home, unable to reach their armories.

The transportation system remained closed on Saturday. Guard and Highway Department bulldozers began punching lanes through drifted-over roads, although stranded autos and trucks frequently delayed operations. By Sunday, many urban-area roads were reopened, and a skeletel statewide network of highways again began to function. However, in several counties rural roads weren't reopened until mid-week.

The most disagreeable duty faced by National Guardsmen historically has been that of activation during labor disputes. Bitter memories linger from past confrontations, especially in the southwestern Indiana minefields, where militiamen and mine workers had been involved in a number of touchy and

197

occasionally violent encounters dating back to the 1870s. However, the consequences of a widespread coal strike have a particularly heavy impact upon Indiana. The state's electric power systems are almost totally dependent upon coal, and nearly 50,000 homes, as well as other institutions and industries, utilize the fuel. The state had experienced a five-week United Mine Workers strike in 1974. It had little impact, although inventories had begun to evaporate in the closing days.

During the summer of 1977, state energy officials began contingency planning for the expiration of the current coal contract, because of a number of trouble signs pointed to the possibility of a drawn-out strike. At that time they secured Governor Bowen's agreement that state government would take whatever steps proved necessary during a prolonged strike—including the activation of Guardsmen. Since the Guard had limited transportation capability, it was agreed that Guardsmen would safeguard the movement of coal by truck or rail if that proved necessary.

The walkout commenced in December, with little immediate effect because utilities had stockpiled coal reserves. However, colder than normal weather eroded inventories at an abnormal rate, and the strike was effective in halting coal movements. In the early weeks cooperation existed between mine union officials and state government, and the union was willing to permit the transport of coal to residents and to essential institutions. On January 16th United Mine Workers leaders agreed privately to haul coal to individuals who could not get it otherwise.

Several days earlier, officials in Spencer County had called for the activation of Guardsmen to forestall violence and to restore coal movement. The governor considered the request to be premature. On January 17 electric power and coal curtailments were enforced for state government facilities. One week later, national coal bargaining negotiations broke down.

Many observers voiced optimism when a tentative agreement was announced on February 6, but state officials had received word from union sources that the rank-and-file would reject the contract. They did. Four days later the union's national bargaining council rejected another contract settlement, giving clear indication that the strike would not end soon. Meanwhile, utility stockpiles were being depleted at a steady rate.

On February 13 Public Service Commission Chairman Larry J. Wallace announced mandatory power curtailments, generally averaging 25 percent, in utility systems whose stockpiles had dropped below a 40-day margin. The governor decided to activate the National Guard, because energy officials had concluded that extraordinary measures were needed to prevent hardship. In an executive order issued the next day, Governor Bowen activated the Guard to provide security for persons engaged in the production or transport of coal.[21]

Guardsmen initially were used to safeguard convoys moving coal from Public Service Indiana's generating station at Petersburg to another generating unit at Cayuga, where stockpiles had dwindled to an 18-day reserve. On February 16 a 90-truck convoy safely moved coal. Adjutant General Alfred F. Ahner decided to maintain a Guard presence at battalion strength, but to rotate units on a weekly basis, because of the extreme demands upon personnel and the tension of the situation. On the 19th and 20th, convoys began moving coal from 13 non-union mines where stockpiles existed. The security system then was altered, since convoys were moving freely, to one emphasizing aerial and ground surveillance and the use of roving patrols in key trouble spots.

Another settlement was rejected on March 5, and President Carter was compelled to invoke a Taft-Hartley injunction the next day, although he left its enforcement to the states. By this time National Guard and State Police security measures were proving effective. As many as 500 truckloads of coal were being transported on a daily basis, and numerous rail movements, under supervision of Guardsmen and police, were completed without incident. The combination of mandatory power curtailments, electricity imports from regions unaffected by the strike, and the security measures provided by the state succeeded in stabilizing the coal supply situation. Another tentative agreement was reached March 14, and a settlement was ratified ten days later. The governor deactivated Guard units on March 26.

For six weeks, Guardsmen and State Police had succeeded in discharging without serious incident their most demanding civil disturbance assignment of the post-war period. Six battalions of the 38th Infantry Division were utilized during the emergency: Second Battalion, 152nd Infantry; First Battalion, 293rd Infantry; Second Battalion, 151st Infantry; First

Squadron, 238th Cavalry; First Battalion, 151st Infantry, and Second Battalion, 293rd Infantry. Later in the year, Governor Bowen paid tribute to the Guard in a special proclamation. It noted:

> . . . by performing the dangerous duty of guarding the coal mines and coal shipments during the longest coal strike in Indiana's history, these men prevented the outbreak of further violence in connection with the strike and guaranteed the safety of drivers and shippers . . . without such valuable services, many communities in our state would have been more severely affected by the energy crisis.[22]

In addition, 12 Guardsmen, including the battalion commanders involved in security operations, were awarded the state's Distinguished Service Medal for their achievements in carrying out this difficult mission.

Although the demands of a major blizzard and prolonged strike would seem sufficient to dramatize the need for citizen soldiers during times of emergency, a number of Guardsmen again were called out for a two-week period in April to combat near-record flooding on the Kankakee River. At no time in recent history had the value of an effective National Guard organization been more graphically demonstrated than during the first four months of 1978.

As the 1970s closed out, the Guard once again was grappling with strength problems, but an intensive emphasis on recruiting and retention was stabilizing personnel at about 90 percent of authorized levels. There were added incentives, including federally sponsored enlistment bonuses for certain categories of non-prior service recruits. Selected units were afforded the opportunity for different types of training, often in association with regular outfits. A maintenance company trained in Germany in 1978 and another unit was scheduled for an encampment in England in 1980. Others scattered to regular Army installations around the country that year.

Many of the organizational issues that had perplexed Guard and regular Army leaders since America's colonial period still frustrated Indiana's citizen soldiers. Guard leaders, supported by the nation's governors, battled renewed attempts by the Pentagon to assert even greater control over the National Guard, but it was clear as the decade ended that these skirmishes would continue into the 1980s. The future of infantry divisions, such as Indiana's 38th, was uncertain because of nationwide strength problems and officer shortages, and because some federal planners continued to press for the incorporation of smaller Guard outfits into regular formations in the event of war.

The Guard's leadership responded with renewed assertions that the dual role of the Guard was recognized by the federal Constitution and was not subject to the types of administrative tampering contemplated by some in the regular establishment. In Indiana, at least, the National Guard continued to receive strong support from the state's governmental leadership, in part because of its performance during domestic emergencies during the 1970s. Governor Bowen, for example, frequently referred to the Guard's involvement in the 1978 coal strike as the citizen soldiers' "finest hour." As a series of international crises in 1980 focused fresh attention on the state of the nation's defense preparedness, Indiana Guardsmen were cautiously optimistic that the Guard might benefit from the growing national realization that defense rated a higher priority.

---

[1] Indianapolis *News*, May 25, 1946.

[2] Indianapolis *News*, May 6, 1948.

[3] Indianapolis *News*, September 12, 1950.

[4] Indianapolis *News*, May 5, 1953.

[5] Indianapolis *News*, August 13, 1954.

[6] Indiana Adjutant General, *Report* (Indianapolis, 1955), p. 34.

[7] Indianapolis *News*, October 5 and October 6, 1955.

[8] Indianapolis *News*, October 10, 1955; Leonard E. Webster, "A Military History of the Indiana National Guard, 1816-1966," typescript, 1967.

[9] Webster, "Military History of Indiana National Guard," pp. 100-101.

[10] Indiana Adjutant General, *Report* (Indianapolis, 1962), p. 22.

[11] Military Department of Indiana, After-action Report (Indianapolis, April 26, 1965).

[12] Military Department of Indiana, News Release, February 5, 1967.

[13] Military Department of Indiana, Daily Staff Journal, July 15, 1966.

[14] Indianapolis *Star*, May 9, 1970.

[15] Indianapolis *Star*, June 10, 1970.

[16] Ibid.

[17] Governor Otis R. Bowen, telegram to President Nixon, April 14, 1974.

[18] Indiana Adjutant General, *Report* (Indianapolis, 1974), p. 91; Office of the Governor, News Release, April 6, 1974.

[19] Governor Otis R. Bowen, letter to President Carter, January 31, 1977.

[20] Indianapolis *News*, January 26, 1978; Indianapolis *Star*, January 27, 1978.

[21] Office of the Governor, Executive Order 7-78, February 14, 1978.

[22] Office of the Governor, proclamation, May 31, 1978.

APPENDIX A

INDIANA ADJUTANTS GENERAL

John Small 1801-1812
Daniel Sullivan 1812
Charles Smith 1812-1813
Daniel Sullivan 1813
General W. Johnson 1813-1814
Waller Taylor 1814
Allen D. Thom 1814-1817
Stephen Ranney 1817-1819
Henry P. Coburn 1819-1822
Stephen Ranney 1822-1823
Thomas Posey 1823-1831
Jacob Landis 1831-1838
Douglas Maguire 1838-1843
David Reynolds 1844-1854
Stephen Tomlinson 1854-1857
William A. Morrison 1857-1861
Lewis Wallace 1861
John M. Wallace 1861
Lazarus Noble 1861-1864
W. H. H. Terrell 1864-1869
James C. Veach 1869-1870
John Greenwalt 1870-1873
William W. Connor 1873-1877
George W. Russ 1877-1881
James R. Carnahan 1881-1885
George W. Koontz 1885-1889
Nicholas R. Ruckle 1889-1893
Irvin Robbins 1893-1897
James K. Gore 1897-1901
John R. Ward 1901-1905
Oran Perry 1905-1909
George W. McCoy 1909-1913
Franklin L. Bridges 1913-1917
Harry B. Smith 1917-1925
William H. Kershner 1925-1929
William G. Everson 1929
Manford G. Henley 1929-1931
Paul E. Tombaugh 1931-1933
Elmer F. Straub 1933-1941
John D. Friday (acting) 1941
Elmer F. Straub 1941-1942
William P. Weimar 1942-1945
William W. Sherwood 1945

Ben H. Watt 1945-1947
Howard H. Maxwell 1947-1949
Robinson Hitchcock 1949-1953
Harold A. Doherty 1953-1957
John W. McConnell 1957-1960
Alfred F. Ahner 1960-1961
John S. Anderson 1961-1969
John N. Owens 1969-1972
Alfred F. Ahner .... 1972—

APPENDIX B

COMMANDERS OF THE 38th INFANTRY DIVISION

Major General William H. Sage was named commanding general of the 38th Infantry Division on August 25, 1917, but held the position for less than a month. He was followed by a series of brigadier generals who served on an acting basis; some held the position for only a few days. In December, Sage reassumed command and held it until April 15, 1918. Again, he was succeeded by a series of acting commanders until August 30, 1918, when Major General Robert L. Howze was designated to lead the Cyclone Division. Except for a ten-day period in October, Howze commanded the 38th until after the armistice.

The division was reorganized in March, 1923, and Major General Robert H. Tyndall was named to command it. He held the position until April, 1941, after the division had been called to active duty for World War II. Wartime commanders were Major Generals Daniel L. Sultan, April, 1941, to April, 1942; Henry L. Jones, April, 1942, to February, 1945; William C. Chase, February to July, 1945; and Frederick A. Irving, August to November, 1945, when the division was inactivated.

The 38th was reorganized in 1946, with Ben H. Watt as its commanding general from June, 1946, until December, 1948. During part of this period, he also functioned as state adjutant general. Although Watt held the "state rank" of major general, he did not receive federal recognition beyond the grade of colonel. His successors were:

Major General Jesse McIntosh, January, 1949-September, 1953.

Major General Carl O. DeBard, October, 1953-January, 1959.

Major General Wendell C. Phillippi, January, 1959-February, 1963.

Major General Howard S. Wilcox, February, 1963-September, 1964.

Major General Noble F. Schlatter, September, 1964-December, 1967.

Major General Kenneth W. Brewer, December, 1967-September, 1971.

Major General Robert G. Moorhead, September, 1971-August, 1976.

Major General Robert D. Weliver, August, 1976—.

APPENDIX C

MAJOR UNIT COMMANDERS
INDIANA AIR NATIONAL GUARD

122nd Tactical Fighter Wing

  Brigadier General Allison Maxwell, 1950-1956
  Brigadier General William Sefton, 1956-1975
  Brigadier General Richard Petercheff, 1975-1978
  Brigadier General Frank Hettlinger, 1978—

113th Observation Squadron

  Major Wilbur Fagley, 1921-1922
  Major James Patton, 1922-1926
  Major Richard Taylor, 1926-1930
  Major Oliver Stout, 1932-1941
  Captain Earl Sweeney, 1941-1942
  Captain Paul Zartman, 1942
  Captain Richard Morrison, 1942-1943

113th Tactical Fighter Squadron

  Captain John Fesenfield, 1947
  Captain William Hoelscher, 1947-1952
  Major C. Peterson, 1952
  Captain George Meyers, 1953-1956
  Captain Richard Petercheff, 1956-1961
  Captain Frank Hettlinger, 1956-1961
  Lt. Colonel Richard Petercheff, 1961-1962
  Major Willard Dunbar, Jr., 1962-1964
  Lt. Colonel Kenneth Merritt, 1964-1971
  Lt. Colonel Victor Bruce, 1971
  Lt. Colonel Alvin Coffey, 1971-1972
  Lt. Colonel Lester Roberts, 1972-1974
  Lt. Colonel Joseph Orear, 1974-1979
  Lt. Colonel Herbert Spier, Jr., 1979—

163rd Tactical Fighter Squadron

  Major William Sefton, 1947-1954
  Major Ervin Bucher, 1954-1956
  Major Robert Hormann, 1956-1957

Captain Vernon Jersey, 1957
Captain Eugene Royer, 1957-1963
Major Howard Stewart, 1965-1965
Major Fredrick Strauss, 1965-1966
Major Richard Hidy, 1966-1971
Lt. Colonel Arthur Schertz, 1971-1974
Major Ronald Farrell, 1974-1975
Major George Bracke, 1975-1977
Major Ronald Farrell, 1977—

APPENDIX D

PRINCIPAL STAFF OFFICERS
MILITARY DEPARTMENT OF INDIANA
(as of January 1, 1980)

Adjutant General:
Major General Alfred F. Ahner

Assistant Adjutant General (Army):
Brig. General Phillips N. Gordon

Assistant Adjutant General (Air):
Brig. General Robert H. Hormann

Headquarters, Indiana Air National Guard:
Colonel Earl L. Higbie

Commander, State Area Command:
Brig. General John J. Dillon

Chief of Staff:
Colonel Byron L. Dukes

Director, Operations & Training:
Colonel John M. Hine

Director, Military Personnel:
Colonel Robert Sharpe

Director, VICAN Personnel Officer:
Colonel Francis E. Cole

Director, State Maintenance:
Colonel Arthur M. Goldman

Director, Supply & Services:
Colonel Fred D. Smith

Comptroller:
Colonel (Ret) John M. Keller

Facilities:
Colonel (Ret) Morris E. Foist

United States Property & Fiscal Officer:
Colonel John N. Owens

Senior Army Advisor:
Colonel William DeWitt

208

APPENDIX E

PRINCIPAL STAFF OFFICERS
38th Infantry Division
(as of January 1, 1980)

Commanding General:
  Major General Robert D. Weliver

Assistant Commanders:
  Brig. General Jay M. Lotz (Indiana)
  Brig. General Jerome J. Mathieu, Jr. (Michigan)

Chief of Staff:
  Colonel Bill J. Abel

Assistant Chiefs of Staff:
  Personnel: Lt. Colonel Turner Nolan
  Intelligence: Lt. Colonel Harold L. Robison
  Operations & Training: (vacant)
  Logistics: Major John W. Foist
  Civil-Military Operations: Major Gary R. Ringlespaugh

Inspector General:
  Lt. Colonel Walter J. Proctor

Chaplain:
  Major Richard E. Lentz (acting)

Chemical Officer:
  Major William H. Huffman

Public Affairs Officer:
  Major Robert F. Morgan

Staff Judge Advocate:
  Major George A. Hopkins

Transportation Officer:
  Major Stephen D. Imel

Race Relations/Equal Opportunity Officer:
  Major James E. Kaiser

Adjutant General:
  Lt. Colonel Larry G. Bruce

Finance Officer:
  Lt. Colonel Harry E. Winklepleck

Provost Marshal:
   (vacant)
Command Sergeant Major:
   Harold L. Hargrave
Army Advisor:
   Colonel Ronald C. Crowley

APPENDIX F

INDIANA ARMY NATIONAL GUARD STATION LIST, 1 JANUARY 1980

ORGANIZATION	STATION	AUTH STR	COMMANDER
State Detachment			
Headquarters & Headquarters Detachment	Indianapolis	188	CPT Dennis G. Hammer
Det 1, Headquarters & Headquarters Detachment	Camp Atterbury	51	CPT Richard L. Haseman
Command & Control Headquarters	Indianapolis	939	COL John M. Hine
Det 1, 38th Adjutant General Company	Indianapolis	58	1LT Richard B. Moorhead
120th Public Affairs Detachment	Indianapolis	13	CPT William J. Watt
1438th Transportation Company	Camp Atterbury	157	CPT Joseph A. Mueller
Atterbury Reserve Forces Training Area	Camp Atterbury	518	COL Clifford M. Brown
1413th Engineer Detachment (Util)	Camp Atterbury	58	CPT Stephen C. Hoffman
128th General Supply Company (GS)	Camp Atterbury	149	CPT Roger T. Arbogast
1313th Engineer Company (Lt Equip)	Camp Atterbury	219	CPT Randall M. Wood
390th Medical Detachment (Gen Disp)	Camp Atterbury	18	1LT Henry L. Mayfield
398th Medical Detachment (Gen Disp)	Camp Atterbury	18	CPT John M. Dietrich
38th Infantry Division	Indianapolis	11,323	MG Robert D. Weliver
Headquarters & Headquarters Company	Indianapolis	158	CPT Michael L. Worrell
38th Military Police Company	Indianapolis	191	CPT Albert L. Hauck, Jr.
Army Aviation Facility	Shelbyville		COL John E. Freeman
38th Aviation Battalion (CBT)	Shelbyville	513	LTC Francis A. Hughes
38th Aviation Platoon (ATC)	Shelbyville	20	CPT John T. Sprecklemeyer
Headquarters & Headquarters Company	Shelbyville	98	CPT Roy M. Umbarger
Company A (CBT)	Shelbyville	209	MAJ Ryland E. Wrede
Company E (CBT)	Shelbyville	206	MAJ Steven A. Strawder

APPENDIX F—Continued

INDIANA ARMY NATIONAL GUARD STATION LIST, 1 JANUARY 1980

ORGANIZATION	STATION	AUTH STR	COMMANDER
1st Squadron 238th Cavalry	Marion	584	LTC John E. Essex
Headquarters & Headquarters Troop	Marion	149	2LT Albert E. Kendra
Troop A	Muncie	145	1LT Ralph Hill, Jr.
Troop B	Bluffton	145	1LT Thomas W. Pett
Troop C	Muncie	145	1LT Louis W. George
113th Engineer Battalion	Valparaiso	733	LTC John F. Pleva
Headquarters & Headquarters Company (–)	Valparaiso	119	CPT William W. Bailey
Det 1, Headquarters & Headquarters Company	Gary	56	2LT James Pressner
Company A	LaPorte	135	2LT Michael D. Matz
Company B	Michigan City	135	2LT Allen R. Schelebo
Company C	Hammond	135	1LT Walter J. Kryszak
Company E (Bridge)	Gary	153	2LT John R. Sabo
138th Signal Battalion	Anderson	646	LTC James H. Dixon
Headquarters & Headquarters Company	Anderson	92	CPT Jerry M. Gill
Company A (Comd Op)	Anderson	217	CPT Joseph W. Boyd
Company B (Spt Op)	Elwood	163	1LT James E. Carpenter
Company C (Spt Op)	Greenfield	174	CPT Jack A. Boes, Jr.
38th Infantry Division Support Command	Indianapolis	1,933	COL Norman E. Miller
Headquarters & Headquarters Company	Indianapolis	94	CPT Michael H. Flannigan
38th Adjutant General Company (–)	Indianapolis	223	CPT Frederick M. Kline
138th Finance Company	Indianapolis	103	1LT Louis J. Dunn III
38th Infantry Division Material Management Center	Indianapolis	127	CPT Robert J. Cole

Unit	Strength	Location	Commander
38th Supply & Transportation Battalion			
Headquarters & Headquarters Company	306	Terre Haute	LTC George L. Meharry
Company A (Sup-Svc)	43	Terre Haute	2LT Max L. Watts, Jr.
Company B (Trans-Mtr Tns)	116	Terre Haute	1LT James E. Abbinett
	147	Brazil	CPT Lawrence C. Bouslog
738th Maintenance Battalion			
Headquarters & Company A (Lt Maint)	725	Indianapolis	LTC Morris R. Crane
Company B (FS)	103	Indianapolis	CPT Linn E. Bostick
Company C (FS)	113	Kokomo	CPT Norman A. Cundiff
Company D (FS)	113	Bedford	CPT David G. Sherfick
	113	Seymour	2LT Dale L. Hall
Company F (Hy Maint)	218	Indianapolis	CPT Floyd F. Branson, Jr.
Company G (−) (Msl Maint)	65	Indianapolis	CPT Gary K. Dent
113th Medical Battalion			
Headquarters & Company A (Spt)	355	Indianapolis	MAJ Cecil P. Deckard
	133	Indianapolis	1LT Margaret A. Schaekel
Company B	74	Boswell	CPT Jerry L. Martin
Company C	74	Remington	1LT William B. Brooks
Company D	74	Lafayette	1LT Michael V. Gigli
38th Infantry Division Artillery			
Headquarters & Headquarters Battery	1,919	Indianapolis	COL Richard L. Chastain
Battery E (Tgt Acq) 139th Field Artillery	201	Indianapolis	CPT Orrice J. Wynn
	143	Indianapolis	CPT Carlton G. Epps
3rd Battalion 139th Field Artillery			
Headquarters & Headquarters Battery	409	Crawfordsville	LTC Robert W. Ferling
	197	Crawfordsville	CPT Robert J. McKeown
Battery A	79	Darlington	CPT Charles W. Alexander, Jr.
Battery B	79	Kempton	CPT Michael B. Montgomery
Battery C	79	Danville	CPT Mark A. Jones
Service Battery	55	Rockville	CPT Darwin E. Floyd
2nd Battalion 150th Field Artillery			
Headquarters & Headquarters Battery	606	Bloomington	LTC Paul L. McCormick
	167	Bloomington	CPT David L. Keys
Battery A	96	Greencastle	CPT Steven J. Baker

APPENDIX F—Continued

INDIANA ARMY NATIONAL GUARD STATION LIST, 1 JANUARY 1980

ORGANIZATION	STATION	AUTH STR	COMMANDER
Battery B	Spencer	96	CPT Jack E. Noel
Battery C	Noblesville	96	CPT Jay R. Brewer
Battery D	Lebanon	86	1LT Patrick M. Carney
Service Battery	Bloomington	65	CPT Johnnie R. Collier
1st Battalion 163rd Field Artillery	Evansville	480	LTC Donald E. Christy
Headquarters & Headquarters Battery	Evansville	188	2LT Phillip W. Stroud
Battery A	Evansville	79	1LT Stephen L. Lynch
Battery B	Evansville	79	CPT David A. Kleug
Battery C	Evansville	79	1LT Michael F. Schafer
Service Battery	Evansville	55	CPT William R. Ochsner
2nd Brigade 38th Infantry Division	Kokomo	2,281	COL Kenneth W. Himsel
Headquarters & Headquarters Company	Kokomo	94	CPT William Myers
2nd Battalion 151st Infantry	South Bend	729	LTC Jerry F. Hoover
Headquarters & Headquarters Company	South Bend	137	CPT Alan J. Doggart
Company A	Warsaw	155	CPT Edward W. Ewing, Jr.
Company B	Angola	155	CPT William W. Bryan
Company C	Plymouth	155	CPT Dennis F. Parr
Support Company	Elkhart	127	CPT Michael A. Blackburn
1st Battalion 293rd Infantry	Fort Wayne	729	LTC William L. Pearl
Headquarters & Headquarters Company	Fort Wayne	137	CPT Robert L. Chadwick
Company A (—)	Hartford City	81	CPT Ronnie G. Withers
Det 1 Company A	Portland	74	1LT Eddy L. Anthony
Company B	Winchester	155	CPT Terrance J. Greene

214

Company C	Fort Wayne	CPT Robert W. Hart	155
Support Company	Huntington	1LT Michael N. Seaman	127
2nd Battalion 293rd Infantry	Logansport	LTC Thomas R. Woods	**729**
Headquarters & Headquarters Company	Logansport	CPT Dewey G. Jones	137
Company A (–)	Delphi	CPT Ernest J. Szasz	81
Det 1, Company A	Attica	1LT Larry E. Dimick	74
Company B (–)	Monticello	CPT Michael E. Nelson	81
Det 1, Company B	Rensselaer	2LT Joseph L. Brady	74
Company C	Peru	CPT Bradford Eschelman	155
Support Company	Frankfort	CPT Richard L. Todd	127
76th Brigade, 38th Infantry Division	Bedford	COL Carl G. Farrell	2,292
Headquarters & Headquarters Company	Bedford	CPT Dan M. Colglazier	94
1st Battalion 151st Infantry	New Albany	LTC Donald J. Smith	729
Headquarters & Headquarters Company	New Albany	CPT Russell L. Marcum	137
Company A	New Albany	CPT Jerry D. Purcel	155
Company B (–)	Scottsburg	CPT Monty D. Marsh	81
Det 1, Company B	North Vernon	2LT Kenneth E. Reguli	74
Company C	Salem	CPT Gerald F. Ramseyer	155
Support Company	Madison	CPT Gerhard Braun	127
1st Battalion 152d Infantry	Jasper	LTC Billie J. Brinkley	729
Headquarters & Headquarters Company	Jasper	CPT Toby C. Yoho	137
Company A	Vincennes	CPT Jay R. Penndorf	155
Company B	Linton	CPT Donald B. Spice	155
Company C	Tell City	CPT Grover L. Miller	155
Support Company	Washington	CPT William E. Burch	127
2nd Battalion (MECH) 152d Infantry	Columbus	LTC Willie M. Prather	**740**
Headquarters & Headquarters Company	Columbus	CPT Charles L. Adams	157
Company A	Richmond	1LT Ardwood R. Courtney	153

APPENDIX F—Continued

INDIANA ARMY NATIONAL GUARD STATION LIST, 1 JANUARY 1980

ORGANIZATION	STATION	AUTH STR	COMMANDER
Company B	Martinsville	153	1LT Billy R. Belevins
Company C	New Castle	153	1LT Richard O. Stamm
Support Company	Connersville	124	CPT Danny L. Slone

INDIANA AIR NATIONAL GUARD STATION LIST, 1 JANUARY 1980

ORGANIZATION	STATION	AUTH STR	COMMANDER
207 Weather Flight	Shelbyville	16	Lt Col Roger T. Winn
122 Tactical Fighter Wing	Fort Wayne	63	B/Gen Frank L. Hettlinger
163 Tactical Fighter Squadron	Fort Wayne	68	Maj Ronald E. Farrell
122 Consolidated Aircraft Maintenance Squadron	Fort Wayne	371	Lt Col Jack H. McNew
122 Civil Engineering Flight	Fort Wayne	121	Maj Wesley L. Holley
122 Resources Management Squadron	Fort Wayne	85	Maj Douglas J. Bauman
122 Communications Flight Support	Fort Wayne	29	Maj Larry G. McManus
122 Tactical Hospital	Fort Wayne	49	Maj Richard C. Spindler
235 Air Traffic Control Flight	Fort Wayne	65	Maj Edward R. Karrmann
163 Weather Flight	Fort Wayne	13	Maj John D. Slagle
122 Combat Support Squadron	Fort Wayne	104	Maj Ronald B. Bennett
122 Weapons Security Systems Flight	Fort Wayne	48	1st Lt Stephen M. Bowland
181 Tactical Fighter Group	Terre Haute	47	Lt Col Joseph Orear
113 Tactical Fighter Squadron	Terre Haute	68	Lt Col Herbert J. Spier, Jr
181 Consolidated Aircraft Maintenance Squadron	Terre Haute	365	Lt Col Samuel D. Dunbar
181 Civil Engineering Flight	Terre Haute	100	Maj Thomas N. Whitt

216

181	Resources Management Squadron	Terre Haute	Lt Col Donald R. Hulsey, Sr
181	Communications Flight Support	Terre Haute	Maj Jerry L. Wookfork
181	Tactical Clinic	Terre Haute	Maj Richard Watson
113	Weather Flight	Terre Haute	Maj David M. Lueck
181	Combat Support Squadron	Terre Haute	Lt Col Francis D. Cramer
181	Weapons Security Systems Flight	Terre Haute	2d Lt Ronald M. Hinsenkamp
	Atterbury Air-to-Ground Gunnery Range	Edinburg	Lt Col Richard M. Pierce
	Jefferson Proving Ground Range	Madison	Maj Lawrence A. Williams

87
29
26
13
104
48
11
5

217

APPENDIX G

INDIANA DISTINGUISHED SERVICE CROSS

The Indiana Distinguished Service Cross is the state's highest award for heroism. It is awarded to officers or enlisted personnel of the militia who perform "at great personal danger and risk of life or limb" acts of heroism designed to protect life or property. In wartime, it can be awarded for acts "over and beyond the call of duty, which, act, danger or risk he could have failed to perform or incur without being subject to censure for neglect of duty."*

The Distinguished Service Cross consists of a metal die embossed medallion of 1/10, 10K gold filled, 14 gauge, 1-11/16 inches wide, 1-11/16 inches high. On the obverse within a circle, the design of the State Banner. A torch in the center, surrounded by an outer circle of thirteen stars, and inner half circle of five stars, the nineteenth star, appreciably larger than the others above the torch, with the word "Indiana" above the nineteenth star. Seven rays emitting from the flame of the torch to the outer top seven stars. Below the circle the words: "Distinguished Service". The medal is suspended by a ring from a silk grosgrain ribbon 1-3/8 inches in length on a concealed bar, attachment pin with jewelers safety catch. Ribbon is 1-3/8 inches in width composed of a gold stripe (1/16 inch), blue stripe (5/16 inch), gold stripe (1/16 inch), blue stripe (1/2 inch), gold stripe (1/16 inch), blue stripe (5/16 inch), and gold stripe (1/16 inch).

INDIANA DISTINGUISHED SERVICE
CROSS RECIPIENTS

Colonel John W. McConnell, 1954

Private Ken Small, 1955

Private James E. Farmer, 1960

Captain Virgil I. Grissom, USAF, 1961

Major Earl L. Higbie, 1963

Master Sergeant Joseph B. Dickerson, 1964

---

* Article IX, Indiana Military Code

Sergeant First Class Richard L. Keller, 1965

Captain Lyman H. Goben, 1965

Airman First Class David J. Brookmyer, 1966

Lieutenant Colonel Virgil I. Grissom, USAF, 1967
(oak leaf cluster, posthumously)

Colonel Frank Borman, USAF, 1969

Sergeant Robert T. Smith, 1969

Specialist Four Charles K. Larkins, 1969 (posthumously)

Platoon Sergeant William E. Butler, 1969

Staff Sergeant David L. Mallory, 1969

Specialist Four Darrel C. Holder, 1969

Sergeant Thomas R. Blandford, 1969

Sergeant James L. Bohanon, 1969

Sergeant Vincent W. Turner, 1969

Sergeant Michael R. Aulbach, 1969

Sergeant Curtis E. Hester, 1969

Sergeant Thomas S. Lilly, 1969

First Lieutenant George L. Kleiber Jr., 1969 (posthumously)

Sergeant Donald L. Jones, 1972

General Mark Clark, 1976

Lieutenant Colonel John Freeman, 1976

Staff Sergeant Charles E. Goolsby, 1977

Second Lieutenant Timothy J. Wright, 1977

Chief Warrant Officer Paul F. Miller, 1977

Specialist Four Archie W. Reynolds, 1977

Staff Sergeant John T. Kelley, 1978

Staff Sergeant Vincent E. Vespo, 1979

APPENDIX H

INDIANA DISTINGUISHED SERVICE MEDAL

The Indiana Distinguished Service Medal is the state's highest award for meritorious service. It is conferred for "unusually distinguished or meritorious service, which to a marked degree is reflected in the increased efficiency of the militia, or which brings exceptional and great honor or credit to the Indiana armed forces and commands the attention and respect of the citizens of the state and of the military establishment throughout the United States."* Although the overwhelming number of recipients have been members of the Indiana National Guard, it occasionally is awarded to state government officials or members of the regular military establishment. On a few occasions, it has been awarded for acts of heroism that do not meet the requirements for granting the Indiana Distinguished Service Cross.

The medal consists of a metal die embossed sterling silver medallion, 14 gauge, octagon, 1-1/4 inches in diameter to the flat sides of the octagon. On the obverse within an inner circle the State Seal of Indiana surrounded by an outer circle, above the State Seal the word "Indiana" and below, the words "Loyal in Peace or War". The medal is suspended by a ring from a silk grosgrain ribbon 1-3/8 inches in length on a concealed bar, attachment pin with jewelers safety catch. Ribbon is 1-3/8 inches in width composed of a yellow stripe (1/8 inch), a leaf green stripe (5/16 inch), orange stripe (1/16 inch), leaf green stripe (1/8 inch), yellow stripe (1/8 inch), leaf green stripe (1/8 inch), orange stripe (1/16 inch), leaf green stripe (5/16 inch), and a yellow stripe (1/8 inch).

INDIANA DISTINGUISHED SERVICE MEDAL RECIPIENTS

1954

Major General Jesse E. McIntosh

Colonel John D. Friday

---

* Article IX, Indiana Military Code

1955

Brigadier General Daniel W. DePrez
Lieutenant Colonel Charlie Y. Talbott

1956

Brigadier General Oliver H. Stout
Lieutenant Colonel John Fissell
Major General Ben H. Watt
Major General Harold A. Doherty

1957

Colonel William R. Sefton
Major General Carl O. DeBard
Lieutenant Colonel Richard G. Stewart
Captain Edward H. Heimbach
Brigadier General Allison Maxwell

1958

Colonel Kenneth P. Williams
Lieutenant Colonel William G. Bray
Lieutenant Colonel Dorris C. Graham

1959

Colonel Robert L. Moorhead
Major George E. Myers
Captain Ola F. Heslar, USNR

1960

Master Sergeant Russell A. Long
Harold W. Handley, Governor of Indiana
Major General John W. McConnell
Colonel Charles L. Kimsey

1961

Lieutenant General Lewis B. Hershey
Colonel Marvin J. Evans

1963

Brigadier General Ivan D. Pogue

1964

Lieutenant Colonel Delbert J. Wolff
Major General Howard S. Wilcox
Chief Master Sergeant Charles M. Buckmaster
Major General John S. Anderson

221

1965

Lieutenant Colonel Stanley J. Urban
Lieutenant Colonel Elmer L. Jackson

1966

Brigadier General Elmer F. Straub
Colonel Jesse C. Drain, Jr.

1967

Brigadier General Kenneth E. Keene

1969

Colonel Alfred F. Ahner
Brigadier General Jack K. Elrod
Major General Noble F. Schlatter
Major General John S. Anderson (oak leaf cluster)
Major Robert L. DeBard
Lieutenant Colonel Varnol G. Farmer

1970

Command Sergeant Major Glenn D. Wolfe
Brigadier General William R. Sefton (oak leaf cluster)

1971

Major General Kenneth W. Brewer
Captain James D. Wolf
Sergeant Murel E. Clark
Colonel Edward A. Costomiris
Major General John N. Owens

1972

Colonel Bernard F. O'Neal
Colonel James M. McFadden
Colonel Norwood R. Hughes
Lieutenant Colonel Stanley J. Urban (oak leaf cluster)

1973

Colonel George S. Blankenbaker
Colonel Ralph E. Spencer
Major General Robert G. Moorhead
Chief Warrant Officer Herbert A. Miller
Colonel Alexander F. Del Bianco
Colonel John J. Dillon
Brigadier General Wendell G. Garrett

1974

Colonel Jack H. Williamson
Lieutenant Colonel Arthur L. Goldman
Colonel Jerome S. Rafferty
Milton M. Mitnick, Indiana Civil Defense Director
Colonel Wilbur O. Stevens
Colonel William A. Scott

1975

Lieutenant Colonel George E. Yockey
Lieutenant Colonel George L. Wilcox
Brigadier General Robert E. Wilson
Colonel Robert D. Weliver
Colonel Paul G. Lewis
Specialist Four Randall B. Merritt
Specialist Four Michael L. Brallier

1976

Sergeant First Class Stanton D. Long
Colonel Robert D. Weliver (oak leaf cluster)
Chief Warrant Officer Carl L. Todd
Colonel Joseph P. Andrews
Major Robert E. Meadows
Sergeant First Class Leroy Hackett
Major Ronald Runyon
Lieutenant Colonel Jack R. Dempsey
Major General Jesse E. McIntosh, IGR (oak leaf cluster)

1977

Chief Warrant Officer Thomas C. Price
Specialist Five Stephen C. Green
Sergeant Rex A. Herb
Lieutenant Colonel Robert L. McAfee
Chief Warrant Officer George R. Smith
Colonel Robert J. Cabiness
Sergeant Major Harry E. Bowman

1978

Colonel Arthur R. Raney
Lieutenant Colonel Charles E. Smith
Colonel John Keller
William J. Watt, assistant to the governor
James T. Smith, assistant to the governor
Colonel Richard H. Huston

223

Major Forrest V. Cooper, Indiana State Police
Lieutenant Colonel Clifford M. Brown
Captain Michael A. Kiefer
Lieutenant Colonel Darvin R. Appel
Lieutenant Colonel Kenneth W. Himsel
Lieutenant Colonel Harold S. Robison
Lieutenant Colonel Wilson P. Dean
Brigadier General Clyde C. Wright
Colonel Charles Maull
Lieutenant Colonel John M. Hine
First Lieutenant Harold M. Goss
Colonel Fred D. Smith
Command Sergeant Major Robert H. Davis
Private Donald R. Bryant
Brigadier General Phillips N. Gordon
Private First Class Ronald E. Groning
Colonel Leland R. Fine
Brigadier General Ervin H. Bucher

1979

Colonel Byron L. Dukes
Colonel William A. Scott (oak leaf cluster)
Captain Floyd Branson
Staff Sergeant Tony R. Barnes
First Sergeant Raymond E. Hinton
Lieutenant Colonel James Franklin
Colonel Wyatt O. Cole
Lieutenant Colonel Claude W. Shields
Chief Warrant Officer Charles W. Griffith
Commander Hollis W. Walls, USNR
Clara J. Green
Command Sergeant Major Harold L. Hargrave
First Sergeant Leland W. Gatewood
Chief Master Sergeant James A. Caldwell
Major Ernest E. Vaught

APPENDIX I

NOTES ON CONTRIBUTORS

Chief Master Sergeant James A. Caldwell retired from the Indiana Air National Guard in 1979, closing out a 40-year career that included service during World War II and Korea. Activated with the 113th Observation Squadron in 1941, he helped to create the 7th Photo Reconnaissance Squadron and later served as line chief of the 23rd Photo Reconnaissance Squadron, which saw duty in Africa, Italy, Sicily, and France. He holds the Indiana Distinguished Service Medal.

Dr. Richard M. Clutter is an associate professor of history at Indiana Central University, Indianapolis. He received a Bachelor of Science degree from Indiana Central and his M.A. and Ph.D. from Indiana University. Dr. Clutter is vice chairman of the Military History Section of the Indiana Historical Society and is editor of the section's publication, the *Indiana Military History Journal.*

Ralph E. Dimmett has maintained a life-long interest in Indiana military history and is an active member of the Military History Section of the Indiana Historical Society. He has contributed reviews and articles to the *Indiana Military History Journal.* In writing the account of the Indiana Guard during the 1920s and 1930s, he interviewed many veterans of that period.

Colonel Robert T. Fischer enlisted in the Indiana Guard in 1949, later commanded a field artillery battery, and served as operations and training officer for the Military Department of Indiana and the 38th Infantry Division. He is deputy commander of the State Area Command and logistics officer for the U.S. Property and Fiscal Office. Colonel Fischer once served as chief of the Reserve Components Division at the Field Artillery School and has been a frequent contributor to the *Field Artillery Journal.*

George W. Geib is professor of history at Butler University, Indianapolis. A specialist in America's early national history, his research interests include urban, regional, and military affairs. Dr. Geib is a past president of the Ohio-Indiana American Studies Association, and is a current board member of the Indiana Historical Society's Military History Section. He is particularly active as a lecturer and planner in state public humanities programming.

Lieutenant Colonel James R. H. Spears, a member of the Army Reserve, was commissioned as an intelligence officer and later commanded a battalion in the 70th Infantry Division. He is a member of the Reserve Officers' Association and the Company of Military Historians and is a board member of the Military History Section of the Indiana Historical Society. He holds degrees from Wabash College and Indiana University.

Captain William J. Watt commands the 120th Public Affairs Detachment of the Indiana Army National Guard and was public affairs officer for the 38th Infantry Division. He is a board member of the Military History Section of the Indiana Historical Society and is a frequent contributor of articles to military publications. Watt has been an executive assistant to Governor Bowen since 1973.

INDEX

228